TWO YEARS TO SERVE

★ ★ ★ ★ ★

RECOLLECTIONS OF A DRAFTED MARINE: HALF A CENTURY AFTER THE VIETNAM WAR

THOMAS ELLIOTT

Charleston, SC
www.PalmettoPublishing.com

Two Years to Serve

Hardcover ISBN: 979-8-88590-940-2
Paperback ISBN: 979-8-88590-941-9
eBook ISBN: 979-8-88590-942-6

"All gave some, some gave all!"

—Howard William Osterkamp

DEDICATED TO AND IN THE MEMORY OF MY FALLEN BROTHERS:

Paul O. Evans: KIA December 22, 1966

Gary G. Schneider: KIA December 31, 1966

Ferrell Hummingbird: KIA January 14, 1967

Patrick S. Cochran: KIA August 21, 1967

Raymond G. Potter: KIA September 10, 1967

Anthony P. Sawicki: KIA September 10, 1967

Ronald L. Black: KIA September 11, 1967

Terrance E. Klaric: KIA May 11, 1967

"Some people live an entire lifetime and wonder if they've ever made a difference in the world. Marines don't have that problem."
—Ronald Reagan, former President of the United States

TABLE OF CONTENTS

Acronyms and Abbreviations · · · ix
Preface/Acknowledgement · · · xi
Chapter 1 My First Encounter with the Marines · · · 1
Chapter 2 Drafted · · · 4
Chapter 3 Arrival at Boot Camp · · · 10
Chapter 4 Boot Camp · · · 15
Chapter 5 The Rifle Range · · · 23
Chapter 6 Ten-Day Leave · · · 28
Chapter 7 Forming the Battalion at Camp Pendleton · · · 34
Chapter 8 Transit to Okinawa · · · 42
Chapter 9 The Philippines · · · 50
Chapter 10 First Time to Vietnam · · · 57
Chapter 11 Welcome to Vietnam, Tom · · · 62
Chapter 12 Dong Ha · · · 68
Chapter 13 Operation Chinook · · · 73
Chapter 14 Operation Chinook: Christmas · · · 81
Chapter 15 Operation Chinook New Year's Eve · · · 87
Chapter 16 Operation Chinook: The New Year · · · 92
Chapter 17 The Graves · · · 97
Chapter 18 The Mule and the Prisoner · · · 102
Chapter 19 C-Rats · · · 105
Chapter 20 Operation Chinook: The VC Sniper · · · 110
Chapter 21 Beer, Bacon, and Eggs · · · 116
Chapter 22 Hill 51 · · · 121
Chapter 23 The Things They Missed · · · 129
Chapter 24 The Fever Blister · · · 132
Chapter 25 Hungry · · · 136
Chapter 26 Phu Bai · · · 140

Chapter 27 Fishing Vietnamese Style · · · · · 149
Chapter 28 Transferred · · · · · 157
Chapter 29 CAP School/Transit to Dong Ha · · · · · 161
Chapter 30 Dong Ha CAP Duty · · · · · 169
Chapter 31 The Job Will Be Yours · · · · · 174
Chapter 32 I Take Over · · · · · 182
Chapter 33 The French Bunker · · · · · 188
Chapter 34 R&R · · · · · 195
Chapter 35 CAP Headquarters, Cam Lo · · · · · 202
Chapter 36 The Icehouse · · · · · 210
Chapter 37 The Poker Game · · · · · 215
Chapter 38 My Birthday · · · · · 223
Chapter 39 Back to the Real World · · · · · 227
Chapter 40 My Last 100 Days · · · · · 233
Epilogue · · · · · 240

ACRONYMS AND ABBREVIATIONS

3/26: 3rd Battalion, 26th Marine Regiment
A.S.A.P: As Soon As Possible
AO: Area of Operation
AWOL: Absent Without Official Leave
BS: Bullshit
C-4: Explosive material
CAC: Combined Action Company
CAP: Combined Action Platoon
CAP: Combined Action Program
CP: Command Post
C-Rations: Combat ready meals
C-Rats: Short for C-Rations
DI: Drill Instructor
DMZ: Demilitarized Zone
EOD: Explosive Ordnance Disposal
Filthy Few: Nickname for Second Platoon
H and S: Headquarters and Service Company
Hooch: Tent or other type of protection/living quarters
HQ: Headquarters
I Corps: Tactical Area South of the DMZ
ITR: Infantry Training Regiment
Klicks: Kilometer
Lt.: Lieutenant
LZ: Landing Zone
M-79: Grenade launcher
MCRD: Marine Corps Recruit Depot
mm: millimeter
MOS: Military Occupation Specialty Code

MP: Military Police
NCO: Non-Commissioned Officer
NVA: North Vietnam Army
OCS: Officer Candidate School
PA: Public Address
PF: Popular Forces
PI: Philippines
PM: Provost Marshal
PRC-25: Portable field communications radio
PT: Physical Training
PTSD: Post Traumatic Stress Disorder
Punji Pit: Sharp bamboo stake booby trap
PX: Post Exchange
R&R: Rest and Recuperation
RVN: Republic of Vietnam
S/Sgt.: Staff Sergeant
Sgt.: Sergeant
Turk: Lt. Dolan Second Platoon Commander
USMC: Unites States Marine Corps
USO: United Service Organizations
VC: Viet Cong
WWII: World War Two
XO: Executive Officer

PREFACE/ACKNOWLEDGEMENT

In January 1966, I was twenty years old, had a job as a draftsman, and attended city college part-time when I was drafted into the United States Marine Corps. My life changed forever. An avid surfer, my transformation from blond-haired, tan-skinned, barefoot, Southern California–beach boy to a U.S. Marine required serious reprogramming. I attended boot camp at the Marine Corps Recruit Depot (MCRD) in San Diego, California. There I learned the true meaning of the phrase, "No pain, no gain."

After boot camp, I received extensive combat infantry training at Camp Pendleton. In May of 1966, the Marine Corps reactivated the former, highly decorated WWII 3rd Battalion, 26th (3/26) Marines to fight in Vietnam. Assigned to Second Platoon Lima Company, I spent a full tour of thirteen months overseas, and ten and a half months in Vietnam. I made and lost close friends and we endured many hardships that tested our resolve. Throughout my time in the Marines, I wrote letters to my family and my girlfriend. Fifteen years after my return from Vietnam, my mother gave me a shoebox containing the letters. She said nothing about them, other than I may want to read them someday. I was not sure if I wanted to relive that time; years passed before I read them.

Thirty-five years after the war ended, I received a phone call from our platoon Navy Corpsman, Bill Miller. We called him Doc. His call to the original members of the Second Platoon was to encourage them to attend the biannual reunion of the 3rd Battalion 26th Marines in Ennis, Montana, in August of 2002. After my talk with Doc, I found the shoebox of letters stored in an old trunk in my garage and began to read them. Correct in my fear of reliving the events, the letters brought back memories—some good, some bad. While I read the letters, I marked the ones with noteworthy events and then decided I would attend the reunion.

Two hundred and fifty members of the battalion attended, including twenty surviving members of the original Lima Company, Second Platoon. A three day event, we spent the evenings drinking beer and telling tall tales of our experiences in Vietnam, some slightly exaggerated over time and the number of beers consumed. My letters helped confirm or amend those experiences.

Our platoon commander, Lieutenant Harry Dolan, who spent twenty-six years in the Marine Corps and retired as a major, also attended the reunion. I was his radio operator in Vietnam. The last night of the reunion, the lieutenant suggested I use the information in my letters to write a journal of the platoon's actions during our tour in Vietnam. I agreed to write the journal, but said I needed help. I received copies of letters the other guys had written home, their story ideas, recollections of events, and pictures. I obtained copies of the declassified daily action reports for the first three months the 3/26 fought in Vietnam. With my letters, the information received from the guys, and notes taken at the reunions, including our own platoon's reunion in 2003, I wrote the journal. Completed in 2005, I printed fifty copies and sent a copy to each of the surviving members of the original Second Platoon and to the relatives of those we lost in Vietnam.

The journal covered the time period from the formation of the 3/26 at Camp Pendleton until the battalion started to mix things up by transferring troops from all the platoons to other battalions in Vietnam. I was transferred to a completely different assignment in a Combined Action Platoon. For me, it was a whole new experience.

Since writing the original journal, I wanted to expand it into a book that covered my entire two years in the Marine Corps. In 2018, I began to attend a memoir writing class for older adults at my local community college. The class instructor and my classmates encouraged me to complete my book. Using my letters, the original journal, the declassified information, and my best recollection of events, I have finished my story.

While I worked on my memoir, I read books by other Vietnam veterans. Often, in the preface or introduction, the authors use, as I have here, the words "To the best of my recollection." After more than fifty years, and many spent trying to not remember, what is the definition of "to the best of my recollection?" I know from my letters and other research that the events depicted in this book actually happened, and I write about them "to the best of my recollection." Where I use dialogues, they may not be the exact words spoken but reflect what happened.

I cannot remember the names of all the men I served with, and where I made up a name, I made a note of it. But know that I am proud, happy, and humbled to have served my country with these men.

As I mentioned above, while I worked on my book, I read recollections of other veterans who served in Vietnam. No matter the service, Military Occupation Specialty Code (MOS), outfit, duty, or area served in-country, each veteran who served in the Vietnam War has a unique story to tell. It is important that veterans tell their stories. I hope more Vietnam veterans will step forward to tell their stories before it is too late.

My two years in the United States Marine Corps were exciting, terrifying at times, happy, sad, and life changing. The Marine Corps taught me the value of discipline and hard work. My time in Vietnam taught me the value of teamwork, friendship, and trust—values that would help guide me throughout my life. "Once a Marine always a Marine." I would not trade the experience for anything. I hope you enjoy my story.

Tom Elliott, Sergeant USMC.

ACKNOWLEDGEMENT

Authoring a book, especially for a first-time writer, is a huge undertaking and cannot be tackled alone. While completing my book, I received help and encouragement from a host of people whom I need to acknowledge and thank.

First, to my wonderful wife, Nanci, for being a writer's widow for the many hours I spent sitting in front of my computer, for her unwavering support, and for making sure I moved around every couple of hours. To Michel

Nellis, for her help in editing the manuscript. To Michele and Jerry Jackman, both experienced writers, for their help and support and for beta reading the manuscript. To Joanne St. John, for her help with editing. To Roger Arden, John Bloomer, and Marc and Joan Hynes as beta readers. Also, I want to thank Shelly Lowenkopf, my writing class instructor, without whose help this book would have not been possible. And to all my classmates who listened as I read in class most of the chapters and then provided excellent feedback and encouragement. I also need to thank Harry Dolan, my platoon commander, for his suggestion that I write a journal, which eventually led to my book. Sadly, Harry passed away before I completed the book. To Jim Strange, Tom Willey, Jaak Aulik, Doug Binkley, Ed Palm and Phil Balint for providing photographs. And thank you to all of the Marines of Second Platoon L/3/26 and CAP Papa for having my back during our experiences in Vietnam.

CHAPTER 1
MY FIRST ENCOUNTER WITH THE MARINES

Corporal Strange crawled past the fighting holes Lieutenant Dolan and I were in. "Evans is dead," he called out to us. Enemy fire erupted from the front of our position; a bullet took a chunk out of the corporal's ear and out through the top of his helmet. He rolled into his fighting hole for cover.

"Radio!" the lieutenant said.

The radio handset was stuffed in the top pocket of my flak jacket; the radio was in a pack on my back. I gave the handset to the lieutenant. With incoming mortars and hand grenades exploding all around us, the lieutenant reported Paul Evans' death to battalion headquarters. We could hear the thump, thump of our own outgoing mortars and heavy machine gun and rifle fire from our forward positions. Now near dawn, I hoped the Viet Cong (VC) would withdraw like they had the past two mornings.

"Three days of this bullshit, sir. You think the VC will give it up for Christmas?" I asked.

"Only if the assholes in Washington negotiate a cease-fire. We can only hope," the lieutenant said.

The shooting died down; the incoming mortars stopped. The lieutenant handed the radio handset back to me. "Stay close," he said. "Looks like the VC withdrew to drag off their dead and wounded."

In country for only two weeks, the first Marine in the platoon was dead and another wounded. Crouched down in our fighting holes, I waited for first light. I pulled my poncho over my head to shield myself from the relentless monsoon rain. I felt as if a wave had washed over and forced me to the ocean's bottom.

I peered out from under my poncho, not sure the attack was over, my rifle at the ready. Wet, cold, and tired, visions of my first encounter with the Marines danced in my head. Over a year and a half ago, my friend Roger and I had sneaked onto Trestles Beach to go surfing. Named for the long train trestle that passed the lagoon behind the beach; this beach part of the Camp Pendleton Marine Corps Base south of San Clemente, California, was off limits for us to surf. Two Marine Military Policemen (MPs) appeared on the beach and signaled us to paddle back to shore. We ignored them and kept surfing, certain they would get tired of waiting and leave like other times when they showed up. They did not leave.

Taking off on a wave, I fell and lost my board. The wave passing over forced me to the ocean bottom. Back on the surface and gasping for air, the MPs were standing on the beach, holding my surfboard. They met Roger and me at the water's edge and took Roger's board. They hassled us about making them wait and trespassing on the base, then threatened us with arrest and jail time. They threw our surfboards in the back of their truck and told us if we wanted them back, we would need to see the provost marshal in Oceanside and would need an adult with us. They let us go.

Two days later, my mother went with us to the base. In his office, the provost marshal did not try to hide his displeasure for using his time to reprimand a couple of surfers who trespassed on his base. He showed respect to my mother. He explained to us why the Marines did not want us on the beach or surfing there. His lecture was over, he reached in his desk drawer and pulled out an eight-by-ten-inch glossy photograph and showed it to my mother. The photograph was of a group of surfers lined up on the beach, bent over mooning the passenger train as it passed over the trestle. Another reason they did not want us on the beach. Mom looked over at me, her eyes glaring a little, but with a curl of a smile on her lower lip. I shrugged and tried to look innocent (which I was not). The provost marshal told us one more time that if we were caught again, we could go to jail.

We picked up our boards and headed off the base. I asked Mom if we could stop at Doheny and go surfing. "No, and don't get caught again!" she said. I went surfing at Trestles two days later, unaware at the time I would eventually end up in the Marine Corps.

Now sitting in my fighting hole, trying to light a cigarette, my hands shook from the cold. A drop of water off my helmet put the match out. I gave up. At first light, the low clouds and light, misty rain gave the battalion perimeter a quiet eerie feeling. "Sir, you think the VC withdrew, or are they waiting for us to stick our heads up?"

"Only one way to find out," he said.

We stood up and left our fighting holes to go check on the platoon. The guys were out of their fighting holes cold, wet, and tired. They checked on one another. Doc was with the corporal, tending to his wounded ear. Nearby, Paul Evans' body lay on the ground covered with a poncho. As we moved along the line, the lieutenant told the squad leaders to reset the claymore mines and trip flares and make sure everyone got reloaded with ammo and grenades, ate, and tried to get a little sleep. "The VC are not done yet," he said. Two days until Christmas.

CHAPTER 2
DRAFTED

During World War Two, drafted meant serving for the duration of the war. During the Vietnam War, drafted meant "Two Years to Serve."

With nothing on but my socks and underwear, I stood in a row with six other guys in their underwear: some in boxers, some in tighty-whities. I was a tighty-whities guy. An older guy with wire-rimmed eyeglasses and a thin mustache and wearing a long white lab coat stood in front of me. He held a clipboard in his hand. With a tiny flashlight, he looked in my eyes and ears. He jammed a flat piece of wood in my mouth and said, "Say ah."

With my head back and my mouth open, my mind raced: "What is happening?" Yesterday I surfed perfectly shaped tubes at my favorite surf spot Stockers. Knowing I was to report for the draft the next morning, I rode every wave like it might be my last. Now I am standing here in my underwear. What started all this?

Out of high school, I worked at a book binding factory during the day and washed dishes at night to earn money. When not hanging out at the fraternity house with my best friend, Roger, I lived at my parents' house in a room Dad, and I built off the side of the garage. I had a steady girlfriend and owned a car and a surfboard. Life was good.

The most important thing in my life at the time was surfing. Roger and I spent the previous summer surfing every day for forty-four days in Mazatlán, Mexico, and points south. We fished and cooked what we caught over a fire on the beach. We bought bread and tortillas from the local vendors and ate tacos and beans from the little palm-frond shack restaurant down the beach from our camp. In town, we drank Corona beer that cost $.08 for a twelve-ounce glass at the Pacifico Corona Brewery. We sneaked into a nearby trailer park at night to take showers. We were living the life of true surf bums and loved every minute of it.

Returning from our surf trip, I was too late to sign up for the architecture class I wanted to take at Pasadena City College. Instead, I signed up for the general education classes I needed and joined the fraternity my friend Roger belonged to.

Being from a blue-collar family, I did not have the money to attend a four-year college. A poor student in high school, I would not qualify anyway. City college was my only choice, and even then, I could not go to school full time. I needed to work. I was ripe for the picking by the draft. I registered for the draft, filled out the papers, and took the preinduction physical and waited for my draft card to arrive.

When my draft card did arrive, I received a classification of 2-S, deferred because of activity in study (a student deferment). A part-time student, I did not expect to get a deferment. Then I read the fine print. The letter said my deferment status would be reevaluated in November. Meanwhile I found a job as a blueprint apprentice. I kept asking the boss to let me do some drawing. By the end of the summer, I worked my way up to draftsman.

Like the small print said, in November, I received a notice of a classification change—reclassified to 1A . . . first to go; just what the Army wanted.

In January, I received the letter, "Uncle Sam Wants You," ordering me to report for induction into the US Army on February 1, 1966. I left the notice of induction on the kitchen table and went straight to the fraternity house. I told the boys the draft got me.

"I need a beer," I said.

"No problem. We just tapped a new keg," Bill, the fraternity president said.

"When do you have to report?" Roger asked.

"First of February."

"Oh shit. You will miss our wedding; you're our best man!"

"Damn, Roger. I didn't think about that. I hate to miss your wedding."

For the rest of the afternoon, I drank beer with the boys to drown my sorrows. *Gloria*, my favorite song, played over and over on the jukebox. I drank too many beers. Roger drove me home.

That night was the first time my mother ever saw me drunk. Dad read the letter I left on the kitchen table. Dad understood but Mom cried. We knew this day would come. Mom was really worried about me going to Vietnam. She gave me a hug. Then turned and grabbed on to Dad. "Don't let him go, Richard, don't let him go!" she pleaded. I hugged Mom and Dad.

"We will get through this one day at a time," Dad said.

I dropped out of school and received an incomplete in all my classes. Not that it mattered much; I never went back to school. I quit work. I planned to surf as much as possible. My boss said to come back when I got out of the service. I never went back. I sold my car, put my surfboards up in the garage rafters, and boxed up all my stuff so my twelve-year-old brother, Tim, could have my room.

We grew up in a nine-hundred-square-foot house with one tiny bathroom. My brother and I shared a bedroom with bunk beds until Dad and I built a room off the side of the garage. When we moved to California from Ohio and my parents bought the house, Dad built a screened-in patio off one side of the garage. He did not realize that in California we did not have the bug problem like in Ohio. When I started high school, I used the patio as a bedroom to get away from sleeping in bunk beds. Dad decided to turn the screened-in patio into a bedroom. He knew a lot about woodwork, and I enjoyed helping Dad build the room. I learned to lay concrete, measure and saw wood, build walls, and use a hammer, complete with a few new choice words that Dad shouted out when he hit his thumb with the hammer. My brother helped and it was a fun time for us with Dad. My brother really wanted my room. He was the only one happy I got drafted.

The day I reported for the draft, Dad dropped me off at the induction center in Los Angeles at 7:30 in the morning. Dad had been a Marine aboard the aircraft carrier U.S.S. *Belleau Wood* during WWII. Before he drove off, he said, "I love you, son." Then he said, "I hope they take you in the Marine Corps." He knew ten percent of draftees were going into the

Marines. I didn't know what to think about that. I told Dad I loved him and to please take care of Mom and Tim.

Inside I presented my draft notice to the clerk behind the desk. He looked at his list and checked me in. He handed me a folder with papers inside and pointed down the hall to a locker room. He told me to find an empty locker, strip down to my socks and underwear, and get in line. "Keep the folder with you," he said. Other guys stood in the line in their underwear, holding folders.

Wait . . . someone is yelling at me. What is he saying? "Drop your drawers! Drop your drawers!" What does that mean? My mind snapped back to the present. I am standing here in my underwear, the guy in the long white lab coat is telling me to pull them down. I hesitated for a couple of seconds not sure what he wanted. He said it again. I pulled down my underwear. As soon as I did, he jammed his finger up next to my balls and said, "Turn your head and cough." I guess he did not do it right the first time; he did it again! He enjoyed his job too much. Done fondling me, he handed me my folder and said, "Pull up your underwear," and pointed the way to the next exam station.

At the next station and still in my underwear, I was checked by another guy for my hearing and vision, including color blindness. He made a bunch of marks in my folder. After answering a ton of questions and being poked and prodded all over, the last guy to check me out kept my folder. He told me to get dressed and take a seat in the room at the end of the hall. There I would sign papers and be sworn into the Army. I had just completed the military induction physical exam—thoroughness questionable. I could have dropped dead at the end, and they would not have known why. If you could walk and talk, you passed.

Dressed, I entered the room at the end of the hall. As the room filled up, I checked out the other guys reporting for induction. From all ethnic backgrounds, there were tall guys, short guys, fat guys, thin guys, guys with long hair, short hair, and no hair. Everyone looked young, some too young. Some looked in good physical shape and some not; they might have trouble in boot camp. Some guys carried small suitcases or backpacks. Guys started to gather in small groups talking about the military and going to Vietnam. There was a great deal of bitching about the draft.

I guess the reality of the draft had not sunk in yet. No way for me to get out of it, so I did not try to fight it; I just let it happen. I planned to go with the flow to see where the adventure took me. The idea of burning my draft card and going to Canada never crossed my mind.

Told to take a seat, 130 of us sat on steel folding chairs behind long rows of tables facing the front of the room. The clerk who checked me in entered the room and set a stack of folders on the front table. He passed out papers we needed to sign when told. A pile of ink pens was on the table, and I picked one up.

Next, a tall Marine in a perfectly formfitting uniform entered the room. His chest was covered with medals, his sleeves covered with stripes. I had no idea what they all meant but he looked impressive. His Smokey-the-Bear hat was tilted exactly right; he looked like the Marine on the recruitment poster.

He walked back and forth in front of the first row of tables as he looked us over with his stone-cold eyes for what seemed like an eternity. Everyone's eyes followed his movements, and the room was dead quiet. When he finally spoke, he announced loudly with a rough voice that he was Gunnery Sergeant Smith (not his real name). "I need ten percent of you for the United States Marine Corps. Who wants to volunteer?" he shouted. Dead silence. He stood there and stared at us. He wanted to dare us or scare us into volunteering. Five guys slowly put up their hands. I was not in the military yet, but I knew enough not to volunteer for anything.

"Okay," the gunnery sergeant said, "I need eight more of you slackers!" When no one else jumped at the chance, he ran his hand up the stack of folders that sat on the table. He pulled out a folder and read the name, "Thomas Richard Elliott."

I stood up, threw the ink pen down, and said, "Fuck!" thought not loud enough for him to hear me.

The guy sitting next to me pointed and said, "Ha, you gotta go in the Marine Corps."

The gunnery sergeant pointed at him and yelled, "What's your name, boy? You're going too!"

During January and February of 1966, the Marine Corps took ten percent of all draftees. Over the duration of the Vietnam War, the Marines drafted 42,633 men. A majority of the draftees served in Vietnam.

A couple more guys volunteered, and the gunnery sergeant chose others to get his thirteen new Marines. Actually, he did not have new Marines, he had a bunch of new recruits. All of us from Southern California, we would require extensive hard-ass training to turn us into United States Marines. My adventure had begun.

CHAPTER 3
ARRIVAL AT BOOT CAMP

The notice of induction said not to bring anything with us when we reported for the draft. Obviously the guys who brought small suitcases and backpacks did not get the memo. The letter said everything we needed the Marine Corps would provide. When I arrived at the induction center, besides the clothes on my back, I brought a pack of cigarettes, matches, and a little cash. When Dad dropped me off, he told me to call later and gave me a handful of change for the pay phone.

The thirteen of us selected for the Marine Corps were moved to another room to wait. Throughout the day, more guys the gunnery sergeant selected joined us.

By noon, my stomach growled. They did not allow us to leave the area to get something to eat. Were they afraid once we knew we were going in the Marines, we might not come back? Judging from the conversations I overheard in the room, that assumption might have been correct. Instead, they handed out box lunches and water to drink.

While eating lunch, I sat with a couple of guys: Albert Drotar and Mike O'Grady. Mike was the guy who was sitting next to me when the gunnery sergeant picked us both for the Marines; we laughed about that. Al and Mike were friends, so when the gunnery sergeant picked Mike, Albert volunteered. They both lived in Yorba Linda, southeast of Los Angeles. They did not surf but we found a lot to talk about, like cars, girls, and smoking dope. Like me, both attended a city college but did not take enough credits to stay out of the draft. We started a friendship that lasted throughout our time in the Marine Corps and after.

Early evening, they loaded us on buses for a ride down the coast to the Marine Corps Recruit Depot (MCRD) in San Diego. With forty guys on the bus, the ride started out noisy—a certain amount of excitement in the air. We were going to be Marines. Not long into the trip, the excitement died down, each guy alone with his thoughts. I worried about Mom being worried about me. Before the bus left, I had called my parents. I was glad Dad gave me change for the pay phone. I told Dad he got his wish. "I am in the Marines," I said. I would get the last laugh about that.

"Boot camp will be tough, but you will be better prepared for what's coming," Dad said. He told me not to worry about Mom; she knew what it was like to have a Marine in a war because of his service in WWII. He knew damned well Mom was worried, afraid, and not happy at all about me going in the Marines. Other guys were waiting to use phones, so I asked Dad to let Phyllis, my girlfriend, know the Marine Corps drafted me and I would call her later.

I thought about Phyllis and what might happen to us if I went to Vietnam. Should we get married before I leave? We talked about marriage the night before I left but made no decision. I was looking out the window and noticed the bus was passing by Trestles, and my thoughts instantly shifted to surfing. Getting dark, the trestle was barely visible alongside the road. I could not see the waves, but in my mind, I relived one of my best days surfing there, and the time the Marine MPs busted me. Would I ever surf there again? By now it was quiet inside the bus; everyone was asleep. Tired, I fell asleep too.

I woke to a Marine in a Smokey-the-Bear hat on the bus screaming at us. "Get off my fucking bus, you maggots. Move! Go, go, go! Get off the bus. Line up with your feet on the yellow footprints! Not in front, not behind, but right on the footprints! Move, move! Go, go, go!" he kept yelling. We scrambled off the bus in record time. Four rows of yellow footprints were on the ground next to the bus. Each set of footprints had the heels touching and the toes forming a forty-five-degree angle. We learned this is how our feet should be when standing at attention. I found a set to stand on, not sure what would happen next.

As we stood on the yellow footprints, the Marine in the Smokey-the-Bear hat yelled, "Attention!" We were not sure what that meant yet, but we all stood up straight. Next, he yelled "Listen up! My name is Sergeant Ahchick. I will be your drill instructor (DI). Your senior drill instructor is Staff Sergeant Quiocho." He stood off to one side. They looked like two Hawaiian guys. We later nicknamed them Pineapple 1 and Pineapple 2. "From now on, the first word out of your mouth is 'Sir!' and the last word out of your mouth is 'Sir!' Got it?" Sergeant Ahchick barked.

We all said, "Yes, sir!" not correctly or loud enough.

He yelled again, "What did I just tell you? You got it now?"

We all yelled, "Sir! Yes! Sir!"

"I can't hear you!"

"Sir! Yes! Sir!" We yelled as loudly as we could.

"Right face!" the sergeant ordered. We turned to the right, except three or four of the guys turned to the left. Sergeant Ahchick yelled out, "You fucking stupid assholes, your other fucking right!" A couple of guys who turned the right way the first time turned around and faced the wrong way. That really set him off. I never heard so many cuss words used at the same time in my life. I tried not to laugh. Actually, it scared me, which is exactly what the sergeant wanted.

With all of us facing in the correct direction, the sergeant ordered, "Forward, march!" Like we knew what that meant. Some guys started on their left foot, others on their right foot. I am sure we looked like a herd of cattle headed for the slaughterhouse, which set the sergeant off again. We became quite good at marching as a unit but that night we were really bad. The sergeant gave up on us marching and was happy to just keep us headed in the right direction. We marched (walked) over to a building. "Platoon halt!" the sergeant ordered. I guess most of the guys knew that halt meant stop. We stopped, except for a couple of guys who ran into the guys in front of them. We had a lot to learn.

Sergeant Ahchick lined us up along the wall of a building, chest to back. "Stand at attention, no talking, eyes forward," the sergeant ordered. With my chest a couple of inches from the back of the guy in front of me, I stared directly at the back of his head. At the head of the line . . . a closed door. As the line moved forward, each guy in front of me disappeared through the door until I was next. What will happen when I pass through that door?

My turn: the door opened. I entered. I heard a range of high-pitched buzzing sounds. Three chairs in the room. A barber standing behind each chair. The drill instructor pointed to an empty chair. "Sit!" he ordered. "Sir, yes, sir," I shouted and took the seat. The barber did not ask me how I wanted my hair cut. For new recruits, only one cut, the Marine Corps "buzz cut."

My hair was already short, but not short enough for the Marines. An expert at cutting recruits' hair, the barber ran his clippers around and over the top of my head. He finished me off with passes up the sides and back. His clippers sounded like a thousand bees buzzing in my ears. In less than a minute, my hair lay on the floor quickly swept up by another recruit.

The barber finished; I reached up to rub the top of my head. My short hair was now no hair. I did not need a mirror, a quick look at the guy next to me and I knew what I looked like. What we all looked like. A short haircut would be the least of my worries in boot camp.

After the haircut, another Marine directed me to a huge warehouse. Inside were rows and rows of shelves full of supplies. At the end of a long counter, I received a large green canvas bag, called a seabag. A Marine behind the counter asked, "What size trousers do you wear?"

"Thirty-two," I said (he does not ask what length). He threw a pair of Marine Corps green trousers across the counter and said, "If they're too long, roll them up." He added a khaki-colored belt with a brass buckle, then a T-shirt (he guessed at my size), and a pair of olive drab green boxer shorts (I wanted to say I was a tighty-whities guy but thought better of it). Next came a yellow sweatshirt.

"Shoe size?" he shouted.

"Eleven," I said. He threw a heavy pair of black boots on top of the pile of clothes along with a pair of green socks. He slapped a hat (the Marines called them covers) on my head and yelled, "Move out!" Does everyone here yell? I put all the stuff he gave me in the sea bag and moved out.

Another Marine directed us to a room with long, high tables. Cardboard boxes sat on top of the table. The sergeant ordered us to stand in front of one of the boxes and change into the clothes we were issued. We were to put our civilian clothes and everything in our pockets in the box. All of us stripped down bare ass naked. I pulled on the boxer shorts, different than my tighty-whities, and my balls were dangling. The trousers fit around the waist but were too long. I rolled them up and put my boots on. I looked like Jethro on the Beverly Hillbillies. The T-shirt fit a little tight. The sweatshirt, with the Marine Corps emblem on the front, was baggy. A couple of guys put them on backwards. Sergeant Ahchick just shook his head.

After getting dressed, I put my clothes and other items in the cardboard box as ordered. With a black marker next to each box, the sergeant ordered us to write our names and addresses on the box. There I was standing in front of the table, with no hair on my head, and everything civilian packed in the cardboard box ready to mail home. Sergeant Ahchick ordered us outside; the night was not over yet. From this point on, my ass belonged to the United States Marine Corps.

CHAPTER 4
BOOT CAMP

What started early in the morning at the Los Angeles induction center ended with no hair on my head and a poorly fitting uniform to wear. In an instant, my entire life changed. Yesterday a carefree surfer doing what I wanted; today I'm a lowly Marine recruit, doing as told.

We arrived at MCRD about ten p.m. By the time we finished getting haircuts and uniforms issued, it was two a.m. We would learn that ten p.m. was 2200 hours, and two a.m. was 0200 hours in the military. Too late for much else, Sergeant Ahchick and Staff Sergeant Quiocho marched us, more like walked us, over to the barracks of half-round, corrugated metal huts left over from WWII and lined up in long rows. The sergeant divided us into two groups and assigned a hut to each group. As we entered the hut, I noticed the number 82 over the door and rows of simple metal frame bunk beds along each side. The sergeant assigned me a bottom bunk, which I wanted because it was easier and faster to get out of. On each bunk sat a rolled-up mattress, sheets, a wool blanket, a pillowcase, a pillow, and a towel. When we were issued our clothes, we also received a small kit with a toothbrush, toothpaste, shaving cream, and a razor. Like the induction letter said, they would give us everything we needed, and right now this was all the Marine Corps thought we needed. I noticed we were not issued a comb, not like we really needed one.

At the foot and head of each set of bunks sat an olive drab wooden box called a footlocker. Inside the box was a tray with divided compartments to organize our uniforms and other gear. We would receive proper instructions on how to pack a footlocker and would stand for inspection on how we did it a thousand times. The box reminded me of my toy box as a kid, but Mom never cared about the order I put the toys away, just that they were all in the box.

Number 82 was my new address and my home for the next two months. I looked around, damn, no place to keep a surfboard. Not funny but I chuckled at the thought.

The drill instructor assigned thirty guys, including Albert, Mike, and me and another guy we met on the bus, Rick Figueroa (Fig), to the same hut. Sergeant Ahchick gave us quick instructions on how to make up our bunks called racks in the Marines. We would learn the proper rack-making technique in the next few days. The sergeant ordered us to make up our racks, use the bathroom (called the head), and then stand at attention at the foot of our racks. When we were all standing at our racks, the sergeant yelled, "Quiet, no talking, hit the rack." He turned out the lights.

Sleep eluded me. Guys were snoring seconds after they hit their racks. I was dead tired, and it was quiet in the barracks, but my mind raced; the events of the day bounced around in my head. What's next? So many new things to learn.

When I was about to doze off, the sound of an airplane engine shook me awake. I realized our barracks were next to the runway for the San Diego airport. Something else we would have to learn to live with.

We did not have to wait long to find out what morning brought. At 0500 hours, the sergeant banged on the bunks and barked orders, yelling for us to get up and, "Move, move, move!" We ran around trying to make our racks, shave, and dress until the sergeant ordered us outside.

Outside, sixty of us stood in four rows in front of the barracks. No yellow footprints to stand on this time, we stood too close together and not in a straight line. Sergeant Ahchick ordered the first man in each row to not move. He then ordered the others to hold their left arm out and touch the right shoulder of the man to his left. After a bit of shuffling to the left, we were all one arm's length apart. This exercise put us in four evenly spaced straight rows—fifteen men in each row. This, we learned, the Marines called "dress right dress" and the first thing we would do when we lined up in formation.

Sergeant Ahchick moved men around by height, short to tall. I was taller than most of the guys, which put me near the end of the line. We looked better when marching in formation that way. Instructions on how to stand at attention and at ease came next. With all of us standing and facing forward at attention, Sergeant Ahchick barked, "Listen up. From this point on, you are Platoon 136. Got it?" he said. We yelled out "Sir! Yes! Sir!" as loud as we could. We were learning fast.

As the platoon stood in our first morning formation, two guys from San Diego spotted their homes on the hillside across from the base. Within the first week, one of them jumped over the fence and went home. The MPs brought him back the next day. He never tried to leave again.

Sergeant Ahchick next ordered, "Right face!" Except for a couple of guys, we all turned to the right. We marched, not very well, over to the mess hall. Sergeant Ahchick ordered us to line up and stand at attention. He said no talking or looking around while we waited to enter the mess hall. Hungry after only two box lunches yesterday, I looked forward to something to eat. Inside the mess hall, I picked up a stamped-out stainless-steel tray with six divided spaces and started down the line. I was not sure how to go through the chow line, as it was not a self-service buffet. I held out my tray and let the chow line guys put food on it. The servers were other recruits on mess duty.

First came scrambled eggs, at least, I think they were eggs, as they were yellow and white. Next some kind of meat, all smashed up in a white sauce and slopped on top of a piece of toasted white bread (the Marines called it "Shit-on-a-Shingle" or SOS, for short). Last along the chow line, oatmeal. I hated oatmeal, even the thought of eating it made me want to puke. Mom always made it for my younger brother, who really liked it, which is why I hated it. Before I could say anything, the chow line guy drops a heaping spoonful of this gooey white stuff on my tray. Unfortunately, I missed the sign at the entry to the mess hall that read, "Take all you want but eat everything you take." I would soon find out what that meant.

I stood by the table at attention with my tray in both hands directly out in front of me. With the table full, the drill instructor stood at one end and ordered, "Sit! Eat!" Eating for the first time at boot camp turned out to be one of the continuing lessons in discipline. Everything we did was a lesson in discipline.

On the table were salt and pepper shakers and two large bottles of ketchup. We learned ketchup went well with about everything the Marine Corps mess hall served, especially the eggs. My wife still gives me the eye when I put ketchup on my eggs.

Not given much time to eat, we learned to eat fast. I finished all the food on my tray except for the oatmeal. From behind me, Sergeant Ahchick yelled, "Do you like oatmeal, Private?"

"Sir. No. Sir," I said.

Wrong answer. He leaned down next to my ear and said, "You have thirty seconds to eat that, Private."

"Sir! Yes! Sir!" I yelled. All the guys at the table, including my new friends Al and Mike, looked right at me, and waited to see what I would do. I put a big spoonful in my mouth, then another. My cheeks began to swell. I could not swallow it. I knew if I puked on the drill instructor, I would be in deep shit and would never live it down. With all the guys watching, I took a big swallow, and somehow managed to keep it down. The guys tried not to laugh. I know they all hoped I would puke. Once I forced the first mouthful down, I finished the oatmeal in the time allotted. Sergeant Ahchick still behind me laughed and said nothing, but I think I was on his shit list after that. I made a mental note to make sure I never let oatmeal land on my tray again.

Our trays all empty, the sergeant yelled, "Attention!" We stood up with our trays in our hands. We lined up and moved to a window to give our trays to the guys on dish washing duty. Out the door, into formation, dress right dress. Now what?

After chow, we marched over to a classroom. Inside we sat at tables facing the front of the room. A chalkboard on the front wall had an address written in white chalk. Sergeant Ahchick introduced us to our junior drill instructor Corporal Tod (not his real name). Recently returning from Vietnam and getting trained as a drill instructor, he turned out to be a real asshole. The power went straight to his head, and he did not know how to manage it. Corporal Tod passed out paper, pencils, and envelopes. He pointed to the address written on the chalkboard and said, "This is your address; you have five minutes to write a letter to your family to let them know." This would be the first of fifty-six letters I wrote to my family over the next two years. Besides letting them know my address, I commented on the food.

The first few days of boot camp, we were issued proper uniforms, endured a more thorough physical exam, and received so many shots in the arm and ass I felt like a pin cushion.

Then the sergeant showed us the proper way to make up our racks and how to pull the sheets and blankets tight all around the mattress. When he finished, the blanket was stretched so tightly around the mattress there were no creases or wrinkles. The sergeant took a dime out of his pocket and held it about a foot above the rack. When dropped, the dime bounced. If the dime did not bounce, you had to make your rack over again. I got really good at making the dime bounce.

Next we received instructions on how to polish our boots and brass. The Marine Corps even wanted us to brush our teeth a certain way, so we received instructions on that—different than what Mom taught me. There was a Marine Corps way to do everything, even how to sing the Marine Corps Hymn.

We each received our military service number, which we memorized. The number differed from our social security number back then. If the DI asked for your service number, you better be able to recite it in an instant or do fifty push-ups. The number is forever registered in my memory; I can recite it in a second even today. I will not say what it is; I use parts of it in my passwords because I know I will never forget the number. I also use the number to play the lottery; so far, no big winners.

We marched in formation everywhere we went on the base. Training to march as a single unit took place daily on a blacktop paved area, called the Grinder, as big as two football fields side by side in the middle of the base. Trouble remembering their left from their right, a couple of guys still turned the wrong way sometimes. They caught all kinds of hell from the sergeant, and each did fifty push-ups. One guy was so bad Sergeant Ahchick put a rock in his right hand and told him when orders were to go right, he should turn to the rock. He did okay after that. Our platoon spent hours on the

Grinder learning to march in formation, first without rifles and then with them. There were other platoons out on the Grinder and eventually we all competed in a marching competition. As bad as we were at marching the night we arrived, by the end of boot camp, our platoon won the battalion boot camp ribbon for the best marching platoon.

Since I was a good swimmer and surfer, I considered myself in good physical condition. I was compared to other guys in the platoon, but not as good as the Marine Corps wanted. An important part of boot camp, when not out on the Grinder marching or in a classroom, was Physical Training (PT) on the conditioning (obstacle) course. We jumped and crawled over and under things, climbed ropes, and went on long runs. We also did pull-ups, sit-ups, squat jumps, and thousands of push-ups. When you screwed up or did not do something as fast as the DI wanted, he ordered you, "Drop and give me fifty." That meant fifty push-ups. I did my share of pushups.

There were guys in the platoon a bit overweight and out of shape, some more than a bit. Not cutting it at physical training, they dragged the entire platoon down on long runs and on the obstacle course. The DI sent them to the "fat farm" to lose weight and increase their physical readiness. After that, those of us in better shape helped the other guys however we could. In a couple of weeks, the platoon's overall physical fitness improved.

In all the training disciplines, the four platoons in our series competed against each other to win a ribbon to fly on the winning platoon's flag staff. Our hard ass DIs pushed us to win the competitions because their previous platoons had won a majority of the ribbons. Our first formal test was a physical fitness test. To pass, each recruit was required to score a minimum of 140 points. I scored 209. Our platoon finished with the highest overall score and won the ribbon. We were off to a good start.

The base Olympic-sized swimming pool was fifty meters long and twenty-four meters wide with black lane lines painted on the bottom. The pool reminded me of my four years on the high school swim team. I competed in the four-hundred-meter freestyle and was number three man on the four-hundred-meter relay. One day, the platoon was at the pool to prove our swim skills. To pass the requirements was no problem for me. We swam two lengths of the pool, floated on our back, and held our breath under water for fifteen seconds. Holding my breath underwater many times while surfing gave me an advantage.

I was surprised how many of the other recruits in my platoon, mostly from Southern California, were not good swimmers. Sergeant Ahchick recognized that I and a couple of other guys were comfortable in the water. He ordered us to help the guys who were not good swimmers until the entire platoon passed the swim requirements.

Helping each other on the obstacle course and teaching the guys to swim better, I realized I had become part of a team. I was no longer the free-spirited surfer dude all on my own. I depended on the other guys in the platoon, and they depended on me. Marching in formation and passing our constant platoon inspections and physical fitness requirements, the platoon improved every day. We all began to understand the need for the discipline our drill instructors pounded into us and recognized that's what it took to make a military unit successful.

I got to know more of the guys and made new friends. Some of the other guys in the platoon came from Southern California and surfed. We talked about surf spots and boards. I talked to a couple of guys busted by the Marines surfing at Trestles. We laughed about that and now here we were in the Marines.

One day after a hard afternoon of PT on the obstacle course, I felt sick and had a fever. Afraid he might send me to sick bay, I did not want to report it to Sergeant Ahchick. If I went to sick bay, they might hold me back and assign me to another training platoon. I did not want to leave my platoon mates or miss any training I might have to take over again. I knew that happened to other guys who reported to sick bay.

After chow, the sergeant ordered us to spend the rest of our time cleaning our rifles and gear and polishing our boots and brass. With help from Al, Mike, and Fig, I managed to make it until lights out. Lying in my bunk, I piled on extra blankets the guys gave me. I soon started to sweat like a stuffed pig, shaking all over and fading in and out of sleep. During the night, the fever broke. By morning, weak and a bit dehydrated, I drank water and ate a big breakfast (no oatmeal) and felt okay. Fortunately, that day we spent most of the time in the classroom. In the afternoon, we found out the platoons were to leave MCRD the next day for Camp Pendleton and rifle range training. I was glad I did not end up in sick bay.

CHAPTER 5
THE RIFLE RANGE

After four weeks in the classroom, marching, PT, and polishing our boots and brass at MCRD in San Diego, I was ready for a change. The platoon moved up the coast to the Camp Hansen rifle range on the Camp Pendleton Marine Base near Oceanside. At Camp Pendleton, I knew we were close to Trestles but there would be no chance for me to surf.

Early in boot camp, we were issued the M-14 rifle. We spent hours in the classroom where we received instructions on how to disassemble, clean, and reassemble the rifle, followed by repeated inspections. I had never fired a weapon in my life. I knew Dad trained to shoot a rifle during WWII, but he never talked about it much. Mom never allowed weapons in our house. A leader in my Boy Scout troop, Dad took me camping, but we never went hunting. I wanted to actually shoot my rifle.

After two days of classroom instruction, the platoon started two days of what the Marines called "snapping in" training. "Snapping in" meant we learned how to use the sling to steady the shot and how to hold the rifle and aim at a target in different shooting positions. I learned a lot, but it was not fun. The sling was wrapped so tightly around my arm I was black and blue from the shoulder to the elbow, and it hurt for days.

After snapping in, each platoon took turns Pulling Butts. Standing in trenches under the targets down range from the shooters, the job required us to staple a target to the holder and raise it up above the trench. The shooter up range fired at the target. We pulled the target down, covered the hole, and put the target back up. We held up a white round marker disc if the shot hit the bullseye or a black disc if the shot hit in the outer rings to indicate where the shot hit the target. The shooter and instructor scored the shot. If a shooter missed the target completely, we waved a red flag, called "Maggie's Drawers." When a red flag came up, everyone on the range knew you missed the target. The instructor would smack you up the back side of the head and later you did fifty or more push-ups. I never got a "Maggie's Drawers."

After we completed the classroom training, "snapping in," and "pulling butts," it was time for prequalification (three days) and final qualification day, which meant we would shoot live ammunition at targets for a score. I looked forward to my turn to shoot, but before we started, we found out one of the guys in our platoon came down with meningitis. Our platoon was quarantined, we stayed away from the other platoons, ate last, and sterilized our utensils. Last on the range every day, we were able to continue our rifle qualifications, and no one else got sick.

I shot left-handed. That put my head on the side of the rifle where the spent cartridge ejected. The first time I fired live ammo and experienced the recoil of the rifle on my shoulder, heard the loud report of the rifle discharge, and felt the hot brass spent cartridge fly by my face, I knew right then I would enjoy shooting.

We were shooting to qualify for one of three badges: Expert, Sharpshooter, or Marksman. Expert was the best. The badge was determined by an overall score from the four shooting positions: standing one hundred yards, kneeling two hundred yards, sitting three hundred yards, and prone five hundred yards. A perfect score of 250 was rarely achieved.

On the three prequalification days, I shot well. On the day before final qualification, I scored Expert. On qualification day, I shot well in standing, kneeling, and prone positions. The sitting position included a couple of additional challenges. In the other three positions, we could take as long as we wanted to aim and fire our rifle. The sitting position included a time limit to complete. In addition to the time limit, we had to change magazines halfway through the ten rounds. My first five shots were in the bullseye. After I changed the magazine, I let my elbow drop a little. The second five shots formed a perfect group but were an inch below the bullseye. I scored one point short of Expert and received a Sharpshooter badge.

The day I fired Expert the instructor talked to me about possibly attending sniper school. Later in Vietnam, I saw what snipers did. Not shooting expert on the day it really counted, may have been a good thing.

With our time at the rifle range completed and the quarantine over, the platoon returned to MCRD to continue preparations for our final tests and competitions prior to graduation. At MCRD, I was assigned as a runner for the day, and the officer in charge of visitors handed me a slip of paper and told me to find a certain Marine. He wanted me to find my friend Doug. Drafted two weeks before me, Doug was now eligible to receive visitors. His mom and dad had come for a visit. I found Doug outside his hut, and we took our time walking back to the visitors' area. He already had orders for Vietnam, where he was assigned to a logistics and supply company. A year later, we would have another chance to see each other in Vietnam. Now many years later, we live only about a mile apart and still see each other for a beer when we can.

A week later, I became eligible to receive visitors. Mom, Dad, Tim, Grandma, and Phyllis came to visit. Mom was glad to see me, and I was happy to see all of them, especially my girlfriend, Phyllis. We had a nice visit; Dad took lots of pictures and I got to smoke a couple of cigarettes. The next weekend, I did not expect to have visitors. I forgot this was the weekend Roger and Jean were getting married. They had wanted me as their best man. Which of course did not happen, but they surprised me when they stopped to visit on Sunday on their way to Ensenada for their honeymoon. Good friends. We enjoyed a nice visit, but I was jealous. I knew Roger would be surfing in Mexico.

As I mentioned earlier, Platoon 136 consisted mostly of Southern California draftees. Known as Hollywood Marines, we caught hell in boot camp. By the end of boot camp, we had developed enormous respect for our two drill instructors: Sergeant Ahchick and Staff Sergeant Quiocho. I credit them for the excellent training we received that helped keep us alive in Vietnam. Their hard-ass training also made it possible for Platoon 136 to win a majority of the competitions. In the end, our platoon of mostly Southern California draftees won Boot Camp Battalion Honor Platoon.

Boot camp lasted nine weeks—normally thirteen weeks but shortened to get us to Vietnam as quickly as possible. After endless days of marching, physical and classroom training, and two weeks on the rifle range, we graduated from boot camp on April 4, 1966. Now we were a bunch of cocky, young Marines ready to take on the world. At least we thought we were.

Before we left boot camp, the Marine Corps assigned us a Military Occupation Specialty Code (MOS). A small number of the guys were assigned to the specialized training but the majority of us received an MOS of 0311, rifleman, grunt Marine, ground pounder.

After boot camp, we returned to Camp Pendleton. There we trained for another forty days. We learned weapon systems and how to work together as fire teams and platoons in combat situations. Not as strict as boot camp, we received weekend liberty, most spent on the beach surfing and drinking beer in Oceanside.

With our training at Camp Pendleton completed, we received a ten-day leave. I was ready to go home. Except for the one visit and boot camp graduation, I had not seen my family or girlfriend in over three months. Of course, surfing was my highest priority on leave.

We got the word that when we returned from leave, we would be assigned to the new battalion the Marine Corps had reactivated at Camp Pendleton. Al, Mike, Fig, and I figured if we all reported in at the same time, we might be assigned together. We agreed to meet at the Camp Pendleton main gate, thirty minutes prior to our assigned time to report. Ten days' leave started the next day. First, we would have to pass morning inspection.

"My Boot Camp M-14 rifle qualification—waiting to shoot."

Taking a break during training at Camp Pendleton.
Al Drotar, Tom Elliott, and Rick Figueroa.

CHAPTER 6
TEN-DAY LEAVE

"Coming down!" I yelled at the guy trying to take off in front of me. He looked over and backed off. I dropped to the bottom of the wave, went around him, climbed back to the top lip, and walked to the nose of my board. The glassy wave peeled off perfectly behind me. Happy to be back in the water, I paddled out for another wave. Saturday morning, Roger had picked me up at 5 a.m. We headed for Ray Bay in Seal Beach. The name, Ray Bay, came from two parallel rock jetties that formed a channel for the cooling water from the upstream power plant. The water was always warm, the sandy bottom home to hundreds of stingrays. Even though I was stung once, I still enjoyed surfing the bay. I surfed until my arms were too tired to paddle back out. Roger and I grabbed a burger, fries, and Coke at the Beach Shack and headed home. I told Roger all about the past three months of training. He told me Jean was pregnant. "That did not take long," I said.

Two days earlier, after we had passed inspection, Albert, Mike, Fig, and I waited in front of the barracks to start our ten-day leave. For the past three months, the United States Marine Corps controlled every aspect of our lives. At boot camp and infantry training, the Marine Corps told us when to get up, when to go to bed, when to eat, where to go, what to do, and how to do it. Everything was the Marine Corps' way. On leave, to surf as much as possible was my top priority. On a wave, I am in control. And I wanted to stay up as late as I wanted, get up when I wanted, eat what and when I wanted, and not say "sir, yes, sir" to anybody (except Dad).

Albert and Mike, a couple of crazy guys, always messing around, never seemed to take anything seriously. Still, I knew I could count on them to always watch my back. Their priority on leave was to stay stoned for ten days. I knew they liked to smoke marijuana, but never saw them stoned while on the base. Most of us were not into smoking marijuana yet, but before we left Vietnam, many of us would try it.

Fig (Rick Figueroa) looked like a cross between an Italian and a Hispanic. A short guy, he made up for it with his never-ending energy. He always tried to be first. I knew, like Al and Mike, I could always count on Fig when needed. He looked forward to his mom's home cooking. We agreed again to meet at the main gate after leave.

A horn honked and looked up. Dad pulled up in front of the barracks. "There's my ride. I'll see you guys next Sunday at 1530 by the main gate check-in," I said. As Dad and I drove off, crazy Albert shouted out, "I hope you get laid!"

Dad came by himself. His boss was a close family friend. He had given Dad the day off to come and pick me up. Mom stayed home; Tim was in school. "You want me to drive, Dad?" Dad did not have trouble driving but with only one eye, he sometimes got tired on long drives. His one eye was burned out a couple of years earlier in an accident where hydrofluoric acid was splashed in his face at the plating shop where he worked. He had a glass eye so no one could tell.

"No, you relax; I'll get you home," he said.

The drive home gave us a chance to compare boot camp training stories and I gave him the rundown on the guys in my platoon. Dad attended boot camp in San Diego also and remembered the base and marching on the Grinder. During WWII, Dad served on board the aircraft carrier *Belleau Wood*. He liked to tell the story about me having a kamikaze pilot to thank for being here. The kamikaze pilot hit his ship right through the flight deck and killed over one hundred men, wounding many more. The ship was so severely damaged, the Navy sent it back to San Francisco for repairs. Mom came out from Ohio, and nine months after the ship sailed back into the war, I came along.

"How is Mom?" I asked Dad.

"She is concerned about you and her concern will probably get worse if you go to Vietnam."

"Dad, I don't think there is an if, only a when. What can I do?"

"Spend as much time with your mother as you can and try not to talk much about Vietnam."

Dad and I made it home in time for dinner. Mom ran out of the house to give me a big hug. She was glad to have me home even for what we knew would be a short ten days. My brother, not far behind, came jumping up and down. He wanted to say hello and tell me I could have my room back while home.

Mom made my second favorite dinner of spaghetti and meatballs. I enjoyed the chance to sit around the dining room table with family. Dinner was served on a plate, not a stainless-steel tray. Dad and Mom always made sure we ate dinner together as a family, no television on. I wanted to know how things were at home and how Tim liked the eighth grade. I tried to steer the conversation in that direction, but Tim kept asking questions about the Marines. Mom sat quietly and listened, simply happy to have me home.

After dinner, I helped clear the table. Tim gave up asking questions. I sat in the kitchen and talked with Mom and Dad as they did the dishes. Dad's job was going well. Since his accident, he worked in the office at the plating shop. They filled me in on events at our church where they were both involved. They both seemed busy and happy, which relieved my worry. I asked if I could have a beer. Mom gave me the look; Dad got me a beer. Mom smiled.

"Just one," she said.

I smiled and said, "Thanks, Dad." Four months until my twenty-first birthday.

Phyllis was in class at nursing school and did not come with Dad to pick me up. She told me to call her at home after 7 p.m. In our little nine-hundred-square-foot house, there was one rotary dial telephone on the wall in the kitchen, a long curly cord hung down to the floor. After I finished my beer, I took the phone into the laundry room, closed the door, and called Phyllis.

I first met Phyllis on the beach in Laguna on spring break. We enjoyed a week of heavy partying and the start of a budding romance. A year later and still together, I worried about what might happen to us if I went to Vietnam. Studying for her registered nurse's license, she knew what she wanted to do in life. I had no idea what I wanted to do after I got out of the Marine Corps, except to surf.

I had seen Phyllis only a couple of times over the past three months. We had lots to talk about and I really wanted to see her. We talked for a while and then decided to go to a movie at the drive-in theater the next night. Next, I called Roger to set up surfing on Saturday.

Friday morning, Dad went to work; Tim went off to school. Mom did not go to her job at the church. She stayed home so we could talk. I knew she was worried about me serving in the Marines. She was upset as the newspapers and television news had started to show graphic pictures from the war along with the daily casualty counts of the killed and wounded soldiers.

I told her about the friends I made in boot camp, how we took care of each other, and that our training would keep us safe. I tried to reassure her everything would be okay. She seemed happier after we talked. She laughed when I told her the story about the drill instructor making me eat the oatmeal.

I borrowed Dad's truck for my date with Phyllis. She lived in Eagle Rock, about a thirty-minute drive from our house. After a short visit with her parents, we headed for the drive-in theater in Pasadena. We parked in the back row. With a camper on the back of Dad's truck, I do not remember much about the movie. After the movie, we went to Bob's Big Boy on Colorado Boulevard for a milkshake and French fries.

After church Sunday morning, Grandma and Grandpa came over for a barbeque. Grandpa, Dad, and I played horseshoes. Grandpa won. Mom and Grandma made a poppy seed roll—my favorite pastry for breakfast.

The rest of the week, I spent time with my family and Phyllis. Roger and I went surfing four more times. After surfing, we went to Roger's house to swim in his pool and drink beer, and a couple of our surfer friends joined us. All of us were under twenty-one but his mom and dad let us drink beer at the house. (His dad was a local cop.) I was the only one in my close circle of friends to get drafted and the guys gave me grief about my high and tight haircut. After drinking too much beer, I jumped off the roof of the house into the pool. If hurt, the Marine Corps would have court-martialed me for the destruction of "government property."

Sitting on my surfboard out in the line-up, the last day I surfed, I realized that surfing was no longer the only thing in my life. The Marine Corps had changed me. Not a loner anymore, I wanted to get back to the base and see what the other guys did on their leave and find out what the Marine Corps had in store for us. They told us when we returned from leave, our training would be nonstop as the new battalion was formed, and we would have little time off. I had no idea what we were about to get into.

The last night of my leave, I picked Phyllis up so she could have dinner with the family. Mom made my favorite meat loaf and mashed potatoes. Grandma and Grandpa were there too. Before they left, I gave them both a big hug. I was glad I did; Grandpa died while I was in Vietnam. I used Dad's truck to drive Phyllis home; I returned late.

Sunday after church, Mom and Dad drove me back to Camp Pendleton. Al, Mike, and Fig were already waiting outside the gate with their sea bags. Al and Mike still looked happy while Fig held both hands over his stomach. His mom had made him all his favorite meals. My big smile gave Al the answer to his earlier question. Our seabags over our shoulders, we walked through the main gate.

Dad and me in August of 1966. I was twenty, Dad forty-one. Dad could still fit into his WWII Marine Corps Uniform. The uniform design had not changed much.

CHAPTER 7
FORMING THE BATTALION AT CAMP PENDLETON

The original 3rd Battalion, 26th Marine Regiment (3/26) was part of the 5th Marine Division during WWII. The battalion was disbanded from the rolls of active Marine Corps divisions on the 5th of March 1946. In response to expanding operations in the Republic of Vietnam (RVN) during the Vietnam War, the Marine Corps reactivated the 3/26 in May of 1966 at Camp Pendleton, California. The battalion consisted of four-line companies: India, Kilo, Lima, and Mike, supported by a heavy weapons company and a headquarters and service (H and S) company.

Once inside the main gate, a bus took us to Camp Las Pulgas, one of the smaller camps within the confines of Camp Pendleton. Our plan to report in at the same time worked. At the camp, the officer in charge assigned Mike, Al, Fig, and me to Lima Company, Second Platoon.

Camp Pendleton is a sprawling Marine Corps base stretching along nineteen miles of coastline between San Clemente and Oceanside and reaching over forty miles inland. There are miles of dusty dirt roads and trails, hills and lowlands covered with heavy brush, and dry creek beds running all through the base. The Marines constructed small villages, specially built for what we might see in Vietnam, to help with training. The battalion would spend the next four months at Las Pulgas while we trained for deployment to Vietnam.

As the officers, noncommissioned officers (NCOs), and troops arrived at Las Pulgas, the battalion established the line companies and training as a combat force began. A majority of the men in the battalion were under twenty years of age, some of the officers not much older. I was twenty and turned twenty-one five days after the battalion left for Vietnam. We were from all parts of the country with diverse backgrounds, levels of education, and ethnicities. As we trained, and later in Vietnam, we discovered that little of this diversity mattered; we all bled the same color red.

The platoon commanders were second lieutenants who came from two sources. One we called Mustangs. Prior to becoming officers, Mustangs were Marine Corps enlisted, noncommissioned officers (NCOs) moving up in rank, men with extensive Marine Corps training and experience. The others we called "Ninety-day Wonders"—college boys who had completed three months of Officer Candidate School (OCS).

The Second Platoon commander, Lieutenant (Lt.). Harry Dolan was a ninety-day wonder. I had hoped to get a more experienced Mustang platoon commander like Lt. Frank McCarthy of the Third Platoon. The two of them became good friends, and though they bickered a lot over whose platoon was the best, they always had one another's back.

Twenty-four years old, Lt. Dolan, the platoon nicknamed him Turk, had graduated from OCS Quantico, Virginia, in December of 1965. He joined the platoon at Camp Pendleton and stayed with the 3/26 during his first tour in Vietnam. He served a second tour in Vietnam and spent twenty-one years in the Marines before retiring as a Major in 1986. He learned fast and turned out as a fine officer. The men of Second Platoon would follow Turk anywhere.

The platoon also included two staff sergeants and three sergeants or corporals as squad leaders. Most had extensive Marine Corps experience; some had already seen action in Vietnam. They helped Lt. Dolan and the other platoon commanders while we trained and in Vietnam. Our platoon sergeant assigned Al, Mike, Fig, and me to different squads in Second Platoon.

A platoon consisted of about forty-four men. The first morning, Staff Sergeant Graham had the platoon form up in front of the barracks. Besides the staff sergeants and squad leaders, the platoon members consisted of privates and private first-class troops who recently completed boot camp and infantry training. The one thing we had going for us was we were all gung ho. The night before, we talked about how we wanted more training. We knew it would not be long before we ended up in Vietnam and wanted to be prepared for it. So far, the war protesters had been unable to undermine our thinking. We wanted to serve our country.

The platoon standing in formation, Lieutenant Dolan introduced himself. He told us we would be training for combat. Right off he did not try to sweet-talk us. He told us we were going to war and there was a good chance not all of us would make it home alive. He told us our best chance to survive would be our training, and we needed to work together as a team. Right after that, we went on a five-mile run. The lieutenant wanted to see what kind of men he had to work with. All our physical training up to that point paid off. We made the run with no problems. Lieutenant Dolan led all the way. I already liked the guy.

To prepare for the hardships we might face in Vietnam, we did physical training (PT) every day, including push-ups, sit-ups, squat jumps, rope climbing, and running up and down the hills around the base. We went on forced marches, ten miles in full combat gear. On one of the forced marches, the platoon took a break on a hilltop close to the beach. I could barely make out the surf break at Trestles. Hot, sweaty, and thirsty from the march, I wished I was out in the cool water, catching a wave. My daydream ended when the platoon sergeant yelled, "Saddle up! We're moving out!" By the time we left for Vietnam, I was in the best shape of my life, at six feet one inch tall, I weighed 207 pounds. When I returned home, I weighed 185. Vietnam had a way of sucking the life out of you.

When not doing PT, we spent our time training for combat. We learned to work together as fire teams, squads, platoons, and as a full company. We trained six days a week, including night operations. One day a week, if we were lucky, we drank beer around a fire on the beach in Oceanside. I surfed whenever possible.

Al, Mike, Fig, and I made more friends during training and on our time at the beach. One guy, Pat Cochran, and I became good friends. Not a California boy, he was from Del Rio, Texas, and he talked with a slight drawl. Built like a brick shithouse, he really liked playing football as a semi-pro before joining the Marines. We talked mostly about football. He was one of the few guys in the platoon bigger than I was, and if something heavy needed moving, the lieutenant called on the two of us. An easy-going guy, Pat got along well with everyone. Sometimes Phyllis joined us around the fire on the beach. Before we left for Vietnam, she made Pat and me promise to always watch out for one another. We told her not to worry; we would always have each other's back.

During combat training, we learned tactics: how to patrol and not bunch up, how to set up and execute an ambush, and how to react if we were ambushed. We learned how to identify booby traps and how to disarm them. The instructors showed us what a booby trap, called a punji pit, looked like and how to fall forward if we stepped in one. The pit is a hole in the ground about two feet square and two feet deep with several sharpened bamboo or metal stakes at the bottom. A camouflaged lid hid the trap. If stepped on, the lid would give way, allowing your foot to land on the stakes and penetrate your boot, sticking you in the foot or leg. The VC shit on the stakes, increasing the chances of infection. We would encounter many punji pit and other type booby traps in Vietnam.

We learned hand signals: move forward, stop, get down, spread out, enemy sighted, trip wire, booby trap. All so we could remain quiet on patrol and in a fire fight and the lieutenant would not need to shout orders over the chaos. We trained over and over until we learned to react without thinking, no matter the combat situation.

In the mocked up Vietnamese villages, we learned to look for tunnels and booby traps. We learned that, unlike WWII movies where a Marine runs up to a doorway or window and throws a hand grenade inside and then uses the wall for protection, you cannot do that when the buildings are made out of bamboo and straw.

We learned how to construct defensive positions, dig fighting holes, fill sandbags, and build bunkers for our protection. We attended classroom training on known enemy tactics, what weapons were available to them, and how they might use them against us. We attended classes on how to deal with the local people we might encounter.

We spent time on the range throwing hand grenades and learned how to set up claymore mines. During rifle training, we learned how to shoot short bursts, not on fully automatic, to conserve ammo. We did crossover training to learn the basics of the M-60 machine gun, mortars, and rocket launchers so we could take over these weapons if needed in a fire fight.

We participated in mock fire fights with other units dressed like Viet Cong and firing blanks with AK-47s (the weapon most of the enemy might carry). We fired blanks from our M-14 rifles. This allowed us to experience what it might be like in a real fire fight. The first time we took part in this type of exercise, the deafening sound of all the shooting confused us, resulting in a great deal of chaos. We did not do very well. But we learned from the experience and improved until we became more confident in our ability to react properly. We learned how we reacted as individuals, what each other's strong and weak points were, and how we needed to trust one another. We needed to know how to react instantly as a team when the shit hit the fan.

While we trained at Camp Pendleton, I received specialized training on how to fire and take care of an M-79. The M-79 is a single shot, shoulder fired grenade launcher that fires a 40-mm round. As a result of this training, the platoon sergeant assigned me to carry the M-79 and spare rounds.

However, sometime before deploying to Vietnam, the platoon commander relieved me as the M-79 man and reassigned me as the platoon radio operator. For whatever reason, memory escapes me or I never knew, but somewhere along the line, one of the platoon radio operators left the platoon. One day, Lieutenant Dolan handed me the radio and said, "Elliott, I want you as the platoon radio operator."

I had no training; I did not even know how to change the battery. Now I was the platoon commander's radio operator. The other platoon radio operator assigned to First Sergeant Graham gave me a crash course on the radio and I picked it up from there.

One can never know how fate can change one's life. Being the radio operator put me in a number of tight spots. The radio operator is number two on the enemy hit list, right behind the officer. Life expectancy in a fire fight is five to seven seconds. The antenna sticking up made me a perfect target. I also carried twenty-two more pounds of gear than the other guys. I will never know if I had remained the M-79 man, how the outcome of my tour in Vietnam might have differed. As it turned out, the lieutenant and I became good friends and always watched each other's back.

From May through the end of August, we trained. Mid-August we had a chance to put all our training to the test. The entire battalion and support personnel, over two thousand Marines, and five thousand Navy personnel on six ships, took part in an exercise called "Operation Silver Point." We made an amphibious landing across White Beach on Camp Pendleton and fought our way into the village of Chu Loi, set up to resemble a Vietnamese hamlet. Over the four-day operation, we made effective use of our training and learned even more. All the brass were happy with our performance and called the training exercise a success. Vietnam, however, would turn out quite differently.

Our training complete, we were now a fighting unit. We were ready, or at least we thought we were, for Vietnam. How wrong we were. Soon all our training would be put to the test, and we would be thrust into manhood and witness events that would test our resolve. We would lose close friends and endure hardships beyond our imagination. Without the outstanding training pounded into us by the United States Marine Corps more of us would not have survived Vietnam.

On the first day of September, we attended a class about Vietnam. We knew it was not long before our deployment. In fact, we were itching to go. We were tired of training and wanted to get into the action, be part of the fight, and make a name for ourselves. We had no idea what we were about to get into.

Two days later, the battalion left San Diego aboard a ship bound for Vietnam. We would endure three more months of combat training in Okinawa and the Philippines before getting our chance to join the fight in Vietnam.

Harry C Dolan (Turk), Second Lieutenant
Second Platoon Commander
The Marines of Second Platoon would follow Turk anywhere.
Photograph Courtesy of Jaak Aulik.

The original Lima Company, Second Platoon 3/26
Taken during training in Okinawa, 1966
By Blackie the Photographer

Front Row: Cpl. Sammie Wynn, Sgt. Kelly Webb, S/Sgt. Thomas Magulick, SLT Harry Dolan (Turk), S/Sgt. Jerry Graham, Sgt. Charles Pratt, Sgt. Jim Strange.

Second Row: "Doc" Graham Tedford, Gary Schneider (KIA), James Helton, Kenneth Saterfiel, William Hartig, "Doc" Michael Tassone.

Third Row: Gregory Bryant, Tom Carey, Robert Wordlaw, Keith (Tbag) TeeGardin, Earnest Hoffman, Gary Toler, Raymond Potter (KIA), Rick Figueroa (Fig).

Fourth Row: Sam Williams, Timothy Sargent, George McDonald, Mike O'Grady, Allen (Al) Drotar, Woodrow (Woody) Allen, Howard Lewis, Unknown, Rolf Richvoldse.

Fifth Row: Thomas Ellison, J. C. McLean, Tom Elliott, Diego Morbioli, Dennis Stecki, Jim Mulhall, Frederick Smith, Sharon Huff.

Last Row: Harry Moore, James (Jim) Cooper, Milton Raschen, Charles Johnson, James Green, Thomas Willey, Dewey Ballinger, Patrick Cochran (KIA).

Not in the Picture: Ronald Black (KIA), Ferrell Hummingbird (KIA).

CHAPTER 8
TRANSIT TO OKINAWA

Towering over us, she looked five hundred feet long. In the late afternoon sun, the ship cast a shadow across the dock where we stood waiting to go aboard. I looked up at the name: USS *Lenawee* (APA) 195. A typical WWII Haskell-class attack transport, the *Lenawee* was one of the oldest troop carriers still in use by the US Navy. She looked old and a bit worn, rust streaks running down her sides. Painted Navy gray, the *Lenawee* was a proud ship with many battle ribbons for her years of service in WWII, Korea, and now Vietnam.

Sailors stood at their duty stations on deck. An officer in dress uniform, maybe the captain, stood on the flying bridge observing the line of Marines in full combat gear, seabags over their shoulders, boarding the ship via the gangway. On the dock, wives and children were saying goodbye to the sailors and naval officers.

On September 3rd, 1966, and five days before my twenty-first birthday, the 3rd Battalion 26th Marines boarded the *Lenawee* at the San Diego Naval Base, for transit to Vietnam via Hawaii, Okinawa, and the Philippines. This would be the last transit the ship would make to Vietnam. Thank God she was a sturdy ship. We did not know it yet, but we were embarking on what turned out to be a wild ride.

We sailed on a Sunday morning at 1000 hrs. A couple of guys were seasick before we left the harbor. By the end of the trip, all of us would experience seasickness.

The Second Platoon was assigned to a berthing compartment near the stern, better than near the bow in rough weather (which we would experience a lot of). Stacked five or six high, the bunks were made of canvas and metal frames: no mattresses, one wool blanket, no sheets. We used our life jackets for pillows. I took a lower bunk that was easy to climb into. With my head next to the bulkhead, no one's feet would be close to my face.

The first night at sea and lying in my bunk, I looked up and noticed drawings on the bottom of the canvas bunk above me. Faded over time, there were scribbled cartoons and other stick figures, random doodling, and a heart with Bob loves Mary written inside. The drawings put there by guys lying in this very spot on their way to someplace during WWII or Korea. Did Bob make it home to Mary? On the trip, I left my own scribblings on the canvas bunk above me. I drew waves and a surfboard and Tom loves Phyllis inside a heart.

With all our gear spread out in the dark, smelly, and cramp compartment, we spent most of our time topside. For us Marines, it was our first time onboard a ship. The first few days we spent trying to find our way around. With the entire battalion of close to 1,200 men, and a full complement of sailors on board, we spent much of our time in line waiting for chow.

Clear skies, warm, calm winds, and a flat sea made the cruise to Hawaii smooth. In Hawaii, the ship moored in Pearl Harbor. The battalion received two days of liberty in Honolulu. After eight days at sea, we were ready to get off the ship to hit the beaches and bars. You only had to be twenty years old to drink in Hawaii. That bummed me out. I turned twenty-one a couple of days after we left San Diego, and no one asked me for my ID. The need to be twenty years old to drink did not make sense to us. Why send eighteen- and nineteen-year-olds to war in Vietnam but not allow them to drink beer on the beach? What a bunch of BS!

Al, Mike, Fig, Pat, and I rented a room in the Edgewater Hotel on the beach next to Fort DeRussy. The room gave us a place for some of the other younger guys to drink beer and use the pool and for us to meet if we got separated. The guys went off to buy beer. Because we were military, beer at the Fort DeRussy exchange cost less than in town or at the bars.

I went straight to Waikiki Beach. I had no idea when we left San Diego if I might have a chance to surf or go swimming but, just in case, I brought along a swimsuit. Near the beach, I found a surfboard rental place. About thirty surfboards were in a rack on the beach. A nice-looking, tanned young blond girl in a tiny bikini told me to pick out a board. I looked over the boards and picked out a 9/6. The beach boy carried it down to the water for me. I paddled out into some nice two-to-three-foot waves that rolled in over the many reef breaks. The sand and colorful coral bottom beneath me, visible through the warm and clear water. I paddled out beyond the surf and sat on the surfboard, enjoying the view of the beach and Diamond Head. Someday I will be back here, I thought. I stayed out surfing until I was too tired to paddle. I surfed one last wave near the beach and managed to paddle the short distance to the shore. The beach boy met me at the water's edge and carried the board back to the rack. Used to carrying my own surfboard, I enjoyed the service.

Later, after drinking too many beers, we ended up on Hotel Street, the red-light district where they told us not to go. Of course, telling us not to go meant we had to go check it out. A couple of the younger guys were not familiar with a red-light district, but it did not take long for them to figure it out. We checked out a couple of bars and the "merchandise" available but few of us indulged in the pleasures offered; we would experience that in the Philippines. We went back to our room at the hotel, finished the beer, and enjoyed the view from our sixth-floor room. We put in a wake-up call for five a.m. so we could get back to the ship to check in by six a.m.

When everyone was accounted for, liberty call started again at nine a.m. The second day we had Cinderella liberty; we needed to be back aboard ship by midnight. I went straight back to Waikiki Beach to rent a board. I knew it might be a long time before I would have a chance to go surfing again, if ever.

We went sightseeing on the open-top bus, walked all around the town, and the guys started drinking beer again in the afternoon. I went out for another surf session. Later, and after more beers, we ended up in a tattoo parlor. Albert got the Marine Corps Emblem (Eagle, Globe, and Anchor) tattooed on his forearm. We made it back to the ship minutes before the midnight deadline. In the morning, Albert was face down in his bunk with his arm hanging out. From under the bandage over the tattoo, the blood and colors ran down his arm and dripped off his fingertips onto the deck. That cured me from getting a tattoo.

From Hawaii to Okinawa, we escorted another ship, the U.S.S. *Belle Grove.* An LSD, (Landing Ship Dock) she carried equipment and supplies for the battalion. Mechanical problems kept her from traveling at full speed, a fact that would cost us.

During the day, we attended training classes up on deck. We took target practice shooting our rifles off the fantail at trash thrown overboard (pre-environmental times). To help pass the time, the usual poker or acey-deucy game was always available somewhere on deck. Like me, most of the guys were novice poker players, a fact taken advantage of by one of the older Marines who ran the game. I lost money, but I learned a lot about playing poker.

We did physical training to stay in shape. A boxing match and a talent show with some good guitar players and singers helped to pass the time. We crossed the International Date Line and lost September 15th forever. That would be one day less we would spend in Vietnam.

During the day, the propellers churned up a white wake on the deep blue ocean as the ship slipped quietly through the calm water. I sat on the stern watching. I wanted to jump in with a surfboard and ride the wake.

At night, the sky was like I had never seen before. In the Boy Scouts, I had learned to find the Big and Little Dipper and the North star. Lying on the deck, I stared up at the stars. Pitch black, the sky dotted with a billion tiny white specks, I had trouble finding anything I recognized. The night sky, so clear and beautiful, seemed peaceful. Too bad it did not stay that way.

The next day when the winds blew, the seas started to build. At first, it was fun to watch the waves smash into the side of the ship and throw white and blue spray up in the air. Soon the ship started to rock and roll beyond the fun part. Orders came for us to return to our berthing compartments. Then the ship stopped making headway, and we really started to rock. A sailor who passed through our compartment told us the ship lost part of the steering gear. That's bad, I thought. Then the sound of the engines revving up and the ship began to make headway again. The sailors must have fixed the problem. Underway again did little to reduce the rock and roll of the ship.

The seas continued to build. Late in the afternoon the ship ran smack into "Typhoon Ida," a Category 3 typhoon with sustained winds over 115 knots. We were only a day away from safety in the port at Okinawa: now it looked like we might not make it. Had we not been escorting the *Belle Grove;* we would have outrun the storm.

"Can this get any worse?" I asked Albert. An alarm went off, then over the PA system we heard, "Fire, fire amid ship's lower deck." Oh, shit it just got worse.

"That's below us," Mike said.

"Isn't the ammo locker below us?" Albert asked. Over the PA system again, "Marines, don your life jackets; prepare to abandon ship." Now it can't get any worse. We scrambled around the compartment trying to get our life jackets on. The loudspeaker sounded off again. "Fire under control. Marines, remain in your compartments." I left my life jacket on.

The ship rocked so much our gear started to slide all over the deck. To keep the ship from pitching me out of my bunk, I tied myself in. Most of the guys were seasick, the deck covered with barf. Too rough to go to the galley to eat. The air conditioning had been off for eleven hours. The temperature in the compartments was over hundred degrees. Only the emergency lights were on, which gave everything a red glow. NCOs stood at the exits with loaded 45s to keep us from trying to get outside.

I lay in my bunk and stared at the drawing I had made of the surfboard and heart with my name and Phyllis. What a bitch it would be to die before I even landed in Vietnam. Will Vietnam be any worse than this? (It would be). I leaned over the side of my bunk and added to the barf on the deck; glad no one above me barfed at the same time. Al was in the bunk across from me, Mike one above him. Albert said, "Man, if only we had some weed, this would be a lot easier to take if loaded." For once I agreed with him.

We learned later the sailors trying to steer the ship lasted about fifteen minutes before needing relief. A number of sailors were injured fighting the fire and doing other things to keep the ship afloat. The sailors did an excellent job to keep the ship from sinking. Later we thanked them for saving us.

During the night, the storm quieted down, and the rocking eased. In the morning, they allowed us back on deck. What an amazing sight: all the landing craft and lifeboats were gone, and the davits twisted up like pretzels. Sailors told us the ship took a wave over the bridge twice. We narrowly missed colliding with the *Belle Grove.* We were lucky to make it through the storm. We learned a couple of days later that the storm was the worst typhoon to hit the area since 1945. In Japan, it caused extensive damage and killed 275 people.

Worn out from the storm, we were happy when the ships arrived in Okinawa. The ships anchored in the harbor, and we disembarked, glad to have our feet on solid ground again. Billeted at Camp Hansen in real barracks with bunks and mattresses, I looked forward to a good night's sleep. We had liberty and went to town for a couple of beers, but we were tired and wanted to rest. We went back to the barracks early and hit the rack.

The Northern Training Area of Okinawa included terrain similar to Vietnam. We spent our days there learning a good lesson about operating in hot humid weather with millions of mosquitoes—our only enemy. The training was meant to give us an idea of what Vietnam might be like. Vietnam would be much worse.

In preparation for leaving Okinawa, we turned in our personal belongings and dress uniforms. We would not need them where we were going. When our time in Vietnam ended, if we survived, we would go through Okinawa to pick them up. We kept our khaki uniforms to use on liberty and R&R.

After a couple of weeks of training in Okinawa, we boarded ship again and sailed for the Philippines. There, we were in for more training and would experience some outrageous liberty in Olongapo City.

U.S.S. *Lenawee* (APA 195)
Transported the battalion to Vietnam
Built in 1944
Length: 455ft. Beam: 62ft. Top Speed: 19 kts.
Navy Complement: Fifty-six Officers, 480 Enlisted
Troop Accommodations: Eighty-six Officers, 1,475 Enlisted
Cargo Capacity: 150,000 cu. ft., 2,900 tons
Landing craft: two LCM, twelve LCVP, three LCPU
Picture from Wikipedia.

Second Platoon berthing compartment aboard the *Lenawee*.
Jim Cooper in his bunk, Rick Figueroa at the back of the compartment.
Photograph Courtesy of Tom Willey.

CHAPTER 9
THE PHILIPPINES

With the *Lenawee* still under repair in the shipyard after Typhoon Ida, the battalion left Okinawa for the Philippines on October 5th, on board the U.S.S. *Henrico.* The *Henrico* was even older than the *Lenawee*, and the battalion again crammed in berthing compartments throughout the ship. At least this time, it would be a short ride and no storm to contend with.

The ship arrived at Subic Bay in the Philippines. Subic Bay was a huge Naval port; other ships sat anchored out in the bay or moored alongside one of the many docks. The *Henrico* anchored out in the bay. We wanted to go ashore but there was no liberty and we had to stay on board ship.

The next day, the ship left Subic Bay for a training exercise called Operation Hill Top on the island of Mindoro. The ship anchored offshore, and helicopters lifted Lima company to another part of the island where we started to work our way inland. The temperature was ungodly hot; there was no real trail and we had to hack our way through the jungle. We worked our way through the jungle and up a ridgeline high above the jungle near the center of the island. The view over the lush green jungle to the ocean beyond was fantastic.

Then we found ourselves in an area of volcanic rock sharp enough to cut our boots. With no place to stop and sit down for a break, we had to keep moving. On the ridgeline, there was no protection from the sun; we were soaking wet from our own sweat and our drinking water supply ran short. We also saw people in loincloths with spears who were rumored to be headhunters who ate people. Only the officers carried live ammo for their pistols.

With darkness closing in on us, we came to an area with a few small clearings between the volcanic rocks. The captain decided to stop for the night. The clearings were too small for all of us to use our air mattresses to lie down. We buddied up and sat back-to-back, leaning against each other. We set up a watch rotation on the only two approaches to our position and tried to sleep sitting upright.

None of the clearings were large enough to land a helicopter. In the morning, a helicopter hovered over our position and used ropes to drop water cans to us. The helicopter flew ahead of us to mark a path with smoke grenades to guide us down the hill off the ridgeline. By the time we got back to the beach, it was late afternoon and the exercise ended.

Back onboard ship, we returned to Subic Bay. We stayed aboard the ship for a couple of days but got liberty. Because a Marine and a sailor were stabbed in a fight while on liberty in Olongapo City the night before we returned, liberty in the area outside the base was denied to all military personnel. The three liberty clubs on the base were our only option to drink beer. The club for the Marine and Navy enlisted men was called the Sky Club. The club offered lots of beer and local girls we could dance and talk with.

After two nights of drunken brawls between the Marine and Navy personnel at the clubs on the base, the base commander decided to open Olongapo for liberty. Al, Mike, Fig, and I decided to go to town and check it out. Before we were released on liberty, they warned us to not go to Olongapo alone and to stay in groups. We quickly learned why. Olongapo made Tijuana look like paradise. The city housed mostly bars and whore houses with tattoo parlors in between. The city's main reason for existence was to separate the Marines and sailors from their money with easy, unlimited access to alcohol and sex. The locals were exceptionally good at it. Many of the guys left the town broke but smiling. After the first night, I only went back to town a couple of times. I preferred to stay on the base and drink beer at the enlisted men's club. At least that is what I wrote home and told my girlfriend.

One thing about Olongapo ladies of the night was, once you went with one, you were not supposed to go with another girl. They called it butterflying. We knew, for their protection, the girls carried what they called a butterfly knife. The knife consisted of a blade between two handles. When swung in a figure eight fashion, the knife opened as fast as a switch blade, and the girls were good at it. They liked to get their knives out and swing them around to let us know if we butterflied on them, they would cut our dicks off. Most of guys did not take a chance and stuck with one girl. There was no requirement for a girl to stick with one guy.

One night in town, after drinking beer for a while, a few of us (no names here for the protection of the guilty) wandered off the main streets into a back alley (off limits), looking for a good time. One of the guys started talking to a girl in the alley. She asked him if he wanted a short time or a long time. "Short time," he said. They made a deal and went inside. No sooner had he gone inside with the girl, Shore Patrol (One Marine, and one Navy) approached us.

"What are you assholes doing back here; you're off limits," one said.

"Just looking for a good time," we said.

"You won't find it back here. Is there anyone else with you?"

"Our friend just went inside," we said and pointed to the door.

The Marine SP bolted through the door. He came back out holding our friend by his collar while our friend was holding his pants up.

"Get back out on the main street, you idiots; you're lucky we came along. That was not a girl; he's a Benny Boy. (A guy dressed like a girl.) They beat you up and take your money. Now get the fuck out of here before we throw you in the brig for being off limits."

We did not go back to the main street; we went back to the Sky Club on the base and never ventured off limits again.

The next day, the battalion left Subic Bay on a four-day training exercise called Operation Mud Puppy, also on the island of Mindoro. This time we landed on a part of the island that was nothing but rivers, rice paddies, and mangrove swamps. On top of that, it rained most of the time we were on the exercise. I guess that's why they called it Operation Mud Puppy.

For three days, we slouched through the mud, waded across rivers, and walked on the rice paddy dikes and hacked our way through the mangroves learning how to move as a unit in such difficult terrain. At night, we set up ambush sites and endured thousands of mosquitoes. We found out later that the training was for a special assignment where the battalion would land at the mouth of the Mekong River in similar terrain. We would move up the riverbanks to clear out Viet Cong units, who were using the area to attack our ships and boats running on the river. That operation never happened.

With the exercise over, we waited on the beach for boats to take us back to the ship. We looked like hell, covered from head to toe with mud and blood from the mosquito bites. All our equipment was covered in mud. Local kids came out of the bushes selling Coca-Cola (warm, no ice). We did not have much money with us, so we traded our leftover C-Rations and other items we did not think the Marine Corps needed for the Coke. Some older local guys started showing up with beer and locally made rum (real rot gut), and we started trading for that as well and making rum and Coke.

Twenty-five years old, Ray Potter was older than most of the guys in the platoon, and we affectionately called him Dad. He had been in the Marine Corps Reserves but had missed too many of the required meetings; for that, the Marine Corps made him go on active duty. A corporal, he led one of the fire teams in the first squad. The three other fire team members were crazy Al Drotar, Jim Cooper from Tennessee with a heavy hillbilly drawl (his nickname was Ridge-Runner), and Tom Willey (nicknamed Williby). Of Slovak descent, Ray preferred the name Peter Potoshnick and called his fire team Potoshnick's Raiders. I think Potoshnick was the real family name shortened to Potter. None of us, especially Ferrell Hummingbird (one of two full-blooded native Americans in our platoon), could pronounce Potoshnick. Every time we tried, Ray corrected us, and we gave him the finger.

Albert did not really like the name Potoshnick's Raiders and preferred to call the fire team "The Filthy Few." Considering our filthy condition from the exercise, Albert said, "Today we are all The Filthy Few." Hearing what Al said, Ray suggested The Filthy Few might be a good name for the entire platoon. We all agreed, and from then on, the Second Platoon became known as The Filthy Few, and we went on to live up to the name.

Sadly, having missed too many of his reserve meetings and then going on active duty cost Ray Potter his life. He was killed in Vietnam on September 10, 1967.

The Filthy Few Flag

With not much to do on board ship and bored a lot of the time, Al, Mike, and I liked to sneak around the ship, trying not to get caught. On one of our sneak-and-peek patrols aboard the *Henrico*, we ended up in the signal flag locker compartment. The flags were rolled up and stuck in little cubby holes. "Let's take a flag for the platoon," I said and grabbed one. I unrolled it and stuffed it down my pant leg and we got out of there. Back in our compartment, I opened the flag to find a gold background with a blue X. We found out later when flown on the ship it meant the combat cargo officer was not on board.

Months later while the company rested in Phu Bai, Mike used a black marker to letter The Filthy Few on the flag and hung it in our hooch. When we left Vietnam, I brought the flag home with me. I took it to all the platoon reunions I attended, and it hangs proudly at my home today. In addition to the flag, Rick Figueroa produced some great Filthy Few artwork.

A born leader, Ronald Black was a well-liked and respected member of The Filthy Few who always looked out for his fellow Marines. He left the platoon when transferred to a CAP unit outside Phu Bai. He was killed in action on September 11, 1967, two weeks before his tour was up.

In 2003, while searching online for platoon members, Tom Willey found Michael Adams, Ron Black's brother-in-law. After hearing stories about The Filthy Few flag, Michael asked for a photograph of the flag. In 2004, Michael attended the 3/26 reunion in Lake Tahoe. He wanted to meet some of Ron's platoon mates. To our surprise, he presented the platoon with his version of our flag: stained glass with acid-etched wording and emblems. A tribute to Sgt. Ronald Black and The Filthy Few. Tom Willey has that piece of artwork in his home.

The Filthy Few Flag
Mike O'Grady in Vietnam

The finished flag displayed at the 2003 Platoon Reunion at Doc Miller's Cabin.

Stained-glass model of The Filthy Few Flag
A gift from Michael Adams, Ron Black's brother-in-law
Ron was killed on September 11, 1967.

The Filthy Few in Phu Bai.
Kneeling: Jack Saterfiel, Tim Sargent, Ron Black, Jim Cooper
Standing: Doc Bill Miller, Greg Bryant, Tom Willey, Doc Cutright, Rick Figueroa
Artwork by Rick Figueroa
Photograph Courtesy of Tom Willey.

CHAPTER 10
FIRST TIME TO VIETNAM

Back in the Philippines, the battalion received orders to prepare to leave for Vietnam in three days as a reactionary force. The next day, the battalion threw a big beer bust out on Grande Island in the middle of Subic Bay. Landing craft boats picked up troops from all the ships and transported them to the island. We were one of the last platoons picked up and when we arrived, someone yelled out, "They are almost out of beer." This caused a near panic. We all grabbed a few cans of beers, took over a nearby table, and started pounding the brews.

The gunny came over to our table and said, "Elliott, Drotar, O'Grady, Figueroa, Cochran, come with me, on a work detail."

"Ah gunny, the beer is almost gone; we wanted to get our ration."

"Follow me," the gunny said.

Like good Marines, we did as ordered. The gunny marched us over to a walk-in cooler behind a building about fifty meters from the party area. He opened the door, pointed inside, and said, "There are forty cases of beer in there; take them to the beer area." Not all of it made it back to the beer area. We got our ration of beer, then went swimming in the warm water and played volleyball on the beach. With the island located inside the harbor, there was no surf. For a brief time, we forgot about the fact that the next day we were leaving for Vietnam.

The next morning, we left for Vietnam still aboard the U.S.S. *Henrico.* We were a reactionary force on standby to support other Marine units if they got into trouble during the expected pre-monsoon season push by the Viet Cong (VC) and North Vietnam Army (NVA) troops in the area near the Demilitarized Zone (DMZ). When we arrived in South Vietnam the *Henrico* anchored in the Da Nang Harbor. The battalion transferred to the aircraft carrier U.S.S. *Valley Forge.* The ship carried helicopters, not fixed wing aircraft.

The entire battalion (except the officers) was assigned to the hangar deck of the *Valley Forge.* We were issued new air mattresses, so we did not have to sleep on the hard deck. The ship left Da Nang and sailed up and down the coast south of the DMZ.

With a full complement of officers and sailors plus our Marine battalion on board (over 4,000 men), we spent a lot of our time standing in line waiting to eat. To stay busy at night as usual, Al, Mike and I sneaked around the ship to places we were not supposed to go, including the flight deck during darkened ship. During one of our patrols around the ship, Mike and I found a way to go down two decks, travel through the sailor compartments, and come up at the head of the chow line. We did not stand in line for chow after that.

While on board ship it was payday, I received $118 (one month's pay), which included $65 in combat pay because the ship sailed in Vietnam waters. Wow! Simply for being in this tropical paradise with a high probability of dying, I earned a whole extra $65. I took $18 in cash and left the rest on the books, hoping to use it for R&R.

After a week on the *Valley Forge,* we transferred again now to the LPD-2 *Vancouver.* The *Vancouver* was a helicopter carrier and only three years old—mattresses on the bunks, music piped into each compartment, air-conditioning, and good chow. The ship was much better than the *Valley Forge* and like heaven compared to the *Lenawee* and the *Henrico.* We were on board the *Vancouver* on November 10, the Marine Corps 191st birthday. The battalion celebrated on the flight deck with speeches and cake cutting. Sticking to an age-old corps custom, the oldest and youngest Marine on board cut the cake. The youngest Marine was eighteen but looked fifteen. According to the rules, eighteen was the minimum age to fight in Vietnam. Eighteen years old, yet can't vote, can't drink, but can go to die in war. Go figure.

After a week on the *Vancouver*, the expected big VC push did not happen. No longer needed in Vietnam, the ship returned to Subic Bay in the Philippines. The first few nights, we stayed on the ship. When we disembarked, the company was billeted at Cubi Point, living in Quonset-type huts, sleeping on air mattresses on the cold concrete floor. The battalion was now a "Special Landing Force," on standby to return to Vietnam at any time.

Returning to the Philippines, we continued daily training around the base. Most of the time, it rained, making our time on maneuvers miserable. One of the few days with no rain, we went by landing craft for target practice at a rifle range near Red Beach on an island out in the bay. As we approached the shore, the bow door of the landing craft was lowered and the sailor standing on the door jumped off to run ashore with a line. The water was so clear he misjudged the depth. The water was over his head, and we passed right by him until the bow door slid up on the beach. The sailor was splashing around yelling for help. Lt. Dolan told me (the platoon surfer dude) to swim out and get him. I only had time to take off my flak jacket and shirt before I went in the water.

On my high school swim team, I learned how to approach a distressed person in the water. As I got close to the guy, he was really flailing around. I dove down, grabbed his legs spun him around, and came up behind him. Once he realized what was happening, he relaxed and let me control the situation.

I started swimming the side stroke back to the beach when for the first time I realized I still had my boots on. Swimming for the both of us became a challenge. Another Marine came out with a life preserver ring. We threw the distressed sailor onto the ring and towed him to the beach. Lt. Dolan put me up for the Navy and Marine Corps medal for saving the sailor, but the paperwork never went anywhere. His report did help my promotion to lance corporal a couple of weeks later.

Early in December, the battalion received orders to return to Vietnam via ship. This time for real. We were going to land in country, no more delays. After months of training, it would not be long before we got our chance to join the fight. After one more night of liberty in Olongapo.

Sky Club in the Philippines – Girls and Beer
Sitting: Saterfiel, Toler, Drotar, Strange,
Hilton, Hoffman, Schneider, O'Grady
Standing: Figueroa, Mulhull, Raschen, Elliott, Woody, Cochran, Carey

Red Beach Philippines, after I saved the sailor.
SSgt. Graham, Woody Allen, Jim Green, Tom Elliott,
Al Drotar, Jack Saterfiel, Greg Bryant

CHAPTER 11
WELCOME TO VIETNAM, TOM

Albert was coming down the stairs, his Filipino girl standing at the top of the staircase laughing. She pointed at Al and yelled to us, "Boy-son crazy, boy-son crazy." The last night before leaving for Vietnam, we all went to town. My head spinning from all the beer, we said goodbye to the girls and stumbled out of the bar and back to the base before the midnight deadline. On our last night of liberty in Olongapo, the girls in the bars knew we were leaving for Vietnam the next day and wanted to show us a good time, which they did. For real this time, no more standby force; we were going to land in country. We partied like it was our last hurrah. For some it would be.

In the morning, hung over, we packed our gear. By afternoon, the entire battalion, 1,100+ officers and enlisted, were back on board the *Lenawee*, the ship refitted after the typhoon. We left Subic Bay early the next morning.

A couple of days earlier, we turned in our ID cards and received Geneva Convention cards, like they would do us any good. We received gamma globulin shots—some kind of stuff to thicken our blood and help stop the bleeding if wounded. The dosage was according to your weight; the shot given in the butt cheek hurt like hell. I swear they used a square needle.

Before leaving the Philippines, a new company commander took over Lima Company. Captain Hines, our captain through training, had been promoted to a battalion staff position. Captain Hines had been a good officer; the troops, and the other officers in the company trusted and looked up to him. We were not happy about getting a new unknown, untested company commander so close to our deployment in Vietnam. Sadly, Captain

Hines was killed by a "Bouncing Betty" land mine two months after the battalion landed in Vietnam.

On board ship, the platoon was crammed into a berthing compartment different from the transit from San Diego. We all knew we might have the same problem of waiting in line to eat. Mike O'Grady, our scrounger, found out that the ship's food storage locker and coolers were on the other side of the bulkhead from our compartment. He checked a hatch in the bulkhead, and found it unlocked, giving us access to the food locker compartment. When assigning the berthing compartments, the officer in charge did not realize he assigned The Filthy Few to the compartment next to the food lockers. Somehow Mike got his hands on a set of keys. On this short, three-day transit from the Philippines, we did not stand in line to eat. We took everything we wanted right out of the food lockers and coolers, including all the ice cream we could eat.

Not long before dark on December 10th, most of the platoon was top-side. The ocean was flat, and the ship moved along at a comfortable speed. Guys sat around engaged in a typical bullshit session, smoked, and enjoyed the cooler evening air. I was playing poker. Orders came over the ship's PA system for all the Marines to return to their berthing compartments. Losing in the poker game, I had no problem with that.

The company captain, briefed earlier by the battalion commander, passed along operation orders for the next day to the platoon commanders. Lt. Dolan gathered the platoon around and told us in the morning the ship would arrive off the coast of Vietnam. He told us the 9th Marine Regiment was battling a division-sized North Vietnamese Army (NVA) unit at the Rockpile west of the Dong Ha Combat Base. The area commander decided not to send our newly arriving and green (no combat experience) battalion to reinforce them. Our battalion would assume responsibility for security of the Dong Ha base, taking over the perimeter defensive positions. The more experienced battalion we relieved would move up to reinforce the 9th.

Lt. Dolan told us the galley would be providing an early breakfast prior to debarkation, and that we should be ready to go by 0800. He told me whatever happened tomorrow, I needed to stay close to him with the radio.

Morale was sky high; the guys organized their gear, cleaned their rifles again, and repacked their packs, each of us wondering what tomorrow might bring. The other platoon radio operator and I checked our radios and went over procedures one more time.

I did not know when I might get a chance to write home again, so I wrote a quick letter to my parents and a note to Phyllis. I knew sometime during my tour I would get a week of R&R. I told Phyllis I wanted to try to take my R&R in Hawaii so we could see each other there, and I could go surfing again at Waikiki.

Conversation in the compartment centered around how long it might be until we saw action, or who might take the first shot. We talked about the company's assignment on the base as the perimeter guard and what it might be like. Lt. Dolan mentioned the base received daily sporadic small arms fire around the perimeter along with incoming rocket and mortar fire, but no all-out ground attack on the base. Even though our job would be on front-line guard duty, it sounded like we would have a chance to at least get our feet wet before getting into a real fire fight.

Clowning around, crazy Al wondered how long until our next beer or his next time with a woman. "The heck with beer," Mike said, "I hope we can find some good weed to smoke." We joked about who might get the first Dear John letter or get the clap on R&R or might already have it from our adventures in Olongapo City.

The guys were excited, ready to go ashore; I know I was. Bored with the months of training and being a reactionary force, merely watching the war from the deck of a ship, we were eager for our turn to get into the fight.

Lying in my bunk, the compartment quiet, only the sound of the water rushing by the hull as the ship took us closer and closer to Vietnam. I stared at the canvas bunk above mine, looking at the heart I drew with Tom loves Phyllis written inside. I wondered if I would make it home, what might happen tomorrow, how would I do? I hoped not to make a stupid mistake, forget my training, or piss my pants at the first sign of any trouble.

Then I said to myself, "Wait a minute, this is not an episode of Gomer Pyle; this is the real Marine Corps. This is what we trained for. The Marine Corps molded us into a fighting unit. We know our responsibilities and capabilities; we trust each other to do our jobs; we are a team." I knew Al, Mike, Fig, Pat, and the other guys in the platoon and I would take care of one another. Confident, I was ready to go.

All the food we had stolen from the food locker was gone. We had no idea how long until our next decent meal so, in the morning, we took advantage of the early breakfast. We filled our bellies with steak and eggs, not something we normally ate as mere troops. Hopefully, it was not the last meal for condemned men.

Back in the compartment, ready to go, we waited. Though we were used to waiting in the Marine Corps, today the waiting was killing us. The ship slowed, and then the anchor chain was rattling as the anchor headed for the bottom. Our anticipation heightened. Finally, over the PA system: "Marines, report to your debarkation stations." We scrambled up the ladders, adrenalin pumping; I went up the ladder right behind the lieutenant.

At our debarkation station, I stood in full combat gear: standard utility uniform and boots, my ten-pound M-14 rifle, a cartridge belt with three rifle magazines, two canteens full of water, and a Ka-Bar knife. I had my flak jacket on; my pack contained extra underwear (hopefully not needed today), two pairs of socks, cleaning gear for my rifle, shaving kit, mess kit, blanket roll, poncho, shelter half, entrenching tool, and bayonet. I also carried in my pack a twenty-two-pound PRC-25 (Prick-25) radio and one two-pound spare battery. Helmet on, I was ready to go.

The ship anchored off the coast of Vietnam at the mouth of the Cua Viet River. In the Philippines, we trained how to climb down the side of a ship on cargo nets like the Marines did in old WWII movies. But this was 1966, and in modern times, we should never have to do this for real. Climbing down a cargo net in full combat gear with a rifle slung over your shoulder was not fun. We quickly learned to hold on to the vertical ropes, not the horizontal ones, so the guy above you would not step on your hand.

The landing crafts were launched, and the cargo nets were over the side. Orders came to climb down the nets into the boats. Climbing down, there was the occasional "goddamn it" or "shit"; somebody had put his hand on the horizontal rope.

To get off the nets at the bottom presented another challenge. The big ship and smaller landing crafts were going up and down in the waves, but not in sync with one another. We learned to step off as the landing craft was coming up and the big ship was going down; otherwise, it could be a long drop. A couple of guys misjudged the step off and landed with a thud on the deck, but overall, we did a decent job of getting off the ship.

On the way upriver to the Dong Ha Combat Base, I took a look over the side at the beach to check out the surf, nothing but the wake of our boats rolling onto the beach. I also got a good look at the terrain where we would be running operations. All along the riverbanks was low flatland, crisscrossing dikes outlined rice paddies. Old men and women were working the rice fields, and young boys were riding on top of the water buffalo plowing the fields. There were cart paths running between small hamlets hidden behind bamboo fences, smoke from the cooking fires drifted up. The Viet Cong definitely had the home field advantage.

The sprawling Dong Ha Combat Base was located about fifteen kilometers south of the DMZ near the junction of Highways 1 and 9. Highway 1 ran north and south. Highway 9 west out to Camp Carroll, the Rockpile, and Kae Sanh. The base included a runway large enough to land C-130 cargo planes and available to jet fighters in an emergency. Medivac, attack, and resupply helicopters operated out of the airfield. A MASH-type hospital and logistical support units were also on the base.

The boats nosed up to the riverbank and we scrambled off to hike the last quarter mile onto the base. While getting off the boats, a C-130 cargo plane flew overhead, landing at the base. The plane came in high and dropped down fast onto the runway at the last minute. The plane did not stay on the ground for long. We found out later the big cargo planes did not stay long at the base because they were too big a target for incoming mortar and rocket fire. Maybe that is why we didn't fly into the base.

The Marines watching us new guys enter the base laughed, pointed at us, and yelled out, "Here comes some new meat" or "Welcome to hell." Other Marines called out, "Ten and a wakeup" or "Thirty and a wakeup." They were telling us the number of days left on their tour in Vietnam. We had over three hundred days to go. Our uniforms were still clean, our boots polished, our weapons new. We looked like a green outfit. That would not take long to change.

Standing in front of the base headquarters office, we waited for the captain to get our orders. My head was spinning as I surveyed our new surroundings. I looked around: rows and rows of sandbag walls and bunkers, lines of tin roof buildings that looked like living quarters, heavy canvas tents, barbed wire everywhere, holes in the ground from exploding rockets and mortars, a crashed jet fighter off the end of the runway. The heat of the sun burned the back of my neck, the thumping from the wop, wop, wop of helicopter blades caused pressure in my ears, the smell of humid air and diesel fuel tickled my nostrils, and the blowing dust made my eyes water and my throat dry. So much happening so fast. What have I gotten myself into? Is this the adventure I wanted? What's next?

Welcome to Vietnam, Tom!

CHAPTER 12
DONG HA

I snapped back to reality when crazy Albert yelled out to a couple of Marines walking by. "Where does one take a dump around here?" Other guys standing around echoed his question; must have been the huge breakfast on board the ship. The Marines pointed to a small tin-roofed building away from everything else with three steps leading up to a screen door and walls. Inside were three toilet seats over holes cut into a plywood platform about two feet high. I wondered if the screen walls were to keep the flies in or out. Not really wanting to know, I looked down through one of the holes—not a pretty picture. Under each seat was the bottom half of a fifty-five-gallon oil drum to catch your business. Next to each seat were rolls of toilet paper, at least there were supposed to be. We learned quickly to bring our own. At the bottom of the steps was a series of holes with sandbag walls to dive into if enemy mortar rounds came in when you were in what we called the shitter.

After checking out and using the shitter, we waited by the side of the road. A cargo truck locked up its brakes and came to a sliding stop right in front of us, creating even more dust for us to breathe. Pointing to the back of the truck, the driver yelled, "Ammo!"

The ship had carried a limited supply of M-14 ammo. Before the landing this morning, we each received only four or five rounds. Albert grabbed a second helping and ended up with eight rounds. We all laughed when Turk told him to put his rifle on automatic. We were not happy about going upriver with so little ammunition. Even worse, the Navy guys driving the landing craft had told us earlier not to worry as they had plenty of ammunition and would protect us. That did not set well with a bunch of Marines.

We cracked open the cases of M-14 ammo from the back of the truck and loaded our magazines.

On the way upriver, the boats dropped Kilo Company off at the river mouth to provide security for the fuel depot. Battalion assigned India, Mike, and Lima Companies to take over the outer perimeter security and defensive positions around the combat base.

By the time we arrived at our assigned locations, the Marines we replaced were gone, the perimeter positions empty. The perimeter positions had been occupied for a long time. Behind each set of fighting holes, we found sandbag-protected places to sleep. The tops normally made from ponchos and shelter halves had been taken by the Marines we replaced. The area was a mess. Old empty C-Ration cases, cans, and empty ammo boxes lay all over the place. The fighting holes needed cleaning out and sandbag walls required repair. The captain assigned each platoon a section of the perimeter to guard. My platoon ended up in front of the artillery battery. We took over our positions and prepared for our first night in Vietnam.

The duty as the platoon commander's radio operator required me to go everywhere he went. While the lieutenant moved up and down the line to check things out, to get the lay of the land, and to assign positions to the platoon, I stayed right behind him with the radio. When he stopped to check his map, talk to the squad leaders, or do a task that needed his full attention, he expected me to act as both our eyes and ears and look out for trouble. Not a problem, as I knew part of my duty as radio operator included protecting the lieutenant. The officer and radio operator were the number one and two targets for the Viet Cong. To make it harder for the VC to identify the officers, we did not salute officers in the field (unless we did not like them).

With the platoon squads all assigned to their perimeter positions, the lieutenant (Turk) and I found the previous platoon command post (CP), which also needed work. Turk ordered me to stay behind and fix up the CP while he and the platoon sergeant went off to check out the area in front of our positions. They were looking for avenues of approach by the enemy and where to set up our listening post.

I jumped down into one of the waist deep fighting hole. The diameter was big enough for me to crouch down. A wall made of three to four layers of sandbags circled the hole. Standing, I could fire my rifle over the sandbags and be as protected as possible. This would do unless a mortar round landed right on me.

Using what we learned in training and my education in architecture and camping experience as an Eagle Scout, I envisioned the best way to improve our position. I filled more sandbags to reinforce the walls around the fighting holes. Using other sandbags, empty wood ammo cases, my shelter half, and poncho, I rebuilt the covered sleeping area, called a hooch, for the lieutenant and me.

Turk retuned from checking out our area of responsibility and told me to get something to eat at the mess tent. The food was not bad, but we found it easier to steal cases of C-Rations and remain in our positions. I returned to our hooch and Turk went to eat. When he returned, we made the rounds to check the platoon positions one more time before dark. Turk wanted to make sure we were well prepared for our first night in a combat zone. He liked the setup and we returned to our hooch. I settled in for my first night in Vietnam.

After dark, the base provided little ambient light, and thick clouds blocked out the moon. I could barely see my hand in front of my face. The sounds around me were unfamiliar; I sat in the opening of our makeshift hooch and stared into the blackness with my radio receiver next to my ear. Turk sent a four-man fire team one hundred meters in front of our position to set up a listening post at a location he and the staff sergeant identified earlier. My friend Mike O'Grady carried the radio. With the post set up, he called me for a radio check. I let the lieutenant know they were in position.

"You want the first watch or the second?" Turk asked.

In the daylight, while improving our position, my mind was busy and clear, in the dark, a different story. Too scared to even know I was scared; I knew I could not sleep. "I'll take the first watch," I said.

"Wake me in two hours so I can check our platoon positions," Turk said as he leaned back against the sandbag wall of our hooch. With light rain starting, I don't think he actually went to sleep.

I continued to stare into the darkness, my eyes darting around looking but not seeing. I listened to the radio receiver to hear if Mike or the company commander called. At least with the radio to listen to and knowing I needed to stay alert, my mind didn't wander too far. What were the other guys thinking on our first night?

Ka-boom! Ka-boom! Ka-boom! I almost jumped out of my skin, the sky now lit up with three new suns, the brightness making me squint my eyes. Turk put his hand on my shoulder; I jumped again.

"Base artillery firing illumination," he said. "Don't worry you'll get used to it."

"Ya think? What was that you said about sleep?" I reached down to see if my pants were wet.

As the illumination faded, it created shadows; every blade of grass, every dirt mound, every bush looked like it was moving. Were they enemy? My eyes stared into the darkness again. I couldn't decide if illumination was good or bad. Artillery fired another volley; I did not jump so much the second time. The rest of the night, artillery fired in support of the Marines at Rockpile and to illuminate the base.

Shots fired off in the distance and incoming mortar rounds that hit the other side of the base confirmed VC were in the area, keeping us on alert. Turk went out to check the platoon positions again. When he returned, he took the watch and I tried to get a little sleep. The combination of first night jitters and artillery going off made cat-naps possible but no real sleep. Turk went to check the platoon position a couple of more times during the night. At first light, Turk and I went out to check the line again. Judging from the expressions on everyone's faces and the bloodshot eyes, no one got much sleep our first night. No action had occurred along our perimeter positions, but our first night in country was long, wet, miserable, and scary.

The next couple of days, Lima Company stayed on the perimeter and continued to improve our fighting positions. The other companies patrolled outside the perimeter. On the third day, we went on our first patrol away from the base perimeter, our first time in enemy territory. The terrain was mostly flat farmland, rolling hills, low bushes, shallow washes, and stream beds. We spread out to cover the area as we had been trained. We searched for lines of approach the VC might use and cleared brush to open our fields of fire. We were always on the lookout for mines and booby traps. We did not venture too far out the first time, and by afternoon we were back in our defensive positions on the perimeter.

Each day, the companies and platoons took turns patrolling, setting up ambush sites at night, and getting to know the lay of the land. On our patrols, we found and destroyed booby traps and punji pits. These were signs of the enemy, but we made no contact. We all wanted something to happen. We wanted to know how we might react, put all our training to use, prove ourselves. We were still untested in a real combat situation.

In country a whole nine days and over the first night jitters, things were getting better. I became used to all of the activity and noise and more confident in my ability to manage any situation, even though I had not seen any real action yet. The battalion suffered two men killed on an ambush while several others were wounded by small arms fire and booby traps. Patrolling during the day, sitting in ambush sites and perimeter guard at night became our routine. That would soon change. Relieved of Dong Ha perimeter security duty, the battalion received orders for an offensive operation called "Operation Chinook." Things were about to get a whole lot more exciting.

CHAPTER 13
OPERATION CHINOOK

I can't hum, I can't sing, I can't dance, I can't do anything to help me to stay awake on watch that may give away our position. After a long day on a three-thousand-meter sweep through the valley, the company stopped to set up perimeter defensive positions around the battalion Command Post (CP). The low thick clouds of the relentless monsoon rains blocked any light from the moon and stars. Standing in six inches of water at the bottom of my fighting hole, a poncho over my head to protect my radio and rifle, I stared into the darkness. In his fighting hole next to me, I could not tell if Turk was asleep or awake. My flak jacket stuck me in the ribs; tired, hungry, I wanted to smoke a cigarette, I needed to piss. I waited for sunrise.

Early that morning, relieved of perimeter guard duty at the Dong Ha Combat Base, a convoy of over one hundred trucks and support vehicles transported the battalion, a force of close to one thousand Marines, forty kilometers south down Highway 1. Intelligence sources warned us of mines along the road. For our protection, two or three layers of sandbags covered the truck beds. A detail of mine sweeping vehicles and engineers led the convoy. For added security, Huey gunships covered our progress from above.

South of Dong Ha, our convoy passed through the city of Quang Tri, one of the largest cities in the northern part of South Vietnam. So far we had only seen life in the open countryside and a few small villages and hamlets around the Dong Ha Combat Base. This was our first look at a Vietnamese city that included government buildings, homes, shops, restaurants, and parks lining the side streets off Highway 1. The civilian population in colorful, more western-styled dress moved freely. Life in the big city appeared to be quite different.

Assigned to "Operation Chinook," a scheduled fourteen-day offensive sweep-and-destroy mission, the battalion received orders to set up a base of operations in the valley to run patrols and ambushes. The goals of the operation were to keep the Viet Cong (VC) and North Vietnam Regular (NVA) troops from using the area for cover and to disrupt their re-supply lines. Before leaving Dong Ha, the captain informed us the Area of Operation (AO) was a free fire zone. Cleared of the civilian population, we could shoot first and ask questions later.

Past Quang Tri, the terrain turned flat, covered with open plains, rice paddies, and dikes. Halfway between Quang Tri and Phu Bai, the convoy came to a stop where a preidentified dirt road intersected Highway 1. More like a muddy cart path of water-filled potholes from the previous night's rain, the road led to an area known as the Co Bi-Than-Than Valley. Lima Company took point to clear a path and led the way into the valley. Mike and Kilo Companies were on our left and right flanks.

The companies spread out and moved slowly into the valley. One hundred meters off Highway 1, we started to find mines and booby traps. Engineers worked the road to identify mines, destroying anything they found. Supply trucks and other support vehicles followed behind us.

Lima Company moved along on both sides of the road leading into the valley. Turk moved back and forth behind the Second Platoon line checking with the squad leaders. I stayed a couple of meters behind him with the radio. Behind us, there was an explosion and I turned to see a cloud of smoke and dust. A supply truck had run over a box mine. The truck was heavily damaged, three marines wounded. A helicopter landed nearby to pick up the wounded men. We slowed our pace to make sure we did not miss another mine.

When shots off to our right, were followed at once by heavy return fire from our guys up ahead, Turk and I moved up to check it out. The squad leader reported two VC fired at us from a distance. Turk told us the VC wanted to see how we reacted. I am not sure the VC were ready for our immediate and heavy return fire. They found out right away we would stand

and fight. Their shots missed but this was the first time we came under enemy fire. We handled it well. Small groups of two or three VC fired on us three more times during the day; no one wounded. Kilo and Mike companies also reported receiving small arms fire.

Three thousand meters out in the valley we stopped to set up the battalion Command Post (CP). Lima Company took responsibility for perimeter guard. We located the CP near the top of a small rise surrounded by rolling hills. Kilo, Mike, and India Companies set up defensive positions one thousand meters out from the CP toward the east, west, and south.

To secure the CP perimeter, we dug fighting holes and threw up simple defensives of trip flares, claymore mines and strung out what little concertina wire was available. Our current location was set in the middle of no man's land, over forty kilometers from the nearest friendly base.

The truck convoy had left Dong Ha early in the morning. We started our sweep into the AO around noon. By the time we arrived at the CP location and set up our defensives, we were casting long shadows. No time to stop and eat all day. Before dark, I fixed quick C-Ration meals for me and the lieutenant. The first day on Operation Chinook, eleven Marines were wounded, but no one was killed. We still had to get through the first night.

I gazed into the darkness, trying to stay awake by telling myself I was watching the horizon for the next big set of waves and did not want to get caught inside. Turk rustled out from under his poncho. "I'll take the watch; get some sleep," he said. Sleep for me would not be a problem except for one thing. I still needed to piss. Dark with a light rain falling, I could not leave my fighting hole. But I couldn't wait until first light. I pissed in the bottom of my hole. Before I could close my eyes, the ground shook from an incoming mortar hitting behind my position. Mortar rounds started landing all around the CP. The dust from the exploding mortar round had not settled when rifle fire erupted from down the hill. Bullets flying by created an adrenaline rush like dropping into an overhead wave while surfing. I had to be ready to react in an instant.

We did not immediately return fire, which would have given our positions away. Then a pop from a tripped illumination flare, and the sky lit up. The forward guys had targets to shoot at, opened fire and threw hand grenades. The VC continued to shoot and throw hand grenades at us. Enemy mortar rounds continued to hit all around the perimeter, followed by our own outgoing mortars.

The attack around our CP positions lasted about thirty minutes before the VC broke contact. The other company positions were getting mortared, and I could hear rifle and machine gun fire. For the rest of the night, the VC continued to probe all our positions. We figured they were trying to see how big a force we were and how we reacted to their attacks. Not knowing if the probing attacks would increase to a full-on attack made for a scary first night, I never did get to sleep. Not getting time to sleep or enough to eat would be the norm on Operation Chinook.

The next morning, all the companies did sweeps around their perimeters. In the area out front of our position we found only blood trails, but no enemy bodies. During the night, the VC dragged off their dead and wounded. We found spent brass from their AK-47 rifles and unexploded Chinese-made hand grenades. The other companies reported the same around their perimeters. During our first night on the operation, the battalion suffered twelve more Marines wounded. Our luck was holding; no Marines were killed.

The next day we worked to improve our defensive positions. We filled sandbags, lots of sandbags, built the walls higher and thicker, dug our fighting holes deeper, laid more Claymore mines and trip flares in front of our positions. After the first night, we wanted the area better prepared if the attacks increased. During the day, we continued to receive occasional incoming mortar rounds and sniper fire. All the companies sent out patrols searching for the VC and looking for signs indicating their approach to our positions. Before dark, all patrols were back in their perimeter positions.

After midnight, the VC hit us again using the same tactics as the first night, with mortars, small-arms fire, and hand grenades. We kept the sky lit up with illumination, returned fire, and threw hand grenades. If it got too quiet, Pat Cochran yelled out, "VC suck," then threw a grenade down the hill, and the fire fight continued. During the night, India Company received the heaviest attack yet. In the morning, we found nothing but blood trails in front of our position again. India Company counted fifty-three enemy bodies around their perimeter. The battalion suffered more wounded but again no Marines were killed. But our luck was about to run out.

Lima Company remained on battalion CP perimeter guard. Kilo, India, and Mike Companies patrolled outside the perimeter. Information from the patrols, reconnaissance reports, and captured civilians helped us to estimate about three hundred VC operated in the area. We were about to find out there were a lot more. By dark, all companies were back in their perimeter positions. During the night, we took more small-arms fire and incoming mortars, and we returned both. Each night the attacks were increasing in intensity and length.

"How long do you think this is going to go on?" I asked Turk.

"They're just getting warmed up; I think the VC are going to hit us a lot harder soon," Turk said.

"You think the VC might stop for Christmas?"

"That's up to the assholes in Washington. Eat something and try to get some sleep. I'll take the first watch; give me the radio."

No argument from me. Hungry, wet, and tired, and with rain falling I pulled a poncho over my head and slumped down in the bottom of my fighting hole. I wanted to sleep, but my mind kept repeating what Turk said, "The VC are going to hit us a lot harder soon."

Turk was right. Before midnight, on December 22nd, the VC hit us with everything they had. Attacking all around the battalion CP perimeter, they tried to sneak in and overrun our perimeter lines. We held them off with heavy rifle and machine gun fire and hand grenades, both sides firing mortars. At times, the shooting stopped, and it got quiet. We hoped the VC were withdrawing. When more illumination went up, we saw the VC were, instead, trying to crawl in closer, and the battle continued.

Turk and I were in our fighting holes behind the front-line fighting positions of the platoon. Lance Corporal Paul Evans, assigned to us from the weapons platoon, was in his fighting hole to my left. "Doc" Bill Miller, one of our Navy corpsmen, was in his hole to the left and behind Evans. During one of the exchanges of heavy fire, Paul stood up to fire his rocket launcher. He made a strange noise as if he were trying to yell out something, then fell back behind the low sandbag wall in front of his fighting hole. Corporal Strange, the squad leader, and Doc crawled over to check on Paul.

Behind the sandbag wall Paul's body lay lifeless. Doc tried to help Paul, but there was no way to stop the bleeding, a bullet had severed his aorta, and he quickly bled to death. Blood everywhere mixed with the rain and the mud.

Doc pulled a poncho over Paul's body and crawled back toward his fighting hole. The corporal crawled near my position and told me to tell Turk that Evans was dead. As he crawled back to his hole, the corporal took a bullet through his ear up the side of his head and out through the top of his helmet. Doc crawled over to help him.

Turk said he heard the corporal say Paul was dead. He asked me for the radio. My hand, covered with mud, was shaking as I handed the radio handset to him. Paul was the first person I had seen killed and it happened right in front of me. Paul was the first person many of us saw killed in combat. He would not be the last.

While we were still taking rifle fire, incoming mortar rounds, and hand grenades, the lieutenant was on the radio giving a situation report to the battalion commander. During the attack, the VC had managed to crawl close enough to the front line, allowing their hand grenades to land inside the perimeter. As an incoming hand grenade flew overhead and landed near our holes, I yelled, "Down." It failed to explode.

"Shit that was close," Turk said.

"Yes, Sir," was the only thing I could think of to say at the time.

About 0400, the VC began to withdraw. We heard the roar of an airplane engine, and then saw a solid red ribbon come out of the clouds. "Puff" was firing on the VC as they retreated. A converted cargo plane we called Puff the Magic Dragon carried three General Electric miniguns, each capable of firing up to six thousand 7.62 mm rounds a minute. Every fifth round, a tracer created a solid red ribbon from the plane to the ground. Impressive to watch, terrible if you were the target.

After Puff arrived on the scene, the attack ended. In the morning, the total count of VC dead bodies we found was forty-three. We found evidence there may have been more, but with it still raining, it was hard to tell. We collected enemy weapons, hand grenades, and other gear left behind when the VC withdrew. We found long pieces of rope with a meat hook–like device on the end. We assumed the VC used them to drag off their dead and wounded.

During the fighting, I did not have time to think about Paul's death. While we were out checking the area in front of our positions, a graves registration detail picked up Paul's body. Later standing over his empty fighting position with Doc, I had a feeling that became all too familiar then and now; that could have been me! Not really a happy feeling that it was him and not me, but more like a "Why him and not me?" I was only a few meters away. To this day, I still wonder, "Why them and not me?" when I think about all the friends I lost in Vietnam.

"Sir, you think the VC had enough yet?" I asked the lieutenant.

"No."

I hoped he was wrong this time. He wasn't.

Before midnight of December 23rd, the VC mounted another heavy attack around all the company positions, and we fought again until early morning.

In country only two weeks, we had gone from a green outfit to a battle-hardened Marine Corps battalion. Lt. McCarthy, the Third Platoon commander, called it, "Baptism by fire!" Now the day before Christmas, we hoped the politicians back home negotiated a cease-fire.

Operation Chinook:

Three rugged days before truce began

By: Cpl. Cal Guthrie

PHU BAI—Waves of Viet Cong soldiers moving behind barrages of enemy mortars pounded Marine lines from dusk to dawn marking the last day of fighting on Operation Chinook before the Christmas truce.

The 3rd Battalion, Twenty-Sixth Regiment, 3rd Division Marines killed more than 50 communist soldiers during the night-long battle. This brought the enemy dead total to 154 in three days of fighting.

Marine casualties were light.

More than 400 rounds of enemy mortar fire pounded the Marine positions during the action, starting at dusk on Dec. 23 and continuing through the early morning hours of Christmas Eve. The communists broke contact and fled at dawn.

Fighting from water-filled holes in torrential rains during the all-night engagement, the Marines drove back an estimated three companies of hard-core VC.

The communists came within 10 yards of the Marine lines at times in attempts to overrun the positions.

A flareship was on station in an attempt to illuminate the battlefield, but thick cloud cover hampered efforts. Marine artillery illumination was fired below the clouds and the battleground suddenly lit up catching enemy soldiers in the open. Rifles and machineguns caught them in a deadly cross-fire as they scurried for cover.

The grey light of dawn uncovered bodies, weapons, blood trails and blood-soaked rags littering the crater-pocked battlefront as the Marines moved through the area.

It ended the third such engagement in as many nights since the battalion took up positions in the rolling hills 12 miles north of Hue.

The battalion had been in Vietnam only two weeks when Operation Chinook began. They have become battle-tested veterans in a hurry.

At the end of three days of intense fighting the Marines have averaged more than 50 enemy kills a day. They captured five Viet Cong and seized more than 40 automatic weapons and light machineguns.

More than 200 Chinese communist-type grenades have been taken from enemy bodies and several rice caches have been seized and destroyed.

"I" Co. alone accounted for more than 50 of the total enemy kills during three hours of savage fighting on the second night of the operation.

As the Christmas truce brought a lull in the fighting, the Marines bailed out their fighting holes, reinforced their positions and tried to catch some needed sleep.

Article about the three-day attack on Operation Chinook
From the *Sea Tiger Magazine*, January 4, 1966

CHAPTER 14
OPERATION CHINOOK: CHRISTMAS

Christmas Eve Day, a cool breeze in the air, a light rain turning the ground to a slick mud. Six deuce and half six-by-six cargo trucks, engines idling, were parked inside the battalion perimeter with the drivers in their seats. A deuce and a half is a two-and-a-half-ton ten-wheel military truck with a flatbed lined with gates and wooden bench seats along both sides.

We had been hanging around the trucks for a couple of hours waiting for orders to move out. I never found out what caused the delay, but it turned out to our advantage. The radio crackled, "Lima 2 actual Lima 6 over."

I answered, "Lima 2 wait one, over," and walked up to the truck where Turk sat in the front seat and handed him the handset from the radio, "The captain, Sir."

Turk keyed the handset, "Lima 2 actual over."

The captain told Turk to move out.

Turk answered, "Roger, out," and passed the handset back to me.

Turk sat in the third truck down the line. In case of mines or ambush attack, the officer never rode in the first truck. Turk stood up on the running board and with his hand held up in the air turning in circles; he signaled the platoon to load up. The diesel engines shook to life, noisy, the exhaust stacks spewing black smoke into the moist air, creating little black droplets everywhere. Six or seven Marines climbed into the back of each truck, while Turk, the staff sergeant, and squad leaders sat in the front seats. I sat in the third truck behind the passenger-side door so I could hand Turk the radio handset if needed.

The captain assigned Second Platoon the duty to ride shotgun on a resupply convoy to Phu Bai. After standing around in the rain all morning, we were happy for the order to move out. To ride on the trucks was a pleasant change from patrolling the hills all day in search for VC.

Somehow our normally useless government officials back home negotiated a forty-eight-hour cease-fire with the North Vietnamese starting at 0700 Christmas Eve Day. Both sides agreed to hold their positions and not attack. After the heavy attacks of the past three days and the loss of Paul, a cease-fire sounded good to us. We learned from battalion headquarters it was the 802d VC battalion of hard-core Viet Cong who had attacked our positions. We endured over nine hundred incoming mortar rounds and an unknown number of hand grenades plus heavy small-arms fire. We killed over 150 VC. Two Marines were killed and forty wounded.

We planned to use the downtime to improve our positions and make a resupply run. We figured the VC were doing the same. Word from recon patrols was a couple of thousand North Vietnamese troops were heading into the valley directly in front of our battalion position. That information, along with the heavy attacks before Christmas, had prompted a decision to send the 2nd Battalion 26th Marines into the Chinook area to reinforce operations.

Phu Bai was a large Marine Corps combat base about thirty-five kilometers south on Highway 1 from our AO. Highway 1, full of potholes, craters, and other debris from mortar attacks and mines, was not exactly a superhighway. The truck suspension system questionable, we were in for a rough ride. That's why they called them Rough Rider Convoys.

We also knew the VC liked to plant mines in the potholes along the road. With the cease-fire in place, we did not worry much about an ambush attack but the ever-present possibility of hitting a mine concerned us. We kept our guard up and rode all the way with weapons locked and loaded. On the operation for thirteen days, fifteen inches of rain so far indicated the monsoon season was well underway. Raining much of the time, our ponchos stayed on most of the way to Phu Bai.

Fifteen kilometers south of the AO, our convoy passed through the old city of Hue. Prior to the Tet Offensive in February of 1968 destroying many areas of the city, Hue was a beautiful place. Along the road, we saw thick stone walls with stone carvings at the corners. Many colorful old buildings of interesting architecture (at least to me) dated back to the 1700s. At one point, Hue functioned as the capital city of the Nguyen Dynasty. As we passed through, people were pushing vegetable carts, riding motor scooters, shopping in the open-air marketplaces, and sitting in roadside cafés along the Perfume River. I was not sure why they called it the Perfume River; it did not live up to the name! The people paid little attention to us as we passed through in our noisy, dirty trucks; you hardly knew there was a war going on.

By the time we reached Phu Bai, thanks to the initial delay in leaving, it looked like we would not have time to load the trucks with supplies and return to the AO before dark. Instead, we would spend the night. Actually, rumors were that a couple of the truck drivers had reported mechanical problems (actual or made up we never knew). We were dirty from two weeks in the field and somehow Turk had arranged for us to get showers and shaved. We had to put our dirty uniforms back on, but it felt good to clean up a bit. After our showers, we went for a hot meal in the mess tent. I enjoyed sitting at a table rather than on the ground to eat. The chow tasted much better than C-Rations, and I did not have to cook or eat out of a can.

The platoon was assigned to a couple of hooches called transit huts reserved for units like ours that were passing through. With rain falling, the huts provided a dry place for us to sleep. The hooches included cots and blankets, and the best part was we did not have to stand watch. I enjoyed my first dry, warm, and full night's sleep in two weeks.

In the morning, we ate breakfast in the mess tent, nothing to write home about, but again, better than C-Rations. A couple of the trucks were still not ready, as the drivers were still tinkering with them. When the trucks were loaded and ready to go, we found out Christmas dinner was being served. Turk said, "We are not leaving until we eat." The mess crew went all out for Christmas dinner with turkey, mashed potatoes, gravy, and all the trimmings, a real feast, but no champagne. A makeshift Christmas tree in the mess tent gave us a little spirit of Christmas. We were thankful for three hot meals in two days. Another hot meal would not come our way for a long time.

At the Phu Bai Base, we also scrounged (a polite way to say we were stealing anything we could get our hands on). Out in the bush, we did not have all the niceties the guys in the rear with the beer were privy to. We grabbed ponchos and blankets, took rolls of toilet paper and a couple of bars of soap out of the head. We lifted any M-14 rifle magazines we did not think the rear area guys needed as badly as we did. Leaving the mess tent, I reached into the kitchen and grabbed a three-cup aluminum measuring cup. I later used the cup to cook many special C-Ration meals for the guys. We pooled what little money we had and bought packs of cigarettes and candy at the PX on the base.

With the trucks loaded down with food (mostly C-Rations), ammunition, stacks of empty sandbags, rolls of concertina wire, and other materials for reinforcing our positions, we climbed on the trucks and the convoy headed back up Highway 1 to the battalion area. No problems encountered on the return except for more rain.

Back at the AO, we moved into our assigned positions on the perimeter, happy for the good meals and a little rest. For most of us, this was our first Christmas away from our families and there were many sad faces. My family tradition on Christmas Eve had been for Grandpa and Grandma to come to our house and decorate the Christmas tree. Mom and Grandma baked my favorite poppy seed rolls with sugary frosting to have when we finished the decorating. I hoped they were making poppy seed rolls again this year even though I would not be there. I really missed Christmas with family.

On the supply run, we picked up the mail and, when we returned, we had mail call. Something, anything from the real world, we considered a treat. The real world is what we called home. Besides enjoying the news from home, we received food and booze. Mom sent me sorely needed socks and underwear, plus a box of chocolate chip cookies. Doc Miller received a tube of Lebanon Bologna from his mom (moldy but edible); his brother sent two half-pints of Seagram's whiskey, packed inside tins of nuts. We drank the whiskey and ate the nuts. Ray Potter's mom sent a home-made

Russian nut roll. Mike O'Grady's mom sent refried beans and corn chips; other guys received cookies and candy. Everybody shared and we enjoyed another makeshift Christmas feast. No action that night, as the Christmas cease-fire held. Actually, Christmas Day turned out not so bad, considering the circumstances.

The next day, the Second Platoon went on another resupply convoy to Phu Bai. With the cease-fire over, we were much more alert for potential trouble. In a hurry this time, the convoy made it down and back in half a day with no problems.

After we returned from the supply run, battalion ordered Lima Company to set up a forward position about two thousand meters outside the main battalion perimeter. We set up along an old cart path near the same location India Company had used when attacked by the VC a week earlier. For the next five days, we improved our positions, ran patrols during the day, and set up ambushes at night. On our patrols (up to ten thousand meters a day), we found lots of punji pits and various booby traps and took occasional small-arms fire but suffered no serious casualties. Rain flooded rice paddies and streams limited our access to certain areas.

On one of the sweeps, as we were advancing toward an abandoned village, three VC fired on us. They missed and we managed to shoot and kill all three. We continued toward the village and spotted four more VC in a hut. The M-79 man sent a couple of rounds their way and destroyed the hut. Two VC ran out and we shot and killed them. Four more VC were too far from us to engage with small-arms fire, so the mortar men sent two rounds their way. They ran off into the tree line; we let them go. We did not take any casualties except for scrapes and bruises from diving for cover. A heck of a way to end the year and our last encounter with the enemy in 1966. We headed back to the company perimeter for the night.

The last day of 1966, New Year's Eve, the battalion had now been overseas for four months, in Vietnam for twenty days and on Operation Chinook for thirteen days. So far, on Operation Chinook, the battalion suffered four men killed and seventy-four wounded. Enemy casualties were 159 confirmed killed, 235 probable kills, and five prisoners captured. We found and destroyed over 350 booby traps, not counting punji pits, and endured over 1,500 enemy mortar rounds. We captured five thousand pounds of rice. We gave the rice to a local village chief who probably sold it back to the VC.

The VC and NVA were not the only thing we battled during the first twenty-one days in country. Guys were out for two or three days at a time due to the screaming shits (shigella dysentery), a couple of cases of malaria, cracking feet (immersion foot), skin infections, burns, self-inflected gunshot wounds, and broken bones. Most returned to action, but it was disruptive with the battalion not at full strength.

Like Christmas, this would be the first New Year's Eve many of us would spend away from our families and friends. Missing all the football games, parades, food, and drinking beer, we sure did not have much to celebrate. Actually, simply being alive was a good reason to celebrate. What happened next made New Year's Eve a night I will always remember but wish I couldn't.

CHAPTER 15
OPERATION CHINOOK NEW YEAR'S EVE

A second forty-eight-hour cease-fire period started at 0700 on New Year's Eve Day. Our politicians did their job again. The monsoon rain along with a chilly wind made life miserable around our company perimeter positions. No one ever told us how cold it could get in Vietnam and the battalion had not properly prepared for it. We had not been issued field jackets. Being wet most of the time, the driving wind chilled us to the bone.

Battalion sent out five-gallon cans of hot soup and tins of potato chips to augment our meager C-Rations. The soup was chicken noodle. Battalion hoped chicken noodle soup might remind us of our mom's loving care for us when we were sick. A canteen cup full of hot soup did create a warm spot in the belly. The potato chips needed beer to wash them down. I kept the lid from one of the potato chip tins and made a frying pan out of it, which I used many times over the next few months to cook C-Ration meals.

A Red Cross package full of cigarettes, candy, and toiletries also arrived. Because most of cigarettes that came from the old World War II–era C-Rations we were issued were moldy and tasted like wet shoe leather when smoked, I was happy to get some fresh cigarettes. Smoking was one of the few pleasures available to us in the field, assuming we could find a dry match.

Away from the battalion command post perimeter, our main protection from mortar and small-arms fire was our fighting hole and if available, a few sandbags around the top. Outside the CP area, we never knew how long we might be in one position. Orders often came for us to move to a new location and dig in. No sooner were we dug in, than orders would come to move back to where we were, requiring us to fill in the holes we just dug, move back, and dig in again. I swore if I made it home, I would never dig another hole in the ground.

We stayed in our fighting hole, to eat, sleep, and stand watch. The monsoon rain constantly filled the holes with water. I fought a never-ending battle to bail out the water with an empty C-Ration can. Standing watch at night, my feet were in the water; crouching to sleep, my ass was in the water. Since the beginning of Operation Chinook, it rained a total of more than fifteen inches. New Year's Eve Day was no different. Low clouds down to the ground made visibility difficult. The rain changed from light to heavy and then back to light but never really stopped. The accompanying wind made the rain go sideways.

The cease-fire in place, we stayed inside the company perimeter. Turk knew we were tired from daily patrols and nightly ambushes for days on end. He set up a rotating day watch, allowing us to get some much-needed sleep. He told me he would take our first watch. Using the dirt, I had shoveled out of my fighting hole, I made a low dirt wall in front of the hole to block the wind, so I did not have to sleep in my water-filled hole. We tried to build makeshift shelters with our ponchos and shelter halves, but the wind quickly destroyed them. Because of the cease-fire, I did not hear the usual sounds of artillery, mortars, small-arms fire, and helicopters flying over. The silence gave me an eerie, uncomfortable feeling, making it hard to fall asleep. I wrapped myself in my poncho, lay on the cold wet ground behind the dirt mound, curled up in the fetal position using my helmet for a pillow, and finally managed to shake myself to sleep.

According to the conditions of the cease-fire, each company received orders to set up a single listening post on New Year's Eve. Our company commander wanted to give a break to the guys who patrolled and set up ambushes every night. He ordered the platoon commanders to put together a patrol of guys from different platoons who had been out sick or recovering from bad feet and other ailments.

My Second Platoon friend, Corporal Gary Schneider, had been out of action for three days because his feet had been cracked and bleeding from being wet all the time, a condition called immersion foot. Other guys from the company suffered the same problem. Gary always talked about the car he wanted to buy when he got home. A cool guy, he was always happy, never complaining, and everyone in the platoon liked him. Gary and other guys who had been out of action for a time, returned to the company perimeter in the afternoon with the soup delivery and were assigned to the patrol. Because he was an experienced corporal, the captain assigned Gary to lead the thirteen-man patrol. We would question later if the number 13 was unlucky.

The corpsman assigned to the patrol was Doc Bill Miller. Minutes before departure, Doc Graham Tedford asked Bill if he could take his place. Doc Miller had no problem with the request but warned Graham to be careful out there.

The patrol moved out after dusk. We hoped the VC would honor the cease-fire as they had at Christmas. But we also worried about the two thousand North Vietnamese Army (NVA) troops recon patrols had reported moving through the area. Gary planned to move the patrol out along an old cart path we had been using for patrols over the past few days. About three to four hundred meters out from the company perimeter, he planned to set up a defensive ambush and listening post. With low clouds and no moon or other ambient light, you could barely see your own feet, let alone the guy in front of you. They moved out cautiously.

The patrol was out for hours and there was little radio contact. When the radio finally came to life, it was not good news. A distressed voice I did not recognize came over the radio. The voice reported that Gary had tripped a booby-trap when setting up the listening post; they asked for help. Unfortunately, the patrol had bunched up during the set-up and everyone was wounded to some extent. Gary and Doc Tedford were seriously wounded and needed immediate medical attention. Two others were also gravely wounded from the explosion and required evacuation as well. The rest of the patrol was less severely wounded.

Turk and I listened to the radio traffic as the captain reported the situation to battalion headquarters. Battalion informed the captain that the dangerous weather and darkness had grounded all helicopter operations.

He would need to send out a rescue patrol. The captain assigned the Third Platoon led by Lieutenant Frank McCarthy to find and bring the wounded men back to the company perimeter.

The lieutenant was concerned his men might be separated in the dark, so he ordered them to sling their rifles over their shoulders and to hold a grenade in one hand and hold on to the man in front of them with the other hand. As they moved out, they were instructed, if attacked, to hit the deck, pull the pins and throw the grenades.

Counting steps to determine the distance and a compass to show the direction, the rescue platoon moved at a slow pace. Because of the possibility of more mines and booby traps, the patrol traveled cross country, staying away from the cart path. They stopped about three hundred meters out from the company perimeter where the wounded patrol should have been. Unable to find them, the patrol moved another one hundred meters out and still no contact. They kept moving about fifty to one hundred meters at a time and still no contact with the wounded patrol.

Knowing he might give away their position to any enemy near, but desperate to find the wounded patrol, Lieutenant McCarthy decided to fire a single shot from his 45-caliber pistol. He fired. Over the radio, the wounded patrol reported they did not hear a shot. At this point, the lieutenant became concerned they might have gone past the wounded patrol. He figured they were out about seven hundred meters from the company perimeter and, this far out, if attacked, they would be in deep trouble. The wounded patrol called to report Gary's condition was getting worse. Determined not to leave the wounded patrol behind, Lieutenant McCarthy decided to try one more time and moved another one hundred meters. He fired his pistol again. The wounded patrol reported hearing the shot and guided the rescue platoon to their location.

Seriously wounded, Doc Tedford was unable to give first aid to Gary or the other wounded Marines. The men less wounded had been giving first aid to the more seriously wounded as best they could. The rescue patrol set up a defensive perimeter around the wounded men. One of the corpsmen on the rescue patrol tended to Gary who was barely alive, as the bottom of his torso was torn to shreds. Other corpsmen tended to Doc Tedford and the remaining wounded.

Two other wounded Marines also needed help walking. The others were able to walk on their own. The rescue platoon and the wounded headed back to the company perimeter on foot. Lieutenant McCarthy and one of the corpsmen took turns carrying Gary. They stopped every ten minutes to check the condition of those wounded. Gary Schneider died one hundred meters from the company perimeter. He would never get the car he talked about so much. He died after midnight, but Doc Miller changed the time on his toe tag to read December 31, 1966. He did not want the family to think of New Year's Day as the day their son died.

Inside the company perimeter, we put the wounded in a first-aid and warming tent set up by other corpsmen. The corpsmen began attending to the wounded. Doc Tedford was barely alive with many shrapnel wounds to his head and body. Doc Miller tried his best to patch up his friend. The corpsmen, in radio contact with the battalion aid station, reported Doc Tedford needed better medical attention than they could give him at the makeshift station. Helicopters were still unavailable, so Captain Andy Debona drove a truck two thousand meters out from the battalion perimeter at 0330, through open territory, and with no concern for his own life, to pick up the wounded and take them back to the battalion aid station for medical attention. Thanks to the courage of Lieutenant McCarthy and the men of Third Platoon, and Captain Debona's dash across open terrain to pick up the wounded, the other twelve men on the patrol, including Doc Tedford, survived their wounds.

Not the best way to spend New Year's Eve. After all that had happened in the past two weeks, we could only wonder what the new year might bring.

CHAPTER 16
OPERATION CHINOOK: THE NEW YEAR

We did not have much time to mourn Gary's death. On New Year's Day, the platoon moved out on patrol at first light. On our way out of the perimeter, we passed by Gary's body lying on the ground covered by a poncho. Each man paused and said his own goodbye. Lieutenant Dolan paused longer; his head hung low. Gary was the first man in his platoon who was killed, and I knew it had a profound effect on Turk. He was determined to do his best to not lose anyone else, though he would not be successful. When I paused alongside Gary, I got that feeling again, "Why him and not me?"

On our first patrol of the New Year, a VC patrol along a trail on the other side of the river spotted us about the same time our point man spotted them. A short fire fight broke out and the VC took off down the trail back into the trees. With the holiday cease-fire over, we were back to business as usual. Since the river was wide and running fast from all the rain, we did not try to cross it and go after them. Turk reported the contact to battalion, and we continued our patrol along the river, hoping to run into the VC again.

Down river, we saw VC off in the distance, but they were too far away to engage them in a fire fight. They must have seen us, as they took off out of sight again.

Patrolling the valley and surrounding areas away from the CP, we found punji pits and other types of booby traps. After the VC realized we would stand and fight, they tried not to engage us in open daytime fire fights.

Booby traps and snipers became the main cause of casualties for the companies operating in the area.

The punji pit made up the majority of the booby traps we dealt with. The VC liked to put the traps in clusters and sometimes put a hand grenade in the pit with a trip wire to the lid. We were always careful when removing the lids of the traps.

Most of the time, we smashed in the tops of the pits and filled in the holes. If we suspected it was more than a simple punji pit, we rolled a grenade in and blew it up. To prevent injury when stepping into a pit, we trained to fall forward on one knee. The knee would catch on the side of the pit and keep one's foot from landing on the stakes. This training saved guys, including me, from getting wounded.

Another type of booby trap we found was left over from when the French were in Vietnam; it included a shotgun shell or rifle cartridge held in place by three nails, the cartridge primer over another nail and buried in the ground. When stepped on, a man's weight slammed the shell down on the nail, setting off the cartridge, and blowing the hell out of his legs. The idea of these crude booby traps was to wound personnel. A wounded man required another Marine to take care of him, putting two or more men out of action.

By the middle of January, we returned to battalion perimeter guard duty. During the day, we patrolled the area around the command post. At night, we set up ambushes. I was getting tired of the monsoon rain. Wet much of the time, the wind made us cold. At night I shivered, in the morning stiff as a board and trying to straighten out and stand up, was often painful. Wet cold hands made it difficult to tie my boots or light a cigarette. The platoon was not always at full strength because guys were out sick. Our socks and boots were wet all the time from the rain and crossing streams and rivers. Guys were out of action for two or three days with immersion foot, which caused the feet to dry up, crack, and bleed. Constant dampness caused our boots to rot and fall apart. We kept asking for new socks and boots, but none ever came. We wrote home asking for socks and underwear. Eventually we gave up wearing underwear.

I discovered the thick plastic bag carrying the spare radio battery was the perfect size to hold a pair of socks. I had two pairs of old socks. At night, I took off the wet pair, squeezed out as much moisture as possible, folded the socks in half, and slid them into the plastic bag. I put the bag inside my shirt and along my stomach above the belt. During the night and next day, my body heat dried the socks. That gave me a dry pair of socks to put on every night and I had no trouble with my feet cracking. When I changed batteries, I gave the plastic bag to one of the other guys and showed him how to dry his socks. I also used the battery plastic bag to slip over the radio handset to protect it from the rain and another one to keep my cigarettes dry. There was a small advantage to being a radio operator.

Our only shower in weeks had been on the resupply run to Phu Bai. As dirty and blood-stained as we were, Doc told us we must get a haircut and a shave. Battalion sent out a guy to give us the typical Marine Corps high and tight haircut. Since no electricity was available, he used hand clippers. The haircut felt like he was pulling the hair out. We could keep our mustaches, but the beards needed to go. Doc said our hair needed to be short and beards gone because of lice. Is that what itched me? We were given only five razors with double-edge blades to shave the entire platoon of forty men. Nothing but peach fuzz on their chins, shaving was easy for the younger guys. For the rest of us, we tried to shave with no shaving cream, and our only mirror was a small piece of shiny metal. Like in the old WWII movies, we put water in our helmet liners, used what little soap we could find as shaving cream, and did our best to shave under the circumstances. By the time we finished shaving, most of the guys had little pieces of toilet paper stuck to several bloody spots on their faces.

To support our patrols and perimeter defensives, battalion assigned a company of Ontos vehicles to our area. The Ontos was a small armored tracked vehicle that carried six 105 mm recoilless rifles, one 30 and one 50-caliber machine gun, all operated by a crew of three Marines riding inside.

We saw patrols go out with three or four Marines riding on top of an Ontos. Battalion sent six Ontos to the Lima Company to use on a patrol. The company commander assigned Second Platoon to the patrol. With not enough room on the vehicles for all of us, the guys not riding spread out to walk the flanks.

Turk and I climbed on top of one of the Ontos. I looked around for some way to hold on but did not find much. I straddled one of the recoilless rifles, riding it like a horse. The first time the Ontos went over a dirt mound and dropped down quickly on the other side, I realized straddling was not a clever way to ride. I wanted to get off and walk.

The Ontos in front of us started up a small hill. One of the Marines riding on top began to fall off the back. He tried to stop his fall by grabbing the handle on one of the rifle breeches. The breech opened and the 105 mm round slid out. The round hit the back of the Ontos, bounced once, and landed on the ground in front of the Ontos Turk and I were riding on. The Marine still holding the breech handle and hanging off the back of the vehicle, let go and landed on top of the round. Fortunately, the round did not explode. Our Ontos managed to stop before running him over. The "loader" jumped out of the back of the Ontos, helped the guy up, dusted off the round, put the round back in the rifle, and slammed the breech closed. The Marine who fell off decided to join the guys who were walking. We were on our way again, just another day at the office.

Nearing the end of our patrol, we had not seen any VC or drawn any small-arms fire. Before returning to the battalion perimeter, the patrol came to a stop on a hillside overlooking the Co Bi-Than Tan Valley. The other side of the valley was mountainous. We knew the VC operated in the valley and used the trails in the mountains to move weapons and personnel into the area and farther south. The commander ordered the six Ontos to line up on the ridgeline and aim across the valley at an open spot where the trail ran through. He told us to get off and lie down between the Ontos before the rifles were fired because a recoilless rifle produces a back blast that can kill anything up to twenty-five meters behind it.

When in position, the commander ordered the six Ontos to fire all six of their recoilless rifles at once (effectively thirty-six rifles at one time). Moments later, we cheered as the other side of the valley disappeared in a fiery cloud of dust and smoke. My ears rang for days.

We continued our patrol. Turk and I decided we had enough riding and walked the rest of the patrol. By dark, we made it back to the company CP and assumed our perimeter defensive positions. The Ontos returned to their positions around the perimeter. We were in for another long night of cold and rain. Before dark and the rain started, I cooked C-Ration meals for the lieutenant and me.

CHAPTER 17
THE GRAVES

The next day, the platoon left the battalion perimeter for a scheduled three-to-four-day patrol. No Ontos to ride on, we humped our asses in the sweltering heat during the day and tried to stay dry under our ponchos at night. Our boots were always wet from wading across streams and tromping through rice paddies. By the end of the first day, we had made little enemy contact. Late in the afternoon, the lieutenant told the squad leaders to find a place to set up for the night. Corporal Strange pointed to an area across the clearing we had just entered. The area looked defendable if attacked. As we moved in that direction, shots rang out. There were two or three VC on their own patrol. Seeing us first, they took a couple of shots hoping to get lucky. They missed. When the squad on point returned heavy fire, the VC broke contact and ran. We fanned out and cleared the area before setting up our defensives for the night.

On patrol early the next morning, the glare from the rising sun created shadows that played tricks on what we saw up ahead. The point man spotted what looked like a tree branch blocking the trail ahead. He halted the platoon. Though hard to tell from a distance it looked like the VC had placed the obstruction across the trail to channel us through a narrow opening, a sure sign of a booby trap. Turk and I advanced to the point man's location, and I told Turk I would check it out. I dropped my radio next to him. Looking along the trail for trip wires and punji pits I carefully moved to look under the tree branch. I found a pipe two inches in diameter and six inches long with a trip wire strung across the trail hidden by the branch.

This type of booby trap was unfamiliar to me, I moved back to report to the lieutenant what I had found.

I pointed out where the pipe was lying, now visible under the tree branch. The point man took a shot at the pipe. The bullet moved the pipe enough to release the trip wire, exploding the device. A blast bigger than a hand grenade, the device would have killed or seriously wounded anyone close by. I moved up to check for more traps around the area. Finding none, I moved the tree branch off the trail and the patrol continued.

Later in the day, the platoon started across an abandoned rice paddy. The mud in the rice paddy kept trying to pull our boots off. From the tree line on the other side, VC opened fired on us. I dove into the rice paddy and used the dike for cover. The guys up ahead returned heavy fire. Turk, about five meters ahead of me, also crouched behind the dike. I crawled through the mud to hand him the radio handset. Before he called for an artillery strike, the VC took off into the trees our guys after them. They managed to kill one and the others got away. The VC knew the terrain better than we did.

One Marine had been wounded during the exchange of fire. Doc Miller tended to his wound and told me to radio for a medevac chopper. I stood up and looked at myself covered with mud and wet from the stagnant water in the rice paddies. On the bright side, I was still alive. I followed Turk across the rice paddy to the tree line where the platoon set up a defensive perimeter while we waited for the chopper to arrive.

We were shot at two more times during the day and managed to kill one more VC in a short fire fight. This became our daily routine: the VC shot at us, and we shot at them. Sometimes they get one of us; sometimes we get one of them. Today we were ahead two to one. Happy to make it through another day, we set up a perimeter and settled in for the night. Turk sent one squad down the trail to set up a listening post and defensive ambush. The night was quiet and uneventful.

The next day, on patrol through an area we had cleared once before, we looked for evidence if the VC had returned. We searched old bunkers and tunnels for recent activity. We looked for new booby traps, a sign the VC were around again. Our goal, as usual, was to keep the enemy from using the bunkers, tunnels, and old villages for cover to attack us. Our constant presence also disrupted their resupply trails through the area.

The rain stopped, the clouds cleared, and the sun came out, raising the humidity level and temperature. It was hot, damned hot. Sweat ran down my back, my utility shirt was soaked under my flak jacket from the weight of my radio. Midday after we checked around for VC, we took a break in an abandoned village. The platoon sergeant set up lookouts, while the rest of us spread out in the village. I found a spot to sit in the shade overlooking the open rice fields. A slight breeze made it almost tolerable. I leaned my rifle on a tree stump, dropped my pack and radio to the ground, flopped down next to them, and reached for my canteen. Albert slumped down next to me. "This sucks," were his only words. Turk came over, I handed him the radio handset, and he reported our location to battalion HQ.

I took a couple of sips of water from my canteen and looked around at what was once a thriving village. What happened to the people who lived here? The South Vietnamese government had forced the villagers to leave before Operation Chinook. Though not Beverly Hills, to the villagers who once lived here, it was home. A lot of arduous work over an extended period of time went into developing the complex of homes, shops, cart paths, and rice fields. Slightly elevated, the village had a pleasant view over the valley. There was a running stream from the hills behind and a stand of trees for shade. A tranquil place for the hardworking villagers.

Now the bamboo and thatched-roof homes were burned to the ground or blown up, a corral for the animals torn down. The rice paddies surrounding the village were mud holes, the dikes in unkept condition, the cart paths overgrown. I imagined all the villagers ever wanted was to raise their livestock and grow rice. I felt sorry for them. Would they ever have a chance to live in their village again? Gung ho and ready to kick ass when we first arrived in Vietnam, now sitting there in the village, I realized my view of the war was changing. I questioned why we were here; what good was all this fighting and dying going to do?

"Saddle up; we are moving out," Corporal Strange yelled. I put my pack on and took my place behind Turk. I turned around for one last look at the village. How sad!

While the Third Platoon was on patrol one thousand meters to our left flank, they reported finding a fresh grave. They dug it up and found a female dressed in a VC uniform, fifteen or sixteen years old they guessed. Five bullet holes in her.

Not one of our favorite duties, battalion often ordered us to dig up the graves for the body count. We did not give a shit about the body count, but it made big news back home. The politicians and the TV news considered it a way of keeping score. Like war was some kind of team sport.

Not long after the Third Platoon reported finding a grave, we found a couple of graves. The VC rarely took time to properly bury their dead after a fire fight. Fresh mounds of dirt usually indicated a grave. Turk did not want to take a lot of time to dig up the graves, so he asked our explosives expert to put a small charge on top of one of the graves and blow some of the dirt off. C-4, the type of explosive we all carried, was a powerful explosive. Our so-called expert used a little too much, causing dirt, mud, and body parts to fly everywhere. I laughed when Turk said, "I guess we won't do that again." (And we never did.) The second grave we dug up held a male VC killed by gun fire and shrapnel from an M-79 grenade.

Before the war, to blow up a grave and mutilate a body would have been horrifying to me. Now as I walked away from the graves, I did not know what to think. We heard (but I never saw) accounts where the VC cut the ears and even the cocks off our guys. I had heard of but did not see any cases where our guys cut the ears off dead VC. Understandable when you have seen your own guys being cut up. I had laughed when we blew up the grave. Now when I thought more about what we had done (even if unintentional), it did not seem so funny. Earlier in the village, I felt sorry for the displaced villagers. The body in the grave was the enemy, killed trying to kill us; why should I care? But he was just a soldier on the other side. He probably did not want to be there any more than I did. How do I separate the two thoughts?

The longer I was in country and the more death and destruction I experienced, the more my attitude continued to change back and forth, back and forth; I was having trouble separating right from wrong, good from bad. At one point, I felt like I might not survive this, so why should I give a fuck anymore. Yet all I wanted to do was survive. All of us just wanted to survive. In fact, we were all fighting to keep one another alive long enough to get home. We were not fighting for a bunch of useless politicians back home, most of whom had no fucking idea what we were going through. This type of confusion is what caused many returning Vietnam War veterans to suffer PTSD.

The patrol continued and we circled back to the company perimeter. We made no enemy contact along the way, and we did not find any more graves. I had enough grave digging for one day. There would be other days. Back in our defensive positions, I tried to push the day out of my mind. I took out the one can of spaghetti and meatballs left in my pack and heated it up for my dinner. Before dark, I enjoyed a smoke. The lieutenant returned from meeting with the captain to get our orders for the next day.

"Are we getting a break tomorrow?" I asked.

"No."

CHAPTER 18
THE MULE AND THE PRISONER

The next day, the platoon left early on a daytime patrol. On patrol for a couple of hours and no contact with the enemy, the trail we were following went near a hill and we entered a ravine. Opposite the hill, a series of trails crisscrossed out into the valley. “This looks like a good place to take a break,” Turk said. The ravine was protected by the hill behind us and wide open to the valley. Turk had Albert and Mike take a radio and go up to the top of the hill to act as lookouts. The rest of the platoon took cover in the rock outcroppings near the bottom of the hill. Turk told us to eat something but not take time to cook. “We won’t be here that long,” he said. I took a can of fruit cocktail out of my pack and quickly ate it. I leaned back against the rock to relax and watch Turk. He did not eat, instead he sat looking at his map.

When Turk folded up his map and put it back in his pocket, I knew we were about to resume the patrol. Before Turk gave the order, Albert called on the radio. Al told Turk they had spotted a VC coming down the trail alone. He said it looked like a female, the one all of the platoons were searching for. We moved quickly to block the trail she was on and fired a couple of shots over her head. She could see she had no chance to escape and gave up without a fight. She was the suspected VC cadre leader we were all searching for. Turk called the company commander and reported the capture. The captain told us to return to the company perimeter and he reported her capture to battalion headquarters.

Back at the company perimeter, a small resupply vehicle called a Mule was getting ready to return to the battalion command post. The Mule is a small open four-wheel drive vehicle with a flat area for cargo in back and one seat for the driver up front. A supply sergeant and driver handled the Mule. Battalion ordered us to send the prisoner back riding on the Mule.

Two Marines who needed to get back to battalion were going along to guard the prisoner. Lieutenant Frank McCarthy, the Third Platoon commander, was experiencing back spasm problems. His corpsman suggested he ride the Mule back to the CP as well to have the battalion surgeon check him out. The lieutenant decided to wait one more day to see if his back pain got better and declined to go. That decision may have saved his life.

When the Mule left our perimeter, the supply sergeant, two Marines, and the prisoner were riding on the flat open cargo space behind the driver. Not long after they left, we heard a short fire fight break out. Second Platoon moved out quickly to check it out. When we reached the Mule, we found two Marines dead and two wounded. The prisoner had escaped. The main goal of the ambush was to free the prisoner. The VC left the two wounded Marines alive. The prisoner must have been valuable to the VC, and they did not want our intelligence people to have a chance to question her.

The sergeant had been shot through his big and index toe and in the lower leg. Knocked off the Mule, he had rolled down the hill and sought cover in the bushes off to the side of the trail, holding two hand grenades. The other Marine lying on the ground near the Mule was more seriously wounded. Doc Miller went to work on him.

The driver was one of the dead Marines, the other was a new guy, an engineer assigned to the company only a couple of days earlier. We hadn't gotten to know him yet. His mother had recently died, and he had received permission to go home for the funeral. That's why he was going back to battalion on the Mule. What a tragedy for the family; now they would have two funerals to attend. Somehow that did not seem fair. Nothing about this fucking war seemed fair.

The Mule was still operational, so we loaded the bodies on it and drove back to the company position. We called in a Medevac for the wounded men. The chopper also took the bodies of the dead Marines.

Two more Marines from the company had died, and those words were in my head again: Why them and not me? But by now, I had seen enough men killed and wounded that the thought no longer lingered. Not my turn, I figured. When drafted, I thought this would be an adventure, and like Dad always said, I should just take it one day at a time. The adventure was over the top now. Taking it one day at a time did not fit the adventure anymore. Now it was surviving one day at a time. I think all of us felt the same. We needed to watch one another's back all the time.

Back on perimeter watch for the night, I hoped we would get a break from patrolling for the next few days. Meanwhile my stomach was growling; I needed to eat. I craved something to eat besides C-Rations. Always hungry, the prospect of eating C-Rations again made me think of times back home sitting in Bob's Big Boy, enjoying a giant cheeseburger, some fries, and washing them down with a cold bottle of coke. Instead, here I was sitting on the edge of my water-filled fighting hole, the sun fading fast, my poncho on and a light rain starting. A can of beans and weenies was my only choice.

Tom Elliott in front of perimeter position bunker on Operation Chinook
Sandbag, ammo boxes, and poncho-covered hooch

CHAPTER 19
C-RATS

A cheeseburger, order of fries, and a coke would not materialize for months. I stared at the can of beans and weenies I held in my hand. Merely thinking of opening the can nearly made me lose my appetite. Hungry as usual, I needed to eat something. No one wanted to trade with me except for one guy, and what he offered was even less appetizing.

How to use a P-38, AKA a John Wayne, was not hard to learn, especially if you wanted to eat in the bush. The P-38 is a small hand-operated device for opening cans. Since C-Rations, (C-Rats) for short, were all we ate on Operation Chinook, I was an expert at opening cans. I finally gave in and opened my can of beans and weenies.

Everything we ate came out of green-colored cans. C-Rations (the real name was Meal, Combat, Individual) came twelve meals to a case. The choices included such mouthwatering gourmet names as Ham and Eggs Chopped, Ham Slices, Turkey Loaf, Boned Chicken, Meat Loaf, Spiced Beef, Beans w/Frankfurter Chunks in Tomato Sauce (we called them Beans and Weenies), Spaghetti and Meatballs, Beefsteak with Potatoes and Gravy, and everyone's favorite Ham and Lima Beans, or as we called them Ham and Mother Fuckers.

Each boxed meal included desserts like cookies, pound cake, crackers and cheese, crackers and peanut butter, pecan roll, and everyone's favorite, fruitcake. One meal even included a can of white bread. Also included in the box was an accessory pack; its contents included a plastic spoon, salt, pepper, coffee (instant), creamer (nondairy), gum, a four-pack of cigarettes, moisture-resistant matches, and the all-important small (often too small) roll of toilet paper. We wrote home and asked for ketchup packets, Tabasco sauce, Lawry's seasoning salt, Cajun spices, and anything else we could think of that would help spice up the meals.

All the guys had their favorite meals and grabbed what they wanted if given the chance. Each individual meal came in a cardboard carton with the contents printed on top. Twelve meals came in a case. To make choosing meals fair, Turk made us turn the case of meals upside down so we could not read the contents of the individual boxes. Each man then chose a couple of boxes. Once the choosing was over, the trading began, and everyone ended up with what they wanted anyway.

I often helped pass out the meals. I discovered even though the twelve meals might be different in each case, the Ham and Lima Beans would always be one of the four boxes in the center of the case. I always tried to grab a box from a corner to not end up with the Ham and Lima Beans.

We received some cases of C-Rations dating back to the early 1950s, left over from the Korean War. We could always tell the older meals because the small pack that held only four cigarettes were moldy and not smokable.

On a five-day patrol, we were issued ten meals, two per day. I could eat two or more at one time. Lieutenant Dolan was not a big eater and often gave me his extra C-Rats. I also discovered that the officers and the Marines who stayed inside the battalion perimeter threw the C-Rats they did not like into the dump inside the perimeter. Al, Mike, and I went to the dump whenever possible and filled a sandbag with discarded C-Rats. A lot of it was Ham and Lima Beans. The extra C-Rats kept us from starving and often gave us good trading material. I also found accessory packs in the dump that supplied extra smokes and the much-needed toilet paper.

We would all voice our own opinion and often argued over what we considered the good and bad C-Ration meals. We agreed none of the meals were bad if they were all you had to eat, and for months C-Rations were all we ate. Ham and Lima Beans was the most hated meal. Opening the can, a half-inch of congealed fat sat on top. If you scraped off the fat before cooking the ham and beans, they tasted even worse. Heat melted the fat into the beans, but after you ate it, all the fat ran through your veins. With a high probability of dying from enemy fire, we did not really worry much about the nutritional value of the meals. The fruitcake tasted horrible and was also hard to get rid of through trading. The best use for it was to throw it at the VC.

With a little ingenuity, two or three guys could combine their meals and cook tastier dishes. Guys in Vietnam even wrote cookbooks about C-Rations. With my large metal cup (the one I stole from the mess hall in Phu Bai), and a frying pan I had made out of the lid from a five-gallon can of potato chips, I cooked up some great combinations when time allowed.

When I had a can of spiced beef, I teamed up with one of the guys who had a can of cheese and crackers. I would spread the cheese on the crackers and stack them back in the can. I opened the spiced beef and heated it, pressing down with a spoon to squeeze out all the juice. I poured the juice over the crackers and cheese. The hot juice melted the cheese and soaked into the crackers. My creation tasted like a mini pizza. Word got out and the guys with cheese and crackers were always asking me to make them a pizza.

When I had a can of beef steak and potatoes, I liked to separate the potatoes out, cut them in slices, and make fried potatoes in my frying pan. The fried potatoes were a pleasant change from eating the beef steak and potatoes together. Sometimes I saved the potatoes until morning and made fried potatoes to go with my Ham and Eggs Chopped for breakfast. We often lamented that no packet of ketchup came in the accessory pack. Ketchup would have helped many of the C-Ration meals, especially the Ham and Eggs.

Pound cake was my favorite dessert. To make it even better, I would find a guy with a can of fruit cocktail. With half the pound cake in the bottom of a can and half the fruit cocktail poured over the cake, we each ate the best dessert going.

To heat C-Rations, special heat tabs were issued with each meal, along with moisture-proof matches. We also learned that a small amount of C-4 explosive rolled into a ball burned extremely hot (and did not explode). The C-4 was especially handy for making a quick cup of coffee or hot chocolate. To make a stove for the heat tabs, we used a church key (we always kept one around in case beer was available) to make vents in the side of an empty

C-Rat can. We put the heat tab or C-4 in the bottom of the stove can and set the meal we were heating on top.

When heated, the C-Ration meals were palatable. The problem was, there were times when we did not have time to heat our meals. During the heavy rains of the monsoon season, it became impossible to get the heat tab to light and keep burning. I ate lots of cold C-Ration meals sitting in six or more inches of water in the bottom of my fighting hole, with a poncho over my head, trying to keep the water out of my food.

Our orders were to never leave empty C-Ration cans in the bush. We were supposed to cut off both ends, smash the cans and bury them or bring them back inside the perimeter. This did not always happen. The reason was to keep the VC from making a booby-trap out of a can. A hand grenade fit perfectly in a C-Ration can. A trip wire across the trail completed the trap. When someone tripped the wire, the grenade slid out of the can, and he was history.

During the chilly weather, we discovered another use for C-Ration cans. When gasoline was available, we filled a C-Rat can with dirt and poured enough gas to saturate the dirt. When lit, it made a small heater. We sat on the edge of our poncho, pulled the poncho over our head, set the can between our crossed legs, and lit the gas. We stayed warm for a brief time and in the morning, our faces were covered with soot. The Black guys in the platoon laughed at us. No telling what our lungs looked like. The lieutenant figured out what we were doing and put a stop to it.

After I finished my beans and weenies, Albert and I split a pound cake and fruit cocktail for dessert, and I smoked one last cigarette. We were hoping we would get a break from patrolling tomorrow. At least, the platoon did not have ambush duty for the night.

C-Ration Carton, cans, and accessory pack.
Can of cheese and crackers on the left.
Open can: beans and frankfurters.
P-38 can opener on top of the can on the right.
Picture taken from Wikipedia.

CHAPTER 20
OPERATION CHINOOK: THE VC SNIPER

There is a saying among Marine snipers: "If you hear my shot, I was not aiming at you."

Early morning, the sun was shining through a hole in the cloud like a spotlight. I wanted the sun to warm my shivering body and dry my damp, rotting uniform. I wanted to smoke a dry cigarette, eat my C-Rations without being under my poncho, sit on dry ground and not in the mud, and write a letter home. A break in the action would be nice. I sat on the edge of my fighting hole, lit my cigarette, opened a can of Ham and Eggs Chopped, and started to heat them.

The lieutenant left our bunker at the first sign of light. My ham and eggs were hot and ready to eat when he returned. I offered him a taste. He shook his head. Not smiling, he said, "Get your gear ready; we are going out again."

"Shit, when are they going to give us a fucking break?"

Turk was already moving down the line to let the squad leaders know. The sky began to darken, the spotlight went out, the monsoon rains were again relentless. At least I got to enjoy a cigarette. We would not see the sun again for weeks.

Our mission for a week was to patrol a new area out in the valley and in between Highway 1 and the hills, up to ten thousand meters away from the battalion command post. I picked up rations of ten meals for the first five days. I filled my canteens and dropped in the iodine tablets to purify the water. They made the water taste bad but kept me from getting the screaming shits (dysentery). I loaded my rifle magazines and grabbed a couple of hand grenades. I picked up a spare battery for the radio. I was ready to go tactically, but really had to concentrate to keep up my mental readiness.

One week turned into two. We stayed in the bush, patrolling during the day, setting up ambushes at night. We never stayed in the same place two nights in a row to avoid mortar attacks. We were fired on daily by snipers or small groups of two or three VC who took off when we returned fire. During the last five days, four Marines had been wounded by small arms fire and three more by booby traps. Each time a man was wounded we had to stop and call for a Medevac chopper. We found and destroyed old, abandoned villages, bunkers, and booby traps, and killed six VC. At night, we called for artillery fire on anything that moved. We captured three suspected VC and turned them over to battalion headquarters. On the go twenty hours a day, our fatigue began taking a toll; we were not always paying proper attention to our surroundings, a fact that would later cost us. Now day thirteen of the patrol, would orders to return to the CP come today?

From the top, Hill 51 provided a commanding view of the valley and surrounding rivers. Anyone up there would see us approaching. We heard rumors that battalion planned to send a company to set up a perimeter on top of the hill and run patrols and ambushes in the area. A couple of days earlier, a company cleared the hill to make sure no VC were there but did not stay on the hill.

Thick brush and small trees covered the hillside, providing perfect cover for an ambush or snipers. Approaching the hill, it was quiet—no wind, heavy clouds threatened rain, the humidity level so high my already salt and blood-stained utility shirt was soaked again. Beads of sweat were running down my ass. The twenty extra pounds from the radio I carried felt like a ton of bricks in my pack.

The platoon moved along spreading out between the bottom of Hill 51 and the river snaking through the valley. My position was closer to the river. I stopped to look up at the top of the hill. The hair on the back of my neck stood up like it did when a fin appeared in the water while surfing. I knew I needed to move. Turk was up ahead of me. Before I moved toward him, a bullet hit the ground next to my right foot and threw dirt on my legs. Then came the sound of the rifle shot. My goddamn radio antenna was sticking up like a sign that said, "Shoot me."

I dove for cover in a nearby shallow ditch. Our M-60 machine gunner was firing away at where he thought the shot had come from, laying down cover fire. The rest of the platoon took cover and fired on the hilltop until the machine gunner moved to better cover. Not sure the ditch gave me good cover while all the shooting was going on, I jumped up and started to run. Turk had taken cover behind a high mound of dirt, and I headed that way, praying the sniper would not shoot at me again. I tripped and landed on my back, knocking the breath out of me. Turk held his hand out. I wasn't sure if he was trying to help me up or he wanted the radio. He wanted the radio. I grabbed the handset out of the pocket of my flak jacket and handed it to him. Then all the shooting stopped. Still on the ground, I tried to catch my breath. Turk put his hand out again, this time to help me up. All our return fire had covered any sound of the sniper shooting. No one was wounded or reported hearing another shot.

Turk reported what had happened and asked battalion for permission to go up the hill to see if we had killed the sniper. He was ordered to continue our mission and start back to the battalion perimeter. I liked hearing that order, but I also wanted to know if we had killed the sniper. Likely, the sniper took his shot and ran off as they usually did.

Too late to get back to the CP before dark, we moved down the valley away from Hill 51. Digging in for the night, and as the sky darkened, I looked back at Hill 51 and thought about how lucky I was. Wasn't my time, I figured. From the top of the hill, the sniper's shot would have been three hundred meters. He had lined up his shot perfectly but had misjudged the elevation and was a couple of inches short. Early on in the war, the VC snipers were poor shots. They did not always have up-to-date weapons or sniper scopes. Thank God this sniper didn't have either or this may have been the end of my story.

The next morning, heading back to the battalion perimeter, we patrolled a tree-covered area looking for VC bunkers and any evidence they were using the area for shelter. From an old VC bunker complex up ahead, a sniper got the drop on us again. There was no way to know if he was the same one who shot at me. There was a single shot followed by rapid fire from the guys up ahead. I was still standing, so I assumed the sniper did not shoot at me this time. Then O'Grady yell out, "Doc! Hummingbird is down." This time the sniper hit his target.

Ferrell Hummingbird was one of two Native Americans in Second Platoon and one of the best-liked guys in The Filthy Few. A small, thin, quiet kid, he kept to himself and never said much. But we could always count on him to have our backs. He was a good friend to Doc Miller and, because Doc loved to talk, Ferrell was a good listener. He got permission to join the Marine Corps at seventeen. He did not even look that old to me now. Eighteen was the minimum age for service in Vietnam.

When we saw Hummingbird coming, we would all sing out in unison, Hummmmmmmmmmmminggggggggggggggggbirrrrrrrrd," holding the "hum" and "ing" for as long as possible and dropping our voices low for the bird part. Then we all cracked up laughing. His Cheshire Cat smile always told us he enjoyed the attention.

Forward of my position, there was occasional small-arms fire and hand grenades going off. The guys were searching around the bunker complex for the sniper. He had taken one shot and then ran off. He had done his job and taken a man down. Now the platoon had to search for him and clear the area while setting up a defensive perimeter so the Doc could check on Hummingbird.

Turk, Corporal Strange and I reached Hummingbird at the same time. Turk was kneeling by his body when Doc Miller arrived and knelt to check Ferrell out. Shot in the head, he was not a pretty sight. Doc looked over at Turk and said, "Sir, there isn't anything I can do for him, sir. He's dead."

The lieutenant tensed up and yelled, "God-damnit, Doc, do something." Doc placed a battle dressing around Ferrell's head and put his helmet over it. I turned away trying not to puke. That feeling hit me again: why him and not me. That could have been me yesterday.

Doc Miller told me later he felt bad about losing his friend, and that even with all his medical training, there was nothing he could have done for Hummingbird. He felt so inadequate. We all felt that way when we lost a fellow Marine. But in no way was Doc Miller inadequate. After seeing him manage the situations with Paul, Gary, and now Hummingbird, to me Doc was a hero. In fact, to me, there were two groups of heroes in Vietnam. First were the corpsmen; we called them Doc out of respect for what they did. Even though the corpsmen were Navy, it did not matter; they were our brothers; to us, they were Marines. They were always there to take care of us, patch our wounds, make sure we treated our water and took our malaria pills, sit with us when we lost a friend, and encouraged us to write home. In combat situations they were always ready to do anything necessary to save a life with little regard for their own.

The other group I considered heroes consisted of the helicopter pilots and crew. They were always ready to come into a hot LZ to recover the wounded and drop off replacements and needed supplies. Although both groups suffered their share of casualties, they saved an even greater number of lives in Vietnam.

The tree cover prevented a chopper from landing to pick up Hummingbird. We used a poncho to make a stretcher and took turns carrying his body until we reached a clearing where I called for a chopper. Doc stayed with Hummingbird's body until the chopper arrived. Corporal Strange came back to tell Turk that the sniper had gotten away. Losing Hummingbird and not finding the sniper pissed Turk off. He stood silently for a minute looking at the ground. He stuck his hand out to me and I handed him the radio handset. He called battalion headquarters to report we lost a man, and we were coming in.

Standing next to Doc, we watched the chopper lift off and then head for the CP; it was over. A couple of hours ago, Hummingbird was our friend; now he was gone. The platoon headed back to the battalion perimeter. We were drained physically and mentally. What a waste!

I was sitting on the sandbag wall of my bunker on the battalion CP perimeter when the rain stopped, and the sky started to clear. I lit one last cigarette before dark. I survived another day. Will we get a break tomorrow?

During January, the battalion suffered eight Marines killed and ninety-one wounded, plus several noncombat injuries, and cases of diarrhea and immersion foot. The battalion was credited for 143 confirmed VC killed, 220 probable kills, and 210 prisoners captured.

CHAPTER 21
BEER, BACON, AND EGGS

"Which beach are you lying on?" the lieutenant asked.

"Doesn't matter, Sir, we haven't seen the sun for weeks; anywhere would be better than here," I said.

"You're right about that; the monsoons have been a bitch. I have never seen so much rain. Well, enjoy the sun while you can; we are going back out in a couple of days."

The lieutenant headed down to the battalion headquarters bunker.

On February first, I had been in the Marine Corps for one year and here I was lying shirtless on a bunch of sandbags, catching some rays, and wishing for a sandy beach someplace. I was also trying not to think about the loss of Hummingbird to a sniper the day before. After I tried to wash out the blood and dirt, my utility and T-shirt were hanging on a makeshift clothesline next to our bunker. The lieutenant was gone and with no one else around, I enjoyed the unusual silence and solitude. My mind was riding waves, not chasing the VC. I could have been lying on the beach anywhere, except for one glaring difference. A loaded M-14 rifle was lying next to me, not my surfboard.

Lima Company was back on battalion perimeter guard duty and not much was happening, other than the occasional small-arms fire and incoming rockets or mortars, to harass us. We were all used to it by now. The other companies patrolling outside the wire made daily contact with the VC. The scuttlebutt was Lima Company would be going out to take over the defensive positions that had been set up on Hill 51 by one of the other companies. Even though we owned the hill now, I was not at all excited about going anywhere near there again.

My bliss of solitude abruptly ended when Albert showed up and yelled, "There's beer coming!!! Let's go." I sat up and looked at Albert; he pointed down the hill. "Come on, come on, let's go!" he said again. I didn't know if he was telling the truth or messing with me, which he did a lot. But the thirst for a cold beer, any beer for that matter, was too much for me to ignore. My T-shirt was dry enough, so I threw it on, grabbed my rifle, and headed down to the battalion supply tent.

A loud cheer erupted as a truck arrived carrying eighty cases of beer: Olympia, Lucky Lager, and Carling's Black Label. I was a Miller High Life guy myself, but today I didn't care who brewed the beer as long as it said beer on the can. A line was already forming around the supply tent, and Mike was holding a place for Albert and me. Eighty cases equal 1,920 cans. We knew the beer would not last long. The supply officer announced only two beers each. I guess they did not want a bunch of guys with loaded weapons running around drunk.

Rarely was beer brought to the CP. The last two times beer was available, our company was in the bush. A beer cost $.15 each. What a bunch of bullshit. We are fighting and dying over here; we should get the damned beer for free. At least there was no requirement to be twenty-one.

The truck carrying the beer came from the base in Phu Bai, about forty kilometers south. Along with the beer, under a heavy canvas cover, the truck also carried two fifty-pound blocks of ice, which were mostly water on the truck bed by the time the truck arrived. The supply sergeant took his sweet time putting the beer in a fifty-five-gallon drum full of water with the ice. The ice melted before the beer had any chance to get cold. The supply officer finally told the sergeant to start passing out the beer.

Waiting my turn, the anticipation of downing a beer was killing me. The line moved from slow to slower. Finally, Mike, Albert, and I received our two beers. We joined other guys from the platoon sitting on a sandbag wall behind the supply tent. I opened my first beer. The beer cans in Vietnam were called flat tops and required a church key to open, which most of us carried.

About to take a swig of my first beer, a guy across the way took a big gulp and spit it out. What's with that? The beer couldn't be that bad. I took a sip; yes, it was warm; I paused for about half a second. After more than two months in the field, warm beer was better than no beer. I swallowed the first sip; my first can was gone in less than a minute. The second beer I savored; it lasted longer as we all sat around laughing and telling beer-drinking stories from back home.

I knew a couple of the guys in the platoon were nondrinkers—a rare occurrence in the Marine Corps. I found them and offered my coffee and sugar, since I did not drink coffee, if they would get me their share of beer. I also had to give up some of my best C-Ration stash and a pack of smokes, but they finally gave in and got me their beer.

Mike O'Grady was the platoon scrounger. Like James Garner in *The Great Escape*, if we needed something, Mike was the guy to see. He also managed to scrounge a few more beers. With beer in hand, we headed back to our bunkers, laughing, and joking like a bunch of high school kids who had scored their first six pack.

I saved one beer for Turk. Albert and Mike went back to their bunker. Alone on top of the bunker again, I took my shirt off to work on my tan and continue to enjoy the solitude. I enjoyed another beer and was thinking about being back home, sitting on a warm sandy beach, drinking an ice-cold beer after a good surfing session. I wanted to be anywhere but here.

The next day was almost as good as yesterday. I took a shower for the first time since Christmas. Man, did I smell bad. But we all smelled bad, so it didn't really matter much. The shower water came from a fifty-five-gallon drum full of water that sat on top of a wooden tower covered on three sides. A pull rope was attached to a valve with a shower head below the fifty-five-gallon drum, supplying the water as needed. A truck pulling a large tank of water (we called them water buffalos) arrived and pumped water into the fifty-five-gallon drum. The water was cold. Makes sense for the Marines: warm beer, cold showers. Everyone wanted a shower, so I got about a minute or two to get wet, soap up, and rinse off, typical Navy shower. We all shared the same few bars of Ivory soap, which we cut into little pieces, but it felt good to get the grunge off.

Some guys went into the shower with their uniforms on, which may not have been a bad idea, as it was a toss-up which was dirtier, our bodies or our uniforms. Since I already had washed my shirt, I stripped down naked. I wanted to feel the water running over me like I was diving under a wave, and I wanted to make sure the places that really needed a good wash got it. I wanted to let the whole fifty-five gallons of water run over me. Since that day, I spend way too much time in the shower.

After the shower, I shaved. For once, we were supplied with real shaving cream and enough razor blades. After the shower and shave, I put the same dirty blood-stained trousers back on. I planned to wash them the next day if time allowed. I had saved my last clean pair of underwear (tighty-whities) Mom sent me just for this occasion. Showered, shaved, and with my new underwear on, I felt almost human again.

Never getting enough to eat, I was out trying to scare up extra chow to replenish my C-Ration stash. After hitting the dump and filling a sandbag full of discarded C-Rations, I discovered the officers at battalion had fresh bacon and eggs in their mess tent. No mess tent for us lowly troops. I told O'Grady (our scrounger), so he, Al, and I made a raid and lifted a couple of small beef roasts, a pound of bacon, and ten eggs. On the way back to our bunker, I carried the eggs in my helmet, trying not to drop them and make scrambled eggs. We showed our take to Turk. He said it was unfair for the officers to have this stuff while we ate nothing but C-Rations. We certainly agreed with him on that.

I made a stove using three rocks evenly spaced in a circle with heat tabs between them. I placed the frying pan I made from the lid of a five-gallon potato chip can on the stove and laid a couple of strips of bacon in the pan. The snap, crackle, and smell of the bacon cooking attracted more guys to our bunker. I poured off some of the bacon grease and cracked a couple of the eggs into the remaining grease. The eggs sizzled and quickly turned white while the edges browned in the grease. Our mouths watering, we were ready to eat. The only thing missing were hash browns or grits, depending on where you were from. I divided up the first two eggs and cooked more until we ate them all. We cut the beef roast into strips, heated them in the frying pan, and ate until they were also gone. Like feeding the multitudes with five loaves, everyone enjoyed a little taste of something besides C-Rats, and it all tasted even better knowing we had stolen the food from the officers.

Turk ate the last piece of bacon and a couple of strips of the roast. He told me to make sure I got rid of all the evidence in case someone from battalion came looking. I poured sand out of a sandbag, poured in the bacon grease, threw in the eggshells, and refilled the sandbag. Early the next morning, I took the sandbag with me to the head, dropped it into the bottom of one of the holes, and did my business on top, sure no one would look for evidence there. Like Turk warned, in the morning, the battalion executive officer (XO) inspected the perimeter looking for evidence of the missing roast, eggs, and bacon. Our reputation as The Filthy Few made us prime suspects. Like Captain Queeg in the movie *The Caine Mutiny* looking for the missing strawberries, the XO did not find a trace of contraband food anywhere. And, of course, we were not going to "fess up" to it. If he found anything, what could he do to us anyway? We were already in Vietnam.

Not long after the XO got tired of looking around, we received the word. The scuttlebutt was correct for once. Lima Company was going back to Hill 51.

CHAPTER 22
HILL 51

August 1985, my breathing labored; my leg muscles screamed in protest with every step. Over 14,300 feet up the mountain, the lack of oxygen made me lightheaded. The top of Mt. Whitney is the highest point in the continental United States. My friend Mark, seven years younger and a former Navy Seal, was already standing on the summit. Doug and Bill were right behind him. They spurred me on, always the last one, to reach my goal. We had waited two years for a permit. No way was I not going to make it to the top. Altitude sickness early in the morning made it touch and go. Now this close, I knew I would make it.

A cloudless day, we could see over two hundred miles in all directions. On the top was a plaque showing the altitude as 14,496 feet. We stood on the edge of the flat rock by the plaque and looked down the two-thousand-foot drop-off. Awestruck by the view, we heard a screaming loud noise coming from behind us; we all ducked. The noise was a USMC jet fighter flying low. The pilot must have seen us make it to the top of the mountain. We watched as he flew out over the valley making a long sweeping turn behind us again. Coming straight at us, the plane screamed over us again; we waved to the pilot. He rolled his wings and sent white smoke streamers out from both wing tips. For a split second, we could see the pilot as he gave us the thumbs up to congratulate us for making it to the top.

While the guys signed the book to prove we had made it to the summit, I stood on the flat rock and watched the jet until it disappeared down the valley. I was envisioning a day in Vietnam long ago when we called for an air strike and watched the pilots as they flew low over Hill 51, rolling their wings back and forth and sending white streamers out from the wing tips just before dropping four two-hundred and fifty pound bombs. Today the plane was not dropping bombs, which made it a lot more enjoyable to watch.

February 2, 1967, early in the morning, the company left the battalion perimeter. The three-hour patrol to Hill 51 was uneventful. We had patrolled near the hill or in the surrounding valley other times, so we were familiar with the area. As we approached the hill, I bent my flexible radio antenna down over my shoulder and stuck it under the strap of my pack. I did not want it sticking up again like a sign that said, "Shoot me." Lima Company had been assigned to take over the defensive positions on top of the hill and to set up ambushes and patrol the surrounding area.

Once on top of the hill, I understood why battalion wanted us up there. We had an unobstructed view overlooking the Co Bi-Than Tan Valley in all directions. Hill 51 was an important strategic location. To the west across the valley were high tree-covered mountains and the Laos border. To the east, rivers ran behind the hill and out into the valley. Anything that moved in the valley or the area around us would be easy to spot.

Dark clouds made it look and feel like rain was on the way. The perimeter defensive positions we were taking over were minimal at best. I made a small hooch behind a couple of fighting holes for Turk and me to use for the night. I cooked a couple of C-Ration meals for us, and we settled in for our first night on the hill. The night was quiet but wet.

The platoons were going to rotate patrolling and setting up ambushes around the hill. At least one platoon needed to stay on the hill at all times. Second Platoon was scheduled to have patrol duty in a couple of days. With time on my hands, I decided to build a place for Turk and me to stay.

With only my entrenching tool to work with, I was glad the dirt was soft and easy to dig. Close behind our fighting holes, I dug a trench seven feet wide, eight feet long, and four feet deep. In the center, I dug the trench eighteen inches deeper, leaving two flat places to lay air mattresses. With sticks and rope, I stretched our shelter halves over the top to make a sloping cover and secured them with sandbags. I was lying on my air mattress, checking out my creation when Turk came in. "What do you think, Sir?" I said.

"A damn outstanding job, Elliott, but bottom line we are still living in a goddamn hole in the ground."

"I think the operative words there, Sir, are We are living."

The lieutenant laughed and said, "If you can call this living."

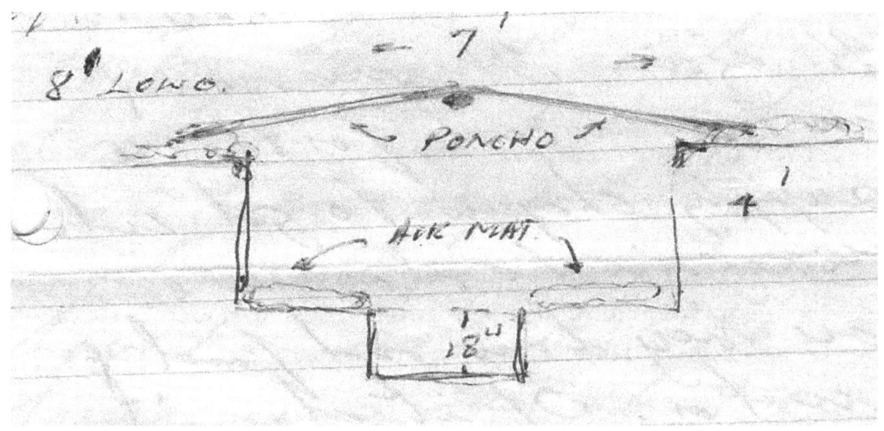

Drawing of the hole I dug for the lieutenant and me to live in on Hill 51. I made this drawing on the back of a letter to Mom and Dad.

Across the valley, the Ho Chi Min trail runs through the mountains along the Laos border. The North Vietnamese Army (NVA) used the trail to move men, equipment, and supplies south. In a couple of open spots, the trail was visible from our position on the hilltop. Using binoculars set on top of a stack of empty ammo crates, we took turns watching the open spots. When we detected enemy movement, we knew about how long it would take for that movement to reach the next open spot. We called in a pre-plotted artillery strike to hit about the same time the enemy should arrive. I think the NVA realized we knew the time and did not always arrive when the artillery rounds hit. We watched the spots at night and, if we saw lights moving, we called in artillery. When an artillery strike hit, we watched and cheered as the other side of the valley exploded into flames and smoke. Did the enemy react the same way when they fired rockets at us? We never knew if or how many VC or NVA we might have killed or how much equipment we had damaged. We certainly disrupted their supply line, even if it was only for a brief time.

Along with artillery, we attacked any movement in the valley with a quad-50 caliber machine gun. The gun had been flown out by helicopter and positioned on top of the hill. A quad-50 is exactly what it sounds like. Four turret-mounted 50-caliber machine guns operated by a crew of three Marines. The gunner sat in a canvas sling seat in between the four guns. Two loaders on a platform next to the guns were on each side.

When we saw movement, the gunner fired all four machine guns at once. Every fifth round was a tracer that created a red ribbon that stretched across the valley into the target. As the gunner fired, the loaders kept reloading each gun.

Each platoon took responsibility to watch the area in front of its position for enemy troop movement. When targets were spotted in the valley, we also had a forward observer assigned to the company. If some jet planes were in the area, he could call for a bomb run. When the planes were to drop napalm, they flew low through the valley to drop the napalm canisters, spreading fire like a fire-breathing dragon. A good thing the VC did not have an air force; napalm is nasty shit. The impressive fireball not only burned everything in its path, but it also sucked the oxygen out of the air. If the VC were in tunnels, which was often, the napalm suffocated them.

Albert was on watch over Second Platoon's area of responsibility when he spotted a VC patrol in an abandoned village deep in the valley and reported it to Turk. We made sure no friendly troops were in that area. The forward observer let us know two planes were close by. The company commander gave the go-ahead for an air strike. We all lined up to watch. The planes, one marked USMC and other US Navy, flew low over the hill on their way to the target. We waved to the pilots as they flew over us rolling their wings back and forth. Diving at the target, at what seemed like the last minute to us, the planes dropped four 250-pound bombs and two canisters of napalm.

"Holy shit," Albert yelled out "Two bombs, and the napalm did not explode."

He didn't really need to tell us that; we were all watching.

"Probably because the Navy pilot forgot to set the triggers," I said. (Marine/Navy humor)

The forward observer told us the planes were flying low when the bombs were released, and there was not enough time for the triggers to set before hitting the target. For safety reasons, when bombs are being attached under the airplane wing, the triggers are not set. When dropped, the bombs need to travel a certain distance before the triggers will set. The two bombs that did explode were short of the target.

Standing behind us to watch the air strike, the company commander looked over at Turk and shook his head. "You called it; you go find the bombs." Of course, that meant the entire Second Platoon would be going on an Easter egg hunt in a mine field, looking out for booby traps and the VC while trying to find two unexploded 250-pound bombs. We needed to destroy the bombs so the VC could not use them for booby traps. Too late in the day to start the search, we waited until the next morning.

In the morning, we each grabbed a couple of pounds of C-4 explosives to carry for the explosives engineer who would go with us. Turk took map readings from the top of the hill to give us an idea where to start our search. At the bottom of the hill, we crossed the river, our boots wet right from the start. We moved down the valley until we reached the search area Turk had identified.

We found where the napalm landed. The two canisters had hit about fifteen meters apart, cracked open on impact but failed to ignite. The gooey mess of napalm gel spread out along the trail. The smell of diesel fuel was in the air. We set up a perimeter guard while other guys covered the stuff with dirt.

We spread out in a line to cover a wide area searching for the unexploded bombs. After an hour, we found one of the bombs buried in the ground with the fins sticking up. The explosives engineer told us to set up a defensive perimeter in a circle about one hundred meters around the bomb location. While we cleared a path of escape for the engineer and set up the perimeter around him, he dug a hole and packed twenty pounds of C-4 plastic explosives around the nose of the bomb. The engineer signaled Turk that he was ready, and Turk signaled back that we were as well. The engineer came running down the path we had cleared for him, yelling, "Fire in the hole! Fire in the hole!" Seconds after he hit the ground behind the small berm where we were, there was a small explosion followed by a much larger one. The C-4 set off the 250-pound bomb. The shock wave passed over us.

Right after the explosion, we started to stand up when all kinds of dirt and rocks came flying everywhere. A few guys suffered cuts and scratches but no serious injuries. Turk said, "Next time we set up two hundred meters away." We walked back to check out the bomb crater. We found a hole in the ground ten meters across and five meters deep.

Up ahead while looking for the second bomb, Mike's fist went straight up in the air, the signal to stop and hold position. He pointed to the ground in front of him to signal a punji pit. One booby trap usually meant others were close by. Turk and I moved to Mike's position while on the lookout for more pits. I had stepped in a punji pit once before but fell forward and managed to catch my knee on the side of the hole to keep from getting injured. I did not want to try that again.

The platoon moved past us looking for more traps. None found, Mike waited until Turk, and I moved to take cover with the rest of the platoon. Mike carefully removed the top from the trap to make sure there was no trip wire with a booby trap inside. He smashed in the top and filled in the hole with dirt. Turk had already noted on his map the locations of the napalm and the first bomb; he added the location of the booby trap to report it all to battalion.

We continued our search but could not locate the other bomb. A couple of days later, one of the other platoons on patrol in the same area found and destroyed the second bomb.

We needed to get back to the top of Hill 51 before dark. Crossing the river on the way back, our boots were soaked again. Back in our hilltop positions, we tried to dry off our feet, eat, and get some sleep. The platoon was scheduled to go back out on patrol the next morning.

Mike O'Grady manning his position on Hill 51.

M51 Multiple 50-Caliber Machine Gun ("Quad Fifty")
Capacity 1600 – 2200 rounds per minute
This is the weapon we had on Hill 51.

Keith (Tbag) TeeGardin
Manning the M-60 Machine Gun in his fighting position on Hill 51.

CHAPTER 23
THE THINGS THEY MISSED

After finding and blowing up the 250-pound bomb that had not exploded, we made our way back to the top of Hill 51. Before dark, six of us sat in a small circle behind our defensive positions about to cook our C-Ration meals for the night. I opened a can of spaghetti and meatballs. Before heating, little white specks of fat floated in the red sauce. Not the most appetizing but, when hungry like always, I did not care. I lit the heat tab and watched the little white specks melt into the sauce.

Sick and tired of C-Rations, we started talking about the food we missed from home. The subject turned into a long discussion, our mouths watering. I visualized sitting at the dining room table, about to devour a big plate of Mom's homemade spaghetti and meatballs, my second favorite dinner after meatloaf and mashed potatoes. We joked and laughed about what we missed. We all missed our moms' cooking; each bragging his mom was the best cook in the world.

Fig shouted out, "I wish I had twenty-five pounds of salami right now."

"I'd rather have twenty-five packages of Oreo cookies," Mike said.

"And five gallons of cold milk to wash them down with," Albert added.

"Wait a minute," I said taking a pencil and paper out of my pack. "Okay, shout out what you miss the most. I'm going to write all of it down and send the list to Mom and ask her to send us a care package."

The following is a verbatim account of my original letter to Mom. I still have the letter.

THOMAS ELLIOTT

Dear Mom:

We are sitting around our position after another long day in the field. We were talking about things we want to eat; we have been eating nothing but C-Rations for over fifty days. Here is what we want.

25 pounds of Hard Dry Salami
10 cases of Chef Boyardee spaghetti
10 cases tuna fish (Star Kist)
10 jars Mayo
5 jars ketchup (Hunts)
5 jars sweet pickles
10 pounds onions
50# Cracker Barrel cheddar cheese
25 packages Nabisco Oreo Cookies
25 packages Vanilla Wafers
35 loaves of French bread
50 boxes graham crackers
10 jars mustard
10 cases canned enchiladas
1000 packs Welsh's lemonade
50 packs beef jerky
50 cans mixed canned fruit
25 jars of onion dip
100 bags of potato chips
5 bottles of black olives
25 boxes Tostem's
10 cases Apple Raspberry Sauce
50 bags dried apricots
25 bags of pretzels
10 jars of peanut butter
And 50 CASES OF BEER

Please send all in one package A.S.A.P.
Your hungry Son and friends!

We did not get it all, but sometime later, I did get a large box of chocolate chip cookies. I shared the cookies with the guys, and we imagined they were all the foods we had missed that day.

Years later, the Santa Barbara County Public Library sponsored an essay contest for students and local veterans related to Tim O'Brien's book *The Things They Carried*. The students and veterans read his book and attended his lecture when Tim came to town. After the lecture, we had two weeks to turn in an essay to the public library. I used my letter to Mom as the basis for my entry into the contest. The title of my essay was "The Things They Missed." I won the veterans' category of the contest.

CHAPTER 24
THE FEVER BLISTER

The next morning, the food discussion still on my mind, I wanted a plate of real bacon and eggs with hash browns, not the cold can of Ham and Eggs Chopped I was about to open. After a quick C-Ration breakfast, we started our patrol along the bank of the Song Bo River. The muddy water quietly twisted and turned down the valley. On the other side, there were old rice paddies surrounded by dikes. Remnants of a burned-out hamlet lay beyond the dikes. Before the war, it would have been a tranquil place. Would it ever be that way again?

Since the monsoon season was not yet over, it was not the best time to patrol along the river. The banks lined with thick stands of bamboo, six to eight inches in diameter and over fifty feet tall, made progress difficult. Spread out, we moved slowly along an old cart path that paralleled the river. Before we started along the riverbank, Turk sent a squad to watch our rear and flank. From behind us, there were shots fired. They sounded like M-14s. The squad on the flank signaled Turk. He moved toward their location, me right behind him. A VC hiding in the tall grass was waiting for us to pass by. He stood up to shoot at us, but before he got his shot off, one of the flank men shot and killed him. The squad on the flank did exactly what they were there for.

Back along the cart path and river, I felt something on the back of my neck and slapped at it with my hand. My hand came back all bloody—a leech. Along the river, small tree leeches dropped out of the bamboo as we passed by. The tree leeches were not the only leech problem we had to deal with. When we waded across a river, we had to stop for a leech check. We all looked like Humphrey Bogart in the scene from *The African Queen* with leeches all over his back. Some guys found up to twenty leeches at one time. Ten were the most for me.

There are two ways to get rid of a leech: one, burn it with a cigarette; the other, squirt it with mosquito repellent. If pulled off, the leech left its stinger behind, making it hard to stop the bleeding and could allow the bite to get infected. I cut an empty sandbag open and wrapped it around my legs at the top of my boots like a set of spats. I sprayed mosquito repellent all over the sandbags to keep the leeches off my legs.

A leech crawled under the eyelid of one of the new guys while he was lying in an ambush site. In the morning, his eye was swollen and bleeding. Doc treated him and I called for a helicopter to take him back to the command post for better medical attention. The tree leeches were small and liked to get into warm places, especially one's crotch. One guy in another platoon had one crawl up the head of his dick. Talk about pain.

Sitting in an ambush site on a night so dark, it did not matter if my eyes were open or shut. I felt a lump on my lower lip and thought it was a fever blister. I licked at it all night. The next morning, Albert asked, "What's that on your lower lip? You look like an Ubangi."

"A fever blister," I said.

"Bullshit, man, it's a leech."

"No shit, burn the damn thing off!" Albert used his cigarette to touch it and it fell to the ground. I squashed the little bastard with my boot. A squirt of blood, my blood, shot out from under the boot. I licked my lips again and tasted my own blood.

The next day while on patrol, we passed an Ontos vehicle completely destroyed when it ran over a booby-trapped bomb. It had been operating in the same area where our platoon had been on a similar Ontos patrol. When the bomb exploded, it also ignited the gas tank and set off the spare rounds carried in the bottom of the vehicle. The three-man crew and four Marines riding on top were killed in the explosion. The blast was so big only five of the bodies were found, and the Ontos was in pieces all over the area. The unit commander was one of the Marines killed. He was a lieutenant and a good friend of Lt. Dolan and Lt. McCarthy. They were deeply hurt by the loss of their friend. Second Platoon never went on another Ontos patrol.

We stopped for a short break in a small ravine near the bottom of Hill 51. A shot rang out, the bullet bouncing off a tree about a foot above Albert's head. Pat Cochran spotted the shooter and wounded him in the shoulder, causing him to fall on top of his rifle. When the VC started to get up, it looked like he was going to shoot at us again. Corporal Strange standing nearby shot and killed him. We cut down a long bamboo pole and tied his body to it. We took turns humping the body up Hill 51. The guy was carrying a Russian-made automatic rifle, two Chinese grenades, and Laotian money. We also found a little book of names and other papers. He was a hard-core North Vietnamese regular, not a typical Viet Cong. The battalion intelligence officer wanted to see the papers and flew out to our location on the helicopter that came to retrieve the body. After examining the papers and other belongings the guy had on him, he let us keep the money. We did not tell him about the little stash of hash we took off the guy.

The next day on patrol, Albert got into a shooting match with a VC along the trail. The gook was down but still alive. Albert wanted to finish the job, but Turk told him no. I called for a chopper, and we sent the prisoner back to battalion. That pissed Albert off; he wanted the kill.

For eighteen days, we carried out company, platoon, and squad-sized operations all around Hill 51. We suffered Marines wounded, mostly by booby traps, but no Marines killed. All the platoons killed VC; Second Platoon killed five.

Now on Operation Chinook for fifty-four days, thirty-nine of which it rained, we were tired of living in holes in the ground, walking ten thousand meters a day, being wet and cold, and eating nothing but C-Rations, all on four hours of sleep a night if lucky. Our gear was rotting from being wet all the time. The weather was often so bad resupply helicopters were unable to get to us. We needed a break.

Late in the afternoon, the captain informed the platoon commanders the company assignment on Hill 51 was over, and we should prepare to leave in the morning. Good news to our ears as we were tired of climbing up and down the damn hill. Heading back to the CP, again I hoped for a break. I always hoped for a break, but it never seemed to happen.

Corporal Jim Strange, Pat Cochran, and Turk looking over the NVA soldier's papers.

Tom Elliott on Hill 51 with weapons taken from dead VC.

CHAPTER 25
HUNGRY

Back on the battalion perimeter after leaving Hill 51, we hoped for a break as we always did. It did not happen. After only two days on perimeter watch, Second Platoon was sent on patrol to work an area at the end of the valley along a river and the foothills. We hoped the monsoons were ending but it looked like they were going to have one more go at us. On and off rain, it was sometimes heavy and sent sideways by the wind. The VC were smart enough to stay under cover; we made no contact. The first day of the patrol, we waded across the river to continue our patrol on the other side. That was a big mistake. The river, now between us and battalion CP, was swelled by heavy rain to the point where ground vehicles were unable to cross. The river was running too fast for us to walk or swim across. Resupply helicopters were not able to reach our position in the harsh weather.

We had left on patrol with only a three-day supply of C-Rations, the usual two meals a day. Before we knew it, we ran out of food. No food, no way for supplies to reach us, and with the severe weather, Turk decided to set up a defensive perimeter and hunker the platoon down until the weather improved. We found an old, partially destroyed VC bunker complex and set up our defensives. I built a small shelter for Turk and me using our ponchos. Cut off in enemy territory, we could not let our guard down. Luckily the rain and cold kept the VC from trying to attack us.

For three days, there was nothing at all to eat. I carried a small bottle of Lawry's seasoning salt Mom had sent me in a care package. I used it to spice up C-Ration meals, but now I sprinkled a little in the palm of my hand and licked it, trying to trick my empty stomach into thinking it was real food. It didn't work. After three days, my stomach growled like a bear coming out of hibernation.

Worse yet, I ran out of cigarettes. Smoking was one of the few pleasures available to us, mostly when back inside the battalion perimeter. In the bush, we could not smoke at night, as lighting a match would give our position away. During the day, it was okay if were out in the open and not sitting in an ambush site. To sit down, lean against a tree or stack of sandbags, and enjoy a smoke helped take the edge off. At least for me it did.

Cigarettes were always hard to get, so I had devised a backup system. When I finished a cigarette, I put it out and saved the butt in a plastic bag. The guys who smoked laughed at me for this habit.

I carried the pipe bowl end of a pipe with the stem broken off. Out of smokes, I opened the butts and put the little bits of tobacco in the pipe bowl, lit up, and enjoyed a smoke. A little harsh without a filter, but better than nothing. The guys begged me for a hit. "Too bad we don't have some good weed to smoke," Albert said. The only problem with that, it would have made us even hungrier.

After three days, the weather let up enough for us to walk about five thousand meters to a resupply point. Walking was difficult after not eating for three days. I fell a couple of times from exhaustion. When we made it to the resupply point, the first thing I did was smoke a cigarette.

Resupplied and our belly's full, battalion made us stay on patrol for three more days. That really pissed us off. We experienced no contact with the enemy. The river finally receded enough for us to cross, and we headed back to the battalion to take up our positions on the perimeter again.

During the time we were cut off, I developed a painful and infected leech bite below the kneecap. Doc Miller tended to it, and, when we were back inside the perimeter, told me to go to the aid station and have it checked out. At the aid station, the corpsman removed the bandage. The infected center was as big as a nickel, and the red around it the size of a silver dollar. The corpsman stretched my leg out on the table and poured hydrogen peroxide on it. When the infected center bubbled up with white foam, I winced from the pain.

That turned out to be the easy part. Next, he took a brush, resembling one of those short, hard-bristled brushes used for cleaning fingernails, and started scrubbing the open wound like he was doing his nails. He kept scrubbing until the skin turned raw and bled down my leg. Then he hit it with the hydrogen peroxide again. Acting like a hard-core Marine, I held it in, but it hurt like hell. I remembered the Marine Corps saying, "Pain is weakness leaving the body." I felt pretty weak! He bandaged up my leg and gave me antibiotic pills to take for seven days. He said, "Have the doc look at it every day, and change the bandage," using the bandages he gave me. The area he cleaned was sore and bothered me for a couple of days, but a week later, it healed up. I still have a scar.

Lima Company was on perimeter guard duty at night and running patrols during the day. There was not much action around the perimeter, but when on patrol, mines, booby traps, and VC patrols were encountered every day. The weather started to get hot—in the nineties, even getting to hundred degrees, during the day. The rain let up, it looked like the monsoons were finally ending. Rumor had it our participation on Operation Chinook was also ending. In the country for eighty-one days and on operation Chinook for seventy three days, we were no longer the new guys. With six more months on our tour, we were not old salts yet either.

Albert came by my position on the perimeter. "We are going to Phu Bai in a few days for a break," he said.

"A break; I'll believe that when I see it." Ten more days went by before we were relieved and reassigned to the base in Phu Bai.

During February, the battalion had suffered seven Marines killed in action and seventy wounded. The battalion was credited with seventy-eight confirmed VC killed, 170 probable kills, and we took forty prisoners.

Lance Corporal Paul O. Evans was the first Marine killed on Operation Chinook, one of the two Marines killed during the fighting on the third night of the operation, and he was the first Marine killed from Lima Company. Assigned to Second Platoon from the Lieutenant Jaak Aulik Weapons Platoon, Paul was a friend and honorary member of The Filthy Few. Battalion had scheduled Operation Chinook to last for fourteen days; we were there for eighty-three days. The Chinook area was eventually turned into a permanent base camp of operations. In Paul's honor, the Marine area commander named it "Camp Evans."

CHAPTER 26
PHU BAI

Warm water ran over my head and down my back. Going without a decent shower for so long, I wanted to stand under the water forever. The water raining down on me made me think of the ocean and surfing, something not on my mind much for the past three months. "Elliott, hurry the fuck up, man; we want to take a shower too," somebody yelled from outside the shower. My daydream of surfing was cut short. Showered and shaved, I put on a clean jungle uniform and boots but no underwear. I felt like a new man, ready to continue the fight.

A military canvas and wood-framed cot is one step above sleeping on the ground, two if you count an air mattress. After three months of sleeping on the ground, much of the time on cold, wet ground, waking up from the best night's sleep I had in three months, the cot I was lying on felt like a thousand-dollar box spring and mattress combo.

Operation Chinook was supposed to be a fourteen-day sweep and destroy mission. We had been on the operation for eighty-three days. During that time, it rained, once for twenty-six days in a row. We went fifty-six days without a shower, a change of clothes, or a hot meal. We saw plenty of action and endured leeches, cold, heat, having not enough to eat, and only a few cans of beer over the entire three months. The battalion suffered twenty-three Marines killed in action and 330 wounded. Guys were also out of action for periods of time due to dysentery, immersion foot, vehicle accidents, a few cases of malaria, and a couple of self-inflicted wounds. We needed a rest.

Finally on March 10, 1967, battalion relieved Lima Company of duty on Operation Chinook, replacing us with the Second Battalion 9th Marines. We were stationed at Phu Bai, a large Marine Corps base south of Hue. Our supplies on Operation Chinook had come from Phu Bai and the platoon rode shotgun on a number of resupply convoys, so we knew a little about the base.

Our company was assigned to live in tin-roofed, screened-in hooches inside the base and away from the perimeter. We would not be required to stand guard duty on the base perimeter. The hooches included cots with pillows and blankets, a pleasant change from sleeping on the ground. Our hooch was close to the mess tent. What a treat to not have to cook our own meals. The mess tent provided tables and chairs; we did not have to sit on the wet ground to eat. The best part was I could eat all I wanted and not be hungry for once. At my first meal in the mess tent my eyes were bigger than my stomach. I ended up with a stomachache after eating too much. A shower, full belly, no guard duty, and a cot with a blanket, I could not ask for much more under the circumstances, except for a cold beer.

The day after we transferred down to Phu Bai, Turk left for R&R in Hawaii. Lucky guy, an officer, he qualified for R&R in Hawaii. The battalion had been in country now long enough, some of the guys from the platoon were going on leave for a week out of country and away from the fight. Most of the guys went to Hong Kong or Bangkok, and most came back with the clap, proving they had a fun time. I wanted to wait to take my R&R in Hawaii so I could meet Phyliss there. As an enlisted man, I would have to wait longer into my tour to be eligible for R&R in Hawaii.

On the base at Phu Bai, we were resting, lying back, playing football and poker, and standing inspection daily by Captain Roller, who took over as the Company Commander halfway through Operation Chinook. We drank a few beers (too few), wrote letters home, and caught up on needed sleep. We knew it would not be long before we were back in the bush.

On the 17th of March, we attended a memorial service for the twenty-three Marines from the battalion killed in action during the eighty-three days we were on Operation Chinook. Second Platoon lost three Marines: Paul Evans, the first man killed on the operation, Gary Schneider, killed during the New Year's truce, and Ferrell Hummingbird, shot by a sniper.

For the service, twenty-three bayonet-fixed rifles were stuck in the ground with helmets on them. A sad day for us all; the saddest part, it would not be the last memorial service we attended in Vietnam. Attending the service, I got that feeling again, why them and not me?

Turk returned from R&R in Hawaii, and the next day The platoon left the base perimeter on patrol. Turk had brought me a T-shirt from one of the surf shops. In the hot weather I cut the sleeves off and wore it under my flak jacket every day until it rotted away. In Hawaii, Turk also bought a fancy new quick-draw shoulder holster for his 45-caliber pistol.

We patrolled our area of operations for a couple of days, sitting in ambush sites at night. We encountered punji pits and other booby traps and got into a couple of quick-fire fights, but no major encounters with the VC. No one was wounded.

The last day of the patrol, we spent hours humping the hills and crisscrossing the area through rice paddies and over the dikes. At the end of the patrol and while coming through the wire of the base perimeter, the gunny checked everyone to get a head count. He noticed Turk's pistol was missing from his fancy new shoulder holster. Like most platoon commanders, in addition to his pistol, Turk also carried a rifle, so he never noticed his pistol was missing. Turk made us backtrack, looking for the pistol. He did not want to report to battalion that he had lost his side arm on patrol. Getting late, it looked like we might never find the pistol. Turk was about to give up and order us back to the perimeter when one of the guys up at the head of the patrol signaled back to Turk. He had found the pistol on the side of a rice paddy dike. The barrel was down in the water and the hand grip was sticking out barely enough to see it. We made it back to the perimeter before dark. Turk spent the evening cleaning his pistol. After that, he carried the pistol in the old, hip-style Marine Corps–issued holster with a flap to hold it in place.

While we were at Phu Bai, General Hochmuth took over command of the 3rd Battalion 26th Marines. He had been our base commander in San Diego when we were in boot camp. He was a good officer, and we were happy about his taking over. Sadly, General Hochmuth was killed in a helicopter crash on November 14, 1967. The Phu Bai Base was renamed Camp Hochmuth in his honor.

Soon we were back in the bush, working an area about thirty-five kilometers north of Pa Nang. The area was a marshy valley with high hills and dense undergrowth. The officers at battalion headquarters expected us to patrol an assigned distance each day. They would look at their map and say move from point A to point B. To them, it was only one inch on the map and the ground looked flat and easy to cross. For us, we were moving across the rice paddies where we sank in mud that nearly pulled our boots off. We crossed rivers with water sometimes up to our shoulders. Leeches were everywhere. We hacked our way through the thick underbrush, carrying sixty pounds packs, watching out for booby traps, and never knowing when the VC might shoot at us—day after day, all with little or no sleep, and not enough to eat. What looked like only an inch on the map to the guys in the rear seemed to us like twenty kilometers. We did not always get from A to B.

The weather changed to extremely hot and humid, not necessarily a pleasant change from the rain and cold. We were really humping our asses when one of the guys passed out from heat stroke. He was so out of it that Doc Miller used a safety pin to secure his tongue to his lip so he would not choke on his tongue. A helicopter took him back to the base for medical attention. He recovered and was back with us a couple of days later. He thanked the Doc for shoving a safety pin through his tongue.

The last couple of days of the patrol, the platoon stayed at a CAP village compound outside Phu Bai. CAP (Combined Action Platoon) was a program of pacification started by the Marines. A small team of thirteen Marines, including a Navy corpsman, lived in the compound with a platoon of South Vietnamese troops. They ran patrols and set up ambushes at night to help protect the nearby village. They collected intelligence on VC movements and helped the people by building water wells and schools. We worked the area for a few days and talked with the Marines in the compound. CAP looked like fairly good duty except for the fact, if attacked, there were only thirteen of them.

At the end of March, the long-anticipated day arrived for Lima Company to receive the new M-16 rifle. The Army had been issued the rifle before the Marine Corps, and we heard stories about jamming problems. I worried about giving up my M-14; in fact, I was having separation anxiety. My M-14 was a part of me; together for over a year and we were inseparable. We went everywhere and did everything together. I knew the serial number by heart. I spent hours cleaning it. I talked to it when no one else would listen. I trusted my rifle with my life. Now they wanted to take it away and give me something new.

The M-16 did have advantages over the M-14. It was lighter and had a selector switch for setting the rifle on full-automatic. Three hundred rounds of ammo weighed the same as one hundred rounds for the M-14 rifle.

At a rifle range outside the Phu Bai base, we turned in our M-14 rifles and received the new M-16 and enough ammo to load two magazines. We took a dozen shots at targets set up one hundred and three hundred meters out. The rifles seemed okay, not much recoil and were accurate up to three hundred meters.

After we were all familiar with the weapon, the captain told us to put in a full magazine and select full-automatic. Standing shoulder to shoulder at the bottom of the hill, we all aimed at the hilltop and fired on full-automatic. A considerable number of rifles jammed due to a spent cartridge caught in the chamber.

The chamber was not lined, and the cartridge wall was too thin for the power load causing the bullet casing to swell in the chamber. The extractor on the bolt pulled off and slammed home on the empty cartridge, jamming it in the chamber.

To clear the jammed cartridge from the chamber required opening the rifle to push the empty cartridge out using a cleaning rod. That meant if the weapon jammed in a fire fight, you had to stop (the enemy did not stop) to get out your cleaning kit, assemble the cleaning rod, which came in three pieces, and clear the jam. In truth, you were fucked.

The officer who issued the M-16 told us we needed to keep the rifle super clean. Tromping around all day in the rice paddies, through wind and rain, and hitting the deck every time we ran into trouble, made keeping a weapon super clean impossible. You could throw an M-14 in the rice paddy for a couple of days, pick it up, and it would still shoot, same with the Russian-made AK-47. All these problems with the M-16 did not instill confidence in us.

Because the M-16s were made of a plastic-looking composite, the saying, "Made by Mattel, they're swell," became our mantra. We, along with other guys in Vietnam, continued to have trouble with the M-16 rifle, and the jamming problems were often responsible for men dying in action. When the problems were eventually fixed, the M-16 became a more reliable and good weapon. But at first, I wanted my M-14 back.

During this time, the battalion was on stand-by to return to Operation Chinook II (now called Camp Evans) because of a big VC build-up in the area. Thankfully we did not have to return. Our next duty assignment would be a little more relaxing and fun.

Tom Elliott: Platoon Radio Operator at Phu Bai Base
M-14 rifle leaning against the sandbag wall
Picture courtesy of Jim Strange

Second Platoon "The Filthy Few"
Resting after Operation Chinook, enjoying a few beers
Phu Bai Marine Base
Sitting: Keith TeeGardin, Doc Graham, Mike O'Grady
Standing: Jim Mulhull, Russ Helton, SSgt Magulick, Ernie Hoffmann, Gary Toler, Sgt. Strange, Pat Cochran, Dennis Stecki
Picture courtesy of Jim Strange

Second Platoon members with our new M-16 Rifles
Front Row: Rick Figueroa, Gary Toler, Garcia, Mike O'Grady, Sharon Huff, Dennis Stecki
Back Row: Sgt Strange, Tom Elliott, Ernie Hoffmann, Tom Carey, Pat Cochran, Keith TeeGardin, unknown

MEMORIAL SERVICES

Invocation.............................. Chaplain Tom Collins

Scripture Reading................. Chaplain Tom Collins

* * * * * * * * * * *

Eulogy............................... Lt. Col. K.L. Hoch

* * * * * * * * * * *

Prayers for the Dead.............. Chaplain Wattigny

* * * * * * * * * * *

End of Memorial Services

TAPPS

....

Lt. Col. K.L. Hoch – Commanding Officer
Major W.J. Woodring, Jr. – Executive Officer
Lt. Bede Wattigny, CHC, USNR – Battalion Chaplain

Men of 3rd. Bn. 26th Marines who have died in Action.

* * * * * * * * * * *

Cpl. R. Ratcliff	I Co
Sgt. S.F. Jalloway	I Co
LCpl. P.O. Evans	L Co
PFC T. W. Shalhoob	K Co
PFC M. Vasquez	K Co
Cpl. G.T. Schneider	L Co
HN R.W. Green	H&S Co
LCpl. J.A. Abrams	I Co
PFC T.A. Greg	I Co
PFC R.B. Painter	K Co
LCpl. F. Hummingbird	L Co
LCpl. K. W. Kraus	L Co
HN C.F. Fincher	H&S Co
HN W.A. Beyer	I Co
LCpl. D.J. Frischmann	M Co
Sgt. L.Robinson, Jr.	M Co
PFC C.M. Swain	H&S Co
Sgt. M.E. Burns	K Co
Capt. R.E. Hines	I Co
Sgt. D.F. Kaufman	M Co
PFC R.L. Thornell	M Co
PFC G.R. Worrell	I Co
LCpl. F.J. Berry, Jr	M Co

* * * * * * * * * * * * * * * * * *

Eternal Rest grant unto them, O Lord. May they rest in Peace!

Program from the Memorial Service
Held on March 17, 1967, at Phu Bai Base for Marines
3/26 lost on Operation Chinook.

CHAPTER 27
FISHING VIETNAMESE STYLE

Damn, our first time near the coast in over five months and there's no surf. I had hoped to at least see waves. The helicopter flew low over the coastline. The ocean water under us was calm and a deep blue. The temperature dropped as cooler air off the ocean blew through the open doors. A pleasant break from the hundred plus degree heat back at the base.

The landing zone (LZ) off in the distance did not look large enough to set a chopper down. But I knew from prior experience, the chopper pilots can land in seemingly impossible places. Approaching the LZ, the rotor blades dug into the air, the nose tipped up, the tail down, and the engine roared. It felt like we were going to shake to pieces. The pilot hovered over a small dirt clearing; the crew chief yelled, "Stand by!" The chopper bounced once and sat down hard. The crew chief yelled, "Go, go!" I jumped off and ran out from under the rotor blades. As soon as Turk and I were off, the crew chief signaled other Marines nearby to get on. The pilot lifted the chopper slightly and rolled off the hill and back out over the water toward the base. The entire process on the ground took about a minute.

We landed on what the map reference called Hill 282, a two-hundred-meter high hilltop at the end of a steep, rocky peninsula sweeping out into the South China Sea, forming a large, protected bay south of Phu Bai.

Our mission was to protect a Navy radio operator in charge of a signal station on the tip of the peninsula. A Navy ship at sea received the signals and used the information to map the ocean bottom. Why we needed that kind of information we were not told. We were simply happy not to be humping our asses in the hills looking for the VC.

The one Navy guy (I will call him Jack), running the station, was stuck there with thirty-five Marines. A good-natured guy, he took a lot of ribbing from us, but gave as good as he got. By the end of the mission, we all became good friends.

Lt. Frank McCarthy's Third Platoon had provided the security for the previous two weeks. We were the replacements. Turk and I flew out on the first chopper so Frank could brief Turk on the operation. As soon as we were off the chopper, Frank signaled us to his location away from the LZ. Before he started to brief Turk, a second chopper came into land, the noise drowning out Frank's words. The LZ on the tip of the peninsula was barely large enough to land a CH-34 transport helicopter. Our platoon flew out in small groups and kept up the rotation with Third Platoon until the transfer was completed. The last chopper was loaded with C-Rations and other supplies we needed for our two-week stay. Oh boy, we get to eat C-Rations again. After the supplies were unloaded, Lt. McCarthy left on the chopper.

The very tip of the peninsula was about 150–200 meters above the water. On the open ocean side, the drop-off went straight down. At the bottom, huge boulders were covered with seaweed gently swaying as small waves rolled over the rocks. On the bay side, the drop-off was less severe, there was what looked like a trail through the rocks down to the water. Except for the space cleared for the LZ and the Navy operator's equipment, rocks, shrubs, and a few trees covered the area. This was going to be our home for a couple of weeks. Away from the base, at least we did not have to listen to artillery going off all night. The monsoons were over so not much chance of rain.

The steep, rocky drop-off around at the end of the peninsula narrowed the land area and was the only approach that needed protection from an enemy attack. Third Platoon had done a very meticulous job of planning and setting up the defensive positions; all we had to do was move in. Frank told Turk that they had no enemy contact, so we did not expect any action. Although the assignment appeared relatively safe, Turk did not want us to lose our edge out here for two weeks. He and the squad leaders set up a day-and-night-watch rotation. Turk also sent a squad to walk the entire length of the peninsula to look for any signs of enemy activity. They reported none but we ran shorter patrols every day to make sure. Turk sent out a listening post every night. We also did daily inspections around the end of the peninsula to make sure the enemy was not trying to approach our position from the water.

With the defensives set up, we kept busy with the patrols, cleaning our weapons, writing letters home, and trying to help Jack when we could. I talked to Jack, who told me that some of the Third Platoon guys had gone down to the rocks at the bottom of the cliff for a swim in the South China Sea. I told Turk, and he said anybody not on watch could go check it out. Not all the guys liked to swim or wanted to climb down the rocks, so only six of us went. I went as often as possible. With no surf inside the bay, I enjoyed diving into the cool, clear water. Jack warned us there were sea snakes in the area, all of them deadly poisonous. One guy stood watch with his rifle while the others swam. After a swim, I lay on the warm rocks to work on my surfer dude tan and daydreamed of surfing.

I was also thinking about a letter I had received days earlier from my surfing buddy Doug. He was also a Marine and had been deployed to Vietnam a couple of weeks before I was. His supply company was stationed at Chu Li further south down the coast. In his letter, he told me about a day the USO showed up with a dozen surfboards and held a surfing contest. Doug won the first international Chu Li surfing championships. I was a much better surfer than Doug; I was really jealous.

Kicking back on the rocks after a swim one day, I watched a fishing boat come around the end of the peninsula and into the bay. The boat was painted the same bright colors as the South Vietnamese flag, yellow and red. Four men were aboard. None appeared armed, but we remained on our guard. The men on the boat spotted us on the rocks and waved; I waved back. The boat headed toward us. The boat had a heavy wooden bow and a shallow draft. The water was deep right up to the rocks. The captain carefully nosed the bow up on the rocks and held it there. He spoke a little English and asked if we wanted to go fishing. Bored, Al, Mike, Pat, and I jumped aboard. The captain backed away from the rocks and headed out to the middle of the bay.

The captain served us tea and told us about his boat and the fishing in the area. The men came from a small village down the coast and enjoyed fishing because the VC did not care to bother them when they were out on the water. Too old for the Regional Forces, they were simple men merely plying their trade.

Sitting on the deck in the shade of the boat's canopy, I looked around as I enjoyed my tea. I did not see any fishing poles, though I did see what looked like rolled up nets near the stern. How did they fish; did they have other gear below deck?

Doing it the proper way with two hands and a slight bow, I held the cigarette pack as I offered the captain a Marlboro. He smiled and bowed his head slightly as he pulled out a cigarette. He used a lighter from his pocket to light the cigarette. He took a long drag and slowly let out the smoke through his nose. He took another drag, savoring the taste and smell of the tobacco, as Vietnamese cigarettes did not have filters, smelled, and tasted like shit when smoked. I had tried smoking a couple. The rest of the crew stared at the captain as he enjoyed his American cigarette. Then they looked over at me. I knew what they wanted. I offered them each a cigarette. They dropped what they were doing, accepted my offer, and lit up. Smiles all around, I became an instant friend.

After enjoying their cigarette, one of the fishermen went below deck. A couple of minutes later, he came up carrying an 81 mm mortar round with a hand grenade taped to the nose. He walked over to show us his creation.

"What the hell is he going to do with that?" I asked.

"I don't know; where did they get the mortar rounds and grenades," Al said.

Before we asked, the fisherman walked to the stern of the boat. The captain moved to the helm and started the engine. When the engine started, the fisherman pulled the pin on the hand grenade and threw the whole thing overboard. The captain hit the throttle, but the boat did not go far. The grenade exploded setting the mortar round off with a powerful thud under the boat. Water sprayed all over us.

Fish started floating to the surface around the boat, killed by the concussion from the explosion. A couple of the fishermen jumped off to get the fish. One by one, they returned to the boat and handed the fish to a man on board. We were laughing as we also helped take fish from the men in the water. With most of the fish on the boat, the captain spotted a sea snake and yelled something in Vietnamese to the men in the water. They just about jumped up and walked on the water to get back on to the boat! That was fishing Vietnamese style.

One of the fishermen cleaned a couple of the fish and cooked them over a small gas grill. We shared the fish and a bowl of rice with the captain and crew as the boat drifted around in the bay. We could have been anywhere in the world. War, what war?

Finally, the guys on the rocks signaled us to come in. Our relaxing afternoon had ended. The captain nosed the boat back on the rocks, I gave him the rest of my cigarettes, and the boat sailed off into the sunset. As we made our way back up the hill, I wondered if the captain would share the cigarettes with his crew. In later years, I often wondered what might have happen to them when the war ended.

Turk was not too happy we had gone out on the boat with no way for him to contact us. I did not have a radio with me. He was concerned when he heard an explosion and saw a plume of water shoot up in the air. I told him about the captain, crew, and fishing Vietnamese style. He laughed and let it go. I went down the hill to swim every day after that, but the fishing boat never returned. There was an extra case of hand grenades on the hill. I had wanted to offer them to the captain for his fishing tackle box.

After two weeks, Jack let Turk know the Navy had completed the mapping process. I hoped a helicopter would come to pick up Jack's equipment. That did not happen. Instead, his ship came around the tip of the peninsula and anchored in the bay. We helped Jack carry his gear, including several heavy batteries, down the hill to the rocks where the fishing boat had picked us up. The Navy ship sent a small boat to pick up Jack and his gear. We made several trips down the hill, and the small boat made several trips out to the ship. On the last trip, the small-boat operator said the ship's captain wanted to invite our lieutenant on board. I sent word up the hill to Turk that the captain wanted to meet him. Turk came down the hill with the platoon sergeant and along with Albert, Pat, and me went out to the ship. We knew the sailors aboard a ship ate decent food. Living on nothing but C-Rations again, we hoped for something better to eat.

The captain welcomed us and thanked us for helping Jack. He gave us a quick tour of the ship ending in the galley. The cook laid out fried chicken, French fries, potato salad, coleslaw, and coke. We topped it off with huge bowls of ice cream.

As we were about to leave, the cook opened his refrigerator to us. Big mistake. We carried off loaves of bread, bags of rolls, bologna, salami, and sliced cheese plus mustard and ketchup—sandwich time for the guys on shore. We even grabbed a gallon of ice cream, which we had to drink from our canteen cups by the time it got to shore. Somehow a case of beer even ended up with us. Back on top of the hill, we told the guys about the meal on board. They were a little jealous but forgot about it when we handed out the food we had brought back and shared the beer.

The hill assignment was over, and we cleaned up the area and got ready to leave. The box of hand grenades I wanted to give to the fishing boat captain and a dozen claymore mines were still on the hill. Turk said he did not want to take them back with us on the chopper and told us to get rid of them. We threw the grenades off the hill and made small rocks out of the big rocks at the bottom of the cliff. We detonated all the claymores into the trees to make a larger clearing at the end of the peninsula. We did not want to leave anything behind for the VC.

Helicopters started flying a rotation to take us off the hill. Everyone but Turk and I went off on the first round of choppers. When the last chopper came in, Turk, the crew chief, and I loaded all the remaining gear on board, mostly left-over C-Rations. The pilot wound up the chopper, which shook like hell inches off the ground. The pilot set it back down and signaled to the crew chief the chopper was too heavy. The crew chief started kicking stuff off the chopper. The pilot wound up the chopper again, the blades were spinning so fast I was sure they were about to come off. The chopper lifted inches above the ground and hovered there. I thought we were going to set back down again when I yelled, "Oh shit." The pilot was now rolling the chopper off the side of the hill, and we started dropping down the cliff. I was holding on for dear life. About the time we were going to hit the water, the chopper came up and leveled off. A wild and scary ride for me and the crew chief was laughing his ass off. He said I should have seen the look on my face when we dropped off the side of the hill. I can laugh about it now. So much for not leaving anything behind; we never went back for the stuff the crew chief had kicked off the helicopter. I hoped whoever found it enjoyed the C-Rations.

Still no surf as we passed over the coastline, and on the return trip, the air coming in the open doors of the chopper was hot. After enjoying a daily swim in the cool ocean water, I did not look forward to going back to the base. As our chopper approached the landing pad at Phu Bai, the platoon waited for us at the air control office. Having recovered from the drop-off the side of the hill, I wanted to know what our next assignment might be. News that transfers were happening throughout the battalion came while we were on the hill. I was worried about the platoon breaking up and that Lieutenant Dolan would be promoted and transferred to another company. What might happen to me?

Living quarters for two weeks on Hill 282
Mike O'Grady, Tom Elliott on the radio

Years later I remembered that wild chopper ride while on vacation in Hawaii. My wife and I went for a helicopter ride on the back side of Lanai to view the two-thousand-foot high waterfalls. Before taking off, I talked to the pilot and found out he was a chopper pilot in Vietnam. I told him I served in Vietnam with the Marines. I told him this would be my wife's first ride in a helicopter. He said, "Okay, I'll try to make it a memorable one." At the waterfalls, he hovered the helicopter at the top so we could get a good look at water cascading over the edge. He looked over at me, winked, and jerked his head to one side. I knew what he was about to do and grabbed hold of the handle near the door. He let the helicopter drop and we fell two thousand feet down the falls, swooping up just as we neared the bottom. My wife's eyes were as big as silver dollars. That's what I must have looked like that day in Vietnam. While the pilot and I were laughing, my wife looked at me and said, "You knew he was going to do that, didn't you?" and then gave me a good, hard sock on the arm. Later she told me she really enjoyed the helicopter ride.

CHAPTER 28
TRANSFERRED

Turk yelled, "Incoming!!!" The base warning sirens sounded before the first mortar round exploded close to our hooch. "Why do the attacks always come in the middle of the night?" I needed a good night's sleep. That night I had hit the rack wearing only my utility trousers, too damn hot for anything else. The sandbag walls around our hooch did not give adequate protection from mortar and rocket attack. Instantly wide awake, I rolled off the cot, half ran, half crawled outside the hooch and dove into the sandbag bunker. I felt bare skin against my own when Al and Mike landed on top of me. Another explosion nearby, shrapnel flew over. There were mortar and rocket rounds exploding all over the base. I wished I was back on Hill 282.

Earlier we had returned to the Phu Bai base via helicopter from Hill 282. We were tired from helping Jack carry his gear down the hill and out to his ship, and we were dirty from two weeks on the hill. The blazing hot sun beat down on us as we walked from the helicopter landing pad to base headquarters to get new orders. The captain assigned us a couple of hooches in the sea of hooches near the center of the base. Lima and other 3/26 company platoons billeted in the same area. Our orders said to take a couple of days to rest, clean our gear, and stand by, in other words, wait. In the hooch, I grabbed a cot near the door hoping a breeze might cool me off. No sign of a breeze.

After a shower, shave, and a needed change of uniform, Al, Mike, Pat, Fig, and I went to the mess tent. We looked forward to eating something besides C-Rations. We talked about what might happen to the platoon. Marines we knew from other platoons told us all the platoons received new replacements while we were gone. We knew troops needed transferring to other units, so the entire battalion did not leave Vietnam at the same time. Together as the Second Platoon and watching each other's back for over a year, we were not happy about the prospect of a transfer to different outfits.

No mortar rounds came in for several more minutes. We sat on the sandbag wall around the bunker hoping the attack had ended. The VC did not attack the Phu Bai Base with mortar or rocket fire very often, not like up at Dong Ha closer to the DMZ, where attacks were more frequent. About ready to go back to our cots, we heard the whistling sound of incoming rounds pass overhead. We dropped to the bottom of the bunker again; boom, boom, boom, three more rounds exploded on the other side of the base. The mortars went silent once more, and we got up and sat on the sandbag wall again.

We heard our own outgoing mortars and the attack on the base was over. There was a lot of activity, fire trucks, and ambulances moving around the base. The base had been heavily damaged, fires had burned up trucks, equipment, and a dozen hooches. The attack destroyed twenty-two aircraft and blew the mess tent to bits, including the new milk machine. What a bummer; at dinner before the attack, I drank my first glass of cold milk in months.

The mortar attack lasted for about thirty minutes. In the morning, we found out around two hundred mortar rounds landed inside the base perimeter. The base reported sixty-eight Marines wounded, none killed. Turk and Lt. McCarthy were among the wounded. While yelling "Incoming," Turk had taken a small piece of mortar fragment in his mouth that cut his lip. He talked with a lisp for a couple of days. Lt. McCarthy took a piece of motor shrapnel in his leg and was out of action for a couple of weeks.

Early the next afternoon, Fig walked into our hooch with Pat right behind him.

"What's wrong, Fig? You look worried," I said.

"Harry, Wardlaw, and I were reassigned to the 1-9."

"Oh man, aren't they called the 'Walking Dead'?"

"Yeh, that's what I'm worried about, we have to go report for duty in one hour. What about you?" Fig asked.

"I don't know; I'm waiting to hear from Turk," I said.

Fig grabbed his gear; we all shook hands and told him to keep his head down. We promised to get together again back home.

I asked Pat about his transfer. He told me that he, Ray Potter, and some of the other guys were staying with the platoon.

"It won't be the same with us all not together," Pat said.

Shortly after Fig left, Turk came to our hooch and told me about my promotion to corporal first class and that I would not be his radio operator any longer. As a corporal, I would be a fire team leader. Tired of carrying the radio on my back all day, the change sounded good to me.

The increase in rank came with a raise in pay of twenty-three dollars a month. Extra money for me to figure out how to spend or save it for R&R if I made it that far.

Knowing I would not stay as Turk's radio operator, I made the decision to volunteer for a Combined Action Platoon (CAP). When our platoon had patrolled around a CAP compound outside of Phu Bai, we learned how the CAPs operated. Al, Mike, and I had talked about volunteering, thinking the duty sounded interesting and different from duty as a grunt in a line company.

Before Turk told me about my promotion, the commanding officer for CAP operations in the area from Phu Bai north to Dong Ha, came looking for volunteers. Evidently CAP was strictly an all-volunteer assignment. Volunteers needed at least three months of combat experience, so we definitely qualified. After Turk told me about my promotion, Al, Mike, Ernie, and I found the commanding officer and told him we wanted to volunteer. He told us if we volunteered, we might go to CAP compounds up around Dong Ha near the DMZ. We went for it, as we were looking for a change. By volunteering we, not the Marine Corps, could choose our new assignment. We also hoped this assignment might keep us all together and watching out for one another.

The evening before starting our new assignments, we were feeling no pain. We sat at one end of our hooch joking, laughing, and trying to forget about the breakup of the platoon. In the morning, the four of us would be off to CAP school, and the rest of the guys would report to their new outfits.

Poor access to beer drove us to occasionally smoke a little marijuana to take the edge off. Marijuana, hash, and an opium derivative were always available from the locals. The VC we killed or captured also carried dope. We never did drugs out in the bush, only back on the base and not on duty. Of course, in reality, in Vietnam we were always on duty. But sometimes we just needed to decompress. Once we scored a Chesterfield unfiltered cigarette with opium paste painted on the outside. We smoked it like a joint. That was the most messed up I have ever been. I never tried it again.

Light from half a moon high in the cloudless night sky cast shadows. When somebody took a hit, the red glow of the joint lit up his face. The door of the hooch swung open, and a figure stepped into the shadows. We did not recognize him. He carried a side arm; he could be an MP or an officer. "Oh shit," I thought. The guy with the joint held it behind him trying to hide the glow of the ash, but the distinct smell of marijuana filled the air.

The unknown intruder in the doorway stood motionless and silent for what seemed like forever. Finally, he said, "How about a hit?" A couple of seconds passed, then the guy with the joint stood up and held it out to the shadowy figure. We watched as he took a big hit and held it in before exhaling in a long slow whisper. The glow of the joint lit up his face but still none of us recognized him. He handed the joint back, turned around, and said "Thanks, you guys be careful out there," and walked out of the hooch. An officer or MP we never knew. Whoever he was, he needed to decompress too.

Later, I lay on my cot staring up at the metal roof of our hooch, my mind raging, the thought of leaving the platoon scared me. Did I make the correct decision to volunteer for CAP duty? Now nine months into our tour, I had survived the adventure one day at a time. Many days were boring, some terrifying, some sad; sometimes I laughed, others I cried. Many days were the same blended together and hard to tell when one stopped and another started. I had seen and done things I hoped to forget. I wondered, have I accomplished anything, other than staying alive? What is this fucking war about anyway?

With 120 days to go, the adventure must continue. CAP duty would be a new experience from our time in the bush with Second Platoon.

CHAPTER 29
CAP SCHOOL/TRANSIT TO DONG HA

"I hear you, Al, and Mike volunteered for CAP," Turk said. The wound on his mouth looked better, and he talked without a whistling sound.

"Yes, sir, if I can't be your radio operator, I might as well try something different," I said. "We're going to CAP compounds outside of Dong Ha. Ernie is going with us."

"You watch your back; that's a hot area up there. But you guys have always watched each other's backs; you'll be okay," Turk said.

"Yes, sir, we hope this will keep us together and watching each other's back."

"Good luck, sir, keep your head down and watch over our friends in Second Platoon."

"My top priority," the lieutenant said and thanked me for being his radio operator and always watching his back. We shook hands and promised to stay in touch. Thirty-five years passed before we would see one another again.

Back at our hooch, Al, Mike, Ernie, and I said goodbye to Pat, Ray, and the other guys staying with Second Platoon. I shook hands with my friend Pat and told him I was sorry I was leaving the platoon. Before we left for Vietnam, my girlfriend Phyllis made Pat and me promise to always watch out for each other. "Watch your back," I said to Pat, "I won't be there."

We all promised to get together back home after our tour. Not everyone would make it.

When Al, Mike, Ernie, and I reported to CAP school, the corporal in charge assigned us to a hooch together. The temperature was getting hotter every day; with the monsoon season over, it rarely rained. The tin roof and screen walls of the hooch did not help much with the heat and it stayed hot inside most of the time. The corporal told us to hang out for the rest of the day, classes would start the next morning at 0900.

With heat waves rippling off the tin roof, I looked for a place outside in the shade to sit and read the surfer magazine my dad sent each month. Always a month behind, the April issue had arrived earlier in the day. I found a rickety, old chair leaning against a sandbag wall. Pictures of the surfer girls on the beach in their bikinis caught my attention! Reading about a surf spot I had surfed many times; I could picture myself riding the perfect wave.

Halfway through the magazine, I came across an article and pictures describing new, innovative surfboard designs by different board builders. I hadn't surfed since our ship stopped in Hawaii over nine months ago; I hoped I remembered how. The sport was evolving fast, and I felt left out. I stared for a long time at a picture of a guy on a glassy, waist-high wave at Malibu, standing on the nose of one of the newer designed boards. The wave peeled off perfectly behind him. I could see myself on that board and liked the idea of a new board waiting for me when I returned home (if I made it home). A new board would be an effective use for my raise in pay.

I wrote a letter to the board builders Hobie, Ole, and Surfboards Hawaii. I told them I was in Vietnam, interested in ordering a new board, and asked them to please send me information and an order form. So excited at the prospect of ordering a new surfboard, I ran all the way to the base post office to mail the letters.

CAP school started in the morning. I don't remember much about it. Before class started, our friend Gary from Second Platoon showed up. That made five guys from Second Platoon going to CAP. There were seven other guys also in the class. They came from other platoons in the battalion, though not all of us were going to Dong Ha.

To start our training, we received a lecture from the captain, telling us about the idea behind CAP. He told us the Combined Action Platoon was started by the Marines as a pacification program. A CAP unit was a squad of twelve Marines and a Navy Corpsman, along with local troops called Popular Forces (PFs), working together to encourage the local population to accept and trust them and turn away from the Viet Cong. The captain told us our number one goal was security for the villagers and we would run patrols day and night and set up ambushes. We would also train the PF troops and help the villagers with civic projects. In turn, we gathered intelligence from the locals.

The captain told us we would change the way we fought the war. Instead of our usual search and destroy operations blowing up and burning everything in sight like we did on Operation Chinook, we would help and protect the villagers. Hell, I thought, Marines were good at destroying stuff, not building things. The duty sounded different than being a grunt in a line company, and we might actually do some good.

For seven days, we attended classes, sometimes into the evening. We learned to appreciate the religions, customs, and mannerisms of the local people. We learned not to cross our legs when we sat in their homes. We learned to bow appropriately and shake hands or present a gift with both hands. If invited to eat a meal in their homes, we learned to always leave a little bit of food on the plate to let them know we had eaten enough. An empty plate would be refilled because the family would think we were still hungry.

We tried to learn basic Vietnamese language, words, and phrases like *co* (yes), *kong* (no), *cam un ban* (thank you), and *dung* (stop). I found the language difficult. A beautiful language when spoken by the Vietnamese, not so much when we tried. Still holding my high school class record of sixteen straight quarters of a D in English (my teacher, the swim coach, did not fail me), learning another language was also not high on my priority list. I remember little of it.

We learned about the obsolete U.S. WWII weapons the PFs carried. We received instructions on running patrols and ambushes with a small team. Used to a platoon or at the minimum a squad, the CAP patrols were smaller. They included only three Marines, a corpsman, and four to six PF soldiers. The patrol classes included map reading and radio procedures, including the use of code books, information I already knew from my months as our platoon radio operator.

The officer in charge of the CAP school became aware of my experience as a radio operator. I told him I had carried the radio but never received formal training in its use. He sent me to a two-day radio school. I learned to set up larger antenna systems for the radios to get better reception, training that came in handy later.

The last day of classes, the captain confirmed what he told us when we volunteered. We were going to CAP compounds up around the Dong Ha Combat Base.

The captain assigned two guys, Tim, and John (not their real names); I did not know well to my fire team. Terrance Klaric was also a fire team leader, and the captain assigned Albert to his team. Mike, Ernie, and Gary did not receive an assignment. Our idea of staying together was not working out the way we had hoped. The captain told us we would find out more about our assignments when we got to Dong Ha. The corporal at CAP headquarters arranged transport to Dong Ha for us the next morning.

We reported to the airstrip terminal in the morning for the flight to Dong Ha. A C-130 cargo plane sat on the end of the runway. I remembered the first day when we arrived in Vietnam, a C-130 flew low over our heads before landing at Dong Ha. I also remembered the plane did not stay on the ground for long because of the possibility of a mortar attack.

Phu Bai airfield waiting for our C-130 flight to Dong Ha
Mike O'Grady, Al Drotar, Gary Tolar, Ernie Hoffman, Tom Elliott, Terence Klaric

At the age of twenty-one, this would be my first time on an airplane. The huge plane sat on the runway with the rear door down creating a ramp. A forklift carrying a pallet of C-Rations drove into the back of the plane and disappeared as if a giant metal monster had swallowed it. After the forklift backed out, two jeeps drove up into the back of the plane. With all cargo loaded and secured, the crew chief signaled us to board the plane. Walking up the ramp, I felt like the plane swallowed me. Inside were canvas sling-type seats lining both sides. I took a seat and buckled the seat belt. I was a little nervous and excited at the same time. There were no windows and we sat sideways with the cargo in front of us.

The door started to close like a coffin lid. Inside the plane it was hot, and I smelled aviation fuel. I looked around, wires and pipes everywhere. How would something this big get off the ground? Albert sat on one side of me, Mike on the other. I turned to talk to Al. Good old laid-back, nothing bothers me Albert was already asleep in his seat. The crew chief came around passing out ear plugs. “This is not good,” I said to Mike.

When the engines started, I knew right away why the ear plugs. The plane started to roll, moving only a short distance, before turning around and coming to a stop. We sat there, the engines idling. Never having flown before, I didn’t know if something was wrong. Why are we sitting here and not taking off? I looked around; no one seemed concerned. The engines began to rev up, then the plane shook as we started down the runway, faster and faster, the plane jumping from side to side, finally the wheels left the ground. I wanted to see outside.

Flying north, the flight to Dong Ha took about thirty minutes. Then I felt the plane dropping. Unable to see outside, I could not tell where we were. Were we over the runway? How far to the ground? I tried to predict the wheels touching down, then bang, the wheels slammed into the ground, the engines reversed, the sound deafening. The plane slowed. Before we stopped, the plane swung around 180 degrees and the rear door started to open. With the door down, the crew chief ordered us to get off and go left. Other crew aboard worked to release the hold down straps on the cargo, and a forklift was ready to remove the pallets. The engines were still running.

Marines on the ground directed us to the airfield office to check in. By the time we checked in, the plane was taking off.

A corporal from CAP headquarters met us at the airfield and introduced himself as Ben Wilson (not his real name). He welcomed us to Dong Ha and CAP Papa. He took us to a tent and told us to find a cot and to stow our gear. He showed us where to find the head and the mess tent and told us the captain would be coming in from Cam Lo tomorrow to give us our assignments.

I grabbed a cot at the end of the tent so I could roll up the side to let air blow through. I later found another advantage to a cot at the end of the tent. The other guys found cots and we stowed our gear. Outside the tent were sandbag bunkers for us to use when the base was attacked by mortars and rockets. The floor of the tent was made of wood pallets. Living in the tents was a step down from our tin roof hooch at Phu Bai, but better than sleeping on the wet ground during Operation Chinook.

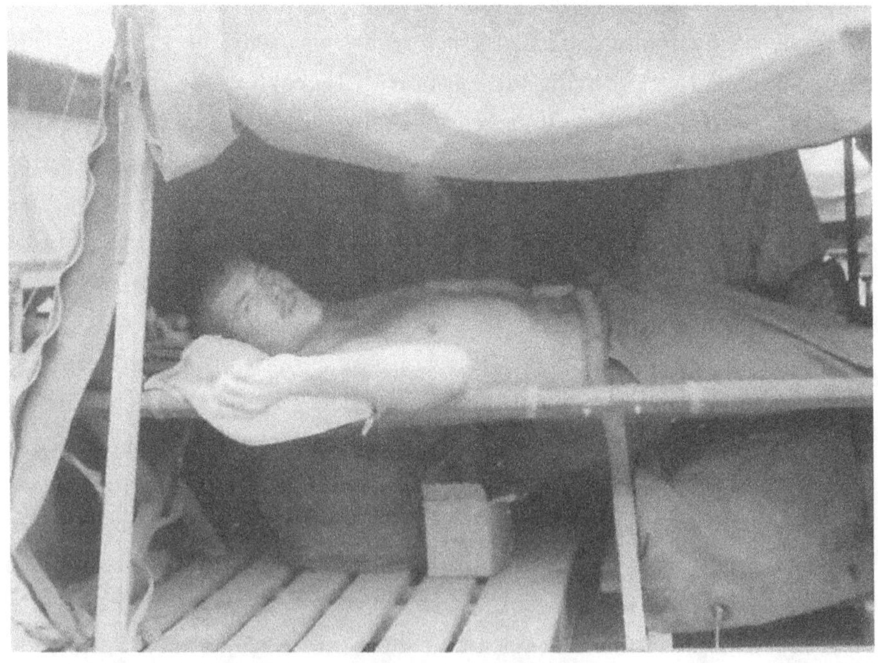

Cot in the CAP tent. Dong Ha Base
Tom Elliott

While playing in a poker game, I noticed Tim and John were not around. I asked if anyone knew where they were. Ernie said they were not feeling well and went to sick bay. When they did not return, I walked over to sick bay to check with the corpsman. He told me he wanted to keep them there for a couple of days. They were suffering from intestinal problems and the screaming shits, perhaps from food poisoning or drinking untreated water. Their illness changed the way I would spend the rest of my tour in Vietnam and may have saved my life.

After chow and a smoke, I relaxed on my cot, enjoying the surfer magazine, hoping the board builders would answer my requests for more information. Later about to nod off, an incoming rocket explode about one hundred meters away. With my cot at the end of the tent and the sides rolled up, I rolled out and ran to the bunker. A short attack, it lasted about five minutes. We took thirteen 140 mm rocket hits. The base suffered minor damage and two Marines were wounded. "Is this what it's like here every night?"

The next morning, after breakfast the captain in charge of CAP operations showed up with a big Hawaiian guy, Gunny Kalani. They lived at CAP headquarters in the village of Cam Lo about twelve kilometers from the base.

The captain was short and young looking, too young for a captain, I thought. No rifle, he carried a standard issued modal 1911 45 caliber pistol on his side. He welcomed us to CAP Papa and thanked us for volunteering.

The captain asked, "Which one of you is Corporal Elliott?"

"I'm corporal Elliott, Sir," I said.

"I want you and your fire team to go to Papa Two."

"Sir, my two guys are in sick bay."

The captain paused for a minute. "Corporal Klaric."

"Here, Sir," Terrance said.

"You take your fire team to Papa Two." That meant Albert would go to Papa Two.

"O'Grady."

"Here, Sir," Mike answered.

"You are going to Papa Four."

"Tolar, you're going to Papa One."

"Hoffman you go to Papa Two also. You guys going to Papa Two get your gear ready, the gunny will drive you out to the compound. O'Grady, Tolar, we will take you out to Papa One and Four when the gunny gets back."

What did the captain have for me?

"Corporal Elliott, stand by here. I may have a job for you. You were a radio operator in a grunt platoon, right?"

"Yes, Sir," I answered not very enthusiastically.

The captain told the gunny to take the guys to Papa Two and come back to pick up him and the other two guys. He turned and walked away.

I looked at Albert, shrugged my shoulders, and repeated what the captain said, "I may have a job for you."

"What the hell does that mean?"

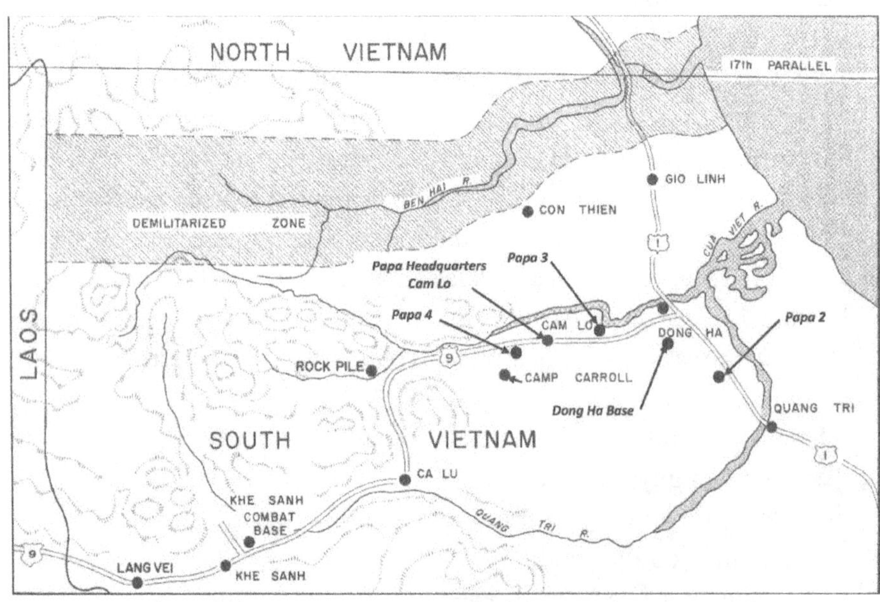

Map of CAP Papa locations around Dong Ha Base
Map from Wikipedia modified to show Papa locations

CHAPTER 30

DONG HA CAP DUTY

A lifer, gunny Kalani looked in his mid-thirties; I'd bet he joined the Marines at sixteen. Six feet tall, stocky, dark skin, darker hair, he welcomed each of us to CAP Papa with a nod of his head and a bone-crushing handshake. I liked the guy right off. He told Al, Ernie, and Terrance to load their gear in his vehicle.

I helped the guys load up. "This isn't working out at all how we planned it," Albert said. "I'm going to Papa Two, Mike to Four, you still don't fuckin' know where you're going. This sucks big time! You talk to the captain, Tom, and get us back together."

I agreed with Al but what could I do about it. Al figured because I could talk to Lieutenant Dolan, I could talk to the captain. After nine months as Turk's radio operator, I could talk to him. The captain I had met only ten minutes ago, and I knew nothing about him. I did not think coming out immediately with a request to change his orders was a wise idea. Going through the chain of command, something Marine Corps training pounded into us, I knew I should talk to the gunny first. He seemed approachable, but I just met him as well. I decided it best to wait and see where the captain assigned me and how things went for Al, Mike, and the other guys.

The guys climbed into the back of the gunny's jeep; I told them to watch out for each other like we always have. "Let us know where you go, Tom," Albert said. Before I answered, the jeep took off in a cloud of dust. Rounding the corner past the end of the tent, the guys gave me a thumbs-up, unaware that in a couple of days they would be in deep shit, and one of them would be dead.

While waiting for the captain to return, I asked Ben if he had any idea what the captain meant when he said he may have a job for me. He told me all the compounds were short personnel, so the captain had lots of options.

Mike and Gary asked him about Papa One and Four. He told us both compounds were beyond Cam Lo headquarters. "Good bunch of guys at both compounds, you'll be okay. I hope you are good at filling sandbags," Ben said.

Mike and Gary laughed, "Yeh, we're experts."

Ben was a lance corporal and I asked him about his job. He told me he stayed in Dong Ha and provided support for all the CAP compounds. "Not bad duty and I am glad I don't leave the base at all. The biggest problem for me is not enough beer, and rocket attacks on the base are more frequent than when I first came here. This close to the DMZ, they can fire rockets at us from North Vietnam."

I looked up and saw the captain walking straight over to me. I stood up as he approached, acknowledging his rank, and said, "Sir." Not sure what to do about Al and Mike, I knew I should let the captain speak first.

"Sergeant Cooper (not his real name) is in charge of running supplies from the base to the CAP village compounds. He is 'short' and headed back to the real world in a few days," the captain said. 'Short' meant Cooper only had a few days left on his tour in country.

I said nothing. I waited for the captain to continue. Why is he telling me this?

When he continued, he said, "Corporal Elliott, I want you to take over for him as the CAP supply NCO (Non-Commissioned Officer). I need at least a corporal for this duty."

"Yes, Sir," I said, not sure what he meant. I looked over at Mike to see his reaction. His head tilted, and shrugging his shoulders, he had the same question I did.

"Sir, can you tell me a little about the duty?"

"Okay, a quick version," the captain said. "You stay here on the base. Work with other non-coms at supply and the sergeants in charge of the compounds to make sure they get what they need from the base. Ben will help you. With a truck and driver, you deliver the supplies to the compounds. That's it," he said.

"Sir, you asked about my radio experience."

"Yes, that is another reason I want you for this duty. You will have a radio with you so you can stay in communication with the compounds and headquarters in case there is a problem."

The job sounded simple enough, but I had one more question on my mind.

"Sir, out on the roads between the base and the compounds, is it only me and the driver with no security detail?" I am sure the captain detected a little concern in my voice.

"That's right," the captain said. "This duty does have a few drawbacks. The biggest problem is the VC like to mine the roads, though Sergeant Cooper hasn't experienced many problems." How did the captain define problems?

"What do you think, Corporal?" The captain asked, looking me in the eye to see my reaction.

"I'll do it, Sir." I tried to sound confident, though still not sure I realized what I was getting into.

"Good, Cooper can show you the ropes on the supply run tomorrow."

"Yes, Sir, I'll be ready."

A couple of days later Tom and John were feeling better and the captain assigned them to different CAP compounds.

The gunny in his jeep came flying around the corner, returning from Papa Two. The captain turned around as he drove up. He told O'Grady and Tolar to throw their gear in the vehicle.

"Any problems?" the captain asked.

"No, Sir. All good at Papa Two."

I helped Mike and Gary with their gear. "Man, you hit the jackpot," Mike said. "You get to stay on the base and eat in the mess tent. No guard duty, no going on patrols or ambushes. Lucky your two guys were sick, or you and your fire team would have gone to Papa Two instead of Terrance and Albert."

Mike was right; I should have gone to Papa Two. The three of us now assigned to separate places was going to make it harder to get us back together, especially with me assigned to stay on the base. I figured at least when I delivered supplies to the compounds where the guys were assigned, I would have a chance to see them. As the guys climbed into the back of the gunny's vehicle, I told them to take care of each other. "Al and I won't be there to watch your backs," I said.

Watching them leave, I felt alone. Al, Mike, and I had been in the same unit since the yellow footprints over a year and a half ago. A good team, we trusted and watched out for one another. Now going to our different assignments, we needed to build that same trust with new guys at CAP. Did we make the correct decision to leave Second Platoon?

After the captain left, Ben and I walked back to our tent. Walking, I asked Ben how the operation worked. He told me the CAP compounds ordered their supplies through the supply office and Dave delivered them like the captain told me. "All we have to do is keep the supplies coming, and nobody bothers us much."

"Dave, is that Cooper's first name?" I asked.

"Yes, but he prefers Cooper, Sergeant Cooper actually."

Ben and Cooper had fixed up the tent with tables and chairs to make it more livable. A backup PRC-25 radio sat on a shelf over a desk made from empty ammo crates. Hanging from the corner of the shelf was a centerfold from *Playboy*, Miss January. Next to the radio was a reel-to-reel tape recorder. Ben flipped the switch and "Gloria" my favorite song at the fraternity house started blaring out of the speakers. "This beats the hell out of being in the bush," I said to Ben. Laughing, he said, "Cooper said the same thing."

Later in the afternoon, it was too hot in the tent, I sat on a couple of sandbags, leaned back against the wall of the bunker in the shade of the tent, and enjoyed a smoke. I was anxious to meet Sergeant Cooper and learn more.

A truck pulled up in front of the tent. A tall, stocky guy with an M-16 rifle in his hand jumped out of the passenger side. He was covered with dust clinging to his sweat-soaked shirt, sergeant chevrons on the collar, and wearing a flak jacket and a helmet. He wore a 45-caliber pistol in a standard issue Marine Corps holster on his hip. Before the truck drove off, he reached back inside and pulled out a pack holding a radio. The flexible flat metal antenna was sticking out of the pack. Same as the one I always carried. Now at least the radio would not be on my back all day.

"Sergeant Cooper?" I asked.

"Yeah, you Elliott?"

"Call me Tom."

"Tom, man, am I glad to meet you; I want out of this hellhole."

Ben came out of the tent and handed Cooper a list of supplies the compounds had ordered for the next day. He quickly looked it over. "This will be a good run for Tom to see how it all works," he said. He told Ben that Papa Two needed water, and to notify the guys at supply a full water buffalo was needed in the morning. Ben turned and walked toward the supply depot.

Cooper definitely sounded like a sergeant, barking orders, no wasted words. I looked forward to working with him.

"Let me clean up and we'll go get chow," Cooper said.

I went to evening chow with Ben and the sergeant. When Ben mentioned to me that Cooper said the same thing I said, about being in the bush, I figured Cooper had also volunteered from a line company. The two of us from different companies, we did not talk much about what happened to us prior to joining CAP. We talked instead about sports, girls, and getting short. Cooper talked about going back to the real world to see his girlfriend. She had stayed with him so far while he was in country. I knew a lot of guys had received Dear John letters. My girlfriend was hanging in there as well. I hoped to see her soon on R&R in Hawaii.

After dinner, Ben took off to check in at the supply office. Back at our tent, Sergeant Cooper took a beer out of an ice chest next to his cot then started to clean his rifle.

"There is one left," he said, and reached in the cooler to pull out the last beer, handing it to me, a Carlings Black Label. "Thanks, I owe you one," I said.

"Be ready to go at 0700, we have a lot to do tomorrow," Cooper said and went back to cleaning his rifle. I opened the beer.

CHAPTER 31
THE JOB WILL BE YOURS

Sitting on my cot, I thought about what O'Grady had said. I guess I did hit the jackpot. A cot to sleep on, a mess tent to eat in, no guard duty, favorite music playing, and a cold beer in hand. After five months of sleeping on the ground and eating C-Rations, this would work for me.

Outside the tent at 0700 with my rifle in hand, wearing my helmet, flak jacket, and web belt with two full magazines, carrying two canteens of water and a Ka-bar knife, I waited for Sergeant Cooper. Cooper came out of the tent with the radio. "Let's go," he said. We walked to the motor pool. On the way, Cooper told me to watch what he did. "If you don't understand something, ask; that's how I learned the job. It's not rocket science." He introduced me to the sergeant in charge of the motor pool and told him I was going to take over the supply runs. The sergeant asked Cooper, "How long?"

"Not soon enough, three days," Cooper said. "Tom should know the job by then."

The sergeant assigned us a truck and driver. The truck, a six-by-six, was capable of carrying up to two and half tons of supplies and equipment. Cooper knew the driver, Mark (not his real name). Cooper introduced me and told me Mark was the usual driver.

Cooper rode shotgun, the radio up front with him. I rode in back, sitting on the bench seat behind the cab on the passenger side. From the motor pool, we drove to the ammo dump. I met another sergeant with whom I would work. We loaded a box of grenades, four cans of ammo for the M-60 machine gun, a box of claymore mines, and two cases of M-16 ammo. At the supply depot, I met the sergeant in charge, and we loaded a pallet of empty sandbags, two rolls of concertina wire, and a food order, mostly C-Rations and a case of SPAM. I was not sure SPAM was any better than eating C-Rations. Behind the supply depot, we hooked up to a tank of water on wheels called a "Water Buffalo."

We left base through the south gate heading down Highway 1. Cooper told me Papa Two was located about seven kilometers south of the base. "Highway" is a misnomer, as the road is narrow, paved in places, dirt, or mud in others, and full of potholes. Cooper told me before we left to hang on because Mark swerved to miss the potholes as much as possible. I remembered the captain told me the VC liked to set mines in the potholes.

Part of the way, rice paddies paralleled the road. In one paddy, a water buffalo was pulling a plow. The animal had a yoke around its neck and thick horns sticking out both sides of its head. Ropes from the yoke led back to the plow with an elderly man behind. Heavy hooves stirred up the mud as the huge animal moved slowly along. A young boy was riding on top. Women and older men in pointed-tip straw hats bent over tending the rice paddies. A hard life was made even harder by the war.

On the first run with Cooper, I experienced what being off base was like with only the three of us and no security detail. If we hit a mine or the VC attacked the truck, we would need to handle the situation with only two of us after Sergeant Cooper left. I was used to all my buddies and a full platoon to watch my back; this would be different.

Off to the left of the road and adjacent to a rice paddy was a village, of a few old whitewashed concrete buildings surrounded by bamboo structures with thatched roofs. I could see smoke from cooking fires, villagers strolling along the cart paths, and others working in the fields. The truck slowed and turned right. Papa Two was located on the other side of the road from the village they protected. A series of sandbag bunkers, trenches, and fighting positions ringed the compound. A couple of tin-roofed hooches were used for living quarters. Row after row of concertina wire surrounded the compound. The gate was already open, and Mark drove the truck into the compound.

Albert was standing in a trench behind a low sandbag wall, working on an M-60 machine gun. When he saw me, he jumped out of the trench and walked over to the truck.

"Are you assigned here?" he asked, a hopeful look on his face.

"No, I am going to take over running supplies. Sergeant Cooper is showing me the ropes."

His look of hope turned to a frown. "You are one lucky motherfucker, Tom. I don't like being here without you and Mike."

Before I could answer Al, Cooper called me over to meet the sergeant in charge of Papa Two. We shook hands and he said he was sorry to see Cooper go. I told him I would do my best to keep up Cooper's excellent work.

Cooper asked the sergeant to unload the trucks; we needed to get back to the base to load up for Papa Three and Cam Lo Headquarters. The sergeant barked his orders and guys from the compound started filling five-gallon cans with water from the "Water Buffalo." Using the five-gallon cans, they filled a Lister Bag, a canvas bag hanging from a tripod with valves around the bottom for filling a canteen or cup of drinking water. The compound had no running water. A fifty-five-gallon drum of water sat on top of a tower to provide a shower, and you did your business in an outhouse. The living conditions were primitive and under constant threat of attack from the Viet Cong.

The guys in the compound unloaded the ammo, claymores, and the rest of the supplies. I handed the M-60 ammo to Al. While unloading the truck, I noticed Terrance and Ernie were not around. I asked Albert where they were. "Out on patrol; I am going on the night patrol," he said.

"Watch your ass out their man," I said, and helped him carry the ammo over to the ammo bunker.

Cooper asked the sergeant if there was anything to go out. The sergeant gave Cooper outgoing mail and said that if they needed anything else, he'd let Ben know at the supply office.

As we were leaving the compound, Albert looked up from loading the M-60. "I'll see you on the next run," I called out to him.

"Bring me some cigarettes," he yelled back.

Back at the base, we loaded supplies for Papa Three. Before leaving, we stopped at our tent where Cooper picked up the empty ice chest. I did not ask why. We headed out the west gate along Highway 9 toward Papa Three and the village of Cam Lo where Papa headquarters and Papa One were located. Highway 9 was in the same poor condition as Highway 1.

We stopped at Papa Three, dropped off supplies and water. The compound was located between the highway and the river. Cam Heiu, the Vietnamese village protected by Papa Three was beyond the compound near the river. Cooper introduced me to the sergeant in charge of Papa Three. He welcomed me aboard and gave me a quick tour of the compound. Papa Three looked more developed than Papa Two. The compound was shaped in a square, with large sandbag bunkers at the four corners connected by sandbag walls. Tin-roofed hooches provided sleeping quarters and a kitchen shack. In the center of the compound was an ammo bunker. Like Papa Two, rows of concertina wire ringed the entire compound with trip flares and claymore mines between the rows of wire. In a couple of days, enemy attacks on both compounds would breach their defenses.

From Papa Three, we continued along Highway 9 to Cam Lo. The terrain was flat, hills and mountains off in the distance made it look like a huge valley. The highway paralleled the river, crossing over several smaller tributaries. Bridges built by our engineers replaced bridges destroyed by the VC. Riding in the back of the truck, I surveyed the surroundings. Plenty of places to set up a roadside ambush. I noticed Cooper always kept his rifle sticking out the truck window.

Highway 9 from Dong Ha to Cam Lo, Camp Carroll, and beyond
Cam Lo River in the Background
Photo courtesy of Ed Palm

The Cam Lo Headquarters compound looked bigger than Papa Two or Three. Two tall concrete pillars with a beam across the top and a closed gate marked the entrance. Two local troops on guard duty opened the gate for us to enter. Twenty or so PF troops stood in formation across the compound. Four tin-roofed buildings were the living quarters and the kitchen shack. The only other buildings were two whitewashed concrete buildings and a tall concrete tower near one side of the compound. Fighting trenches and sandbag bunkers with rows of concertina wire all around completed the defensives. A single tall flagpole in the center flew the American and South Vietnamese flags.

The captain I had met the day before came out of one of the buildings and walked over to the truck. "How is it going?" he asked Sergeant Cooper.

"No problem, Sir," Cooper answered.

"Good, when do you leave?"

"Three more days, Sir!"

"You think Corporal Elliott can manage the supply runs?"

"No problem, Sir, besides, I am leaving no matter what." The captain laughed and handed Cooper a list of supplies needed and the outgoing mail.

"What do you think, Corporal Elliott?" the captain asked me.

"No problem, Sir, I can do it; Sergeant Cooper's a good teacher."

After our talk with the captain, we drove out of the compound and turned left toward Dong Ha base. Across the way sat five houses with small shops attached. We stopped in front of the last one. Cooper came to the back of the truck. "Come on and bring the ice chest with you," he said. The ice chest. Finally, I would find out why we brought the empty ice chest. Out in front of the place was a porch with a couple of tables and chairs and covered by an overhang.

"Sit down; let's have a beer," Cooper said.

"I am up for that," I said. Mark sat down across the table from me.

"Tiger piss or 33?"

"What do you drink?" I asked.

"They both suck, but I go for the 33."

I had tried both before and preferred the 33. Tiger Piss was our nickname for Tiger beer.

"Okay, 33," I said.

Cooper said hello to an old man coming out of the house and said, "Two 33s and a soda." The soda was for Mark. Cooper pointed to the ice chest. The old man nodded and took it. A couple of minutes later a woman came out and gave us our drinks. As I remembered, the beer tasted skunky, but like I always said, in Vietnam any beer is better than no beer, and I was surprised that the beer was cold.

Enjoying our beer, it sounded like a generator was running out back. "What is this place?" I asked Cooper.

"This is the local icehouse."

Ah, that explains the cold beer and the ice chest. The old man was the owner of the place and the woman who served us our drinks was his wife. The old man came out of the house, laboring to carry the ice chest full of ice. Cooper took it from him and put it in the back of the truck. He paid the old guy and told me I owed him a beer. I nodded. "Next trip," I said.

Real American dollars were extremely valuable to the Viet Cong, so the Marine Corps paid us in MPC's (Military Payment Certificates). This paper money in $.25–$10 bills was worthless outside Vietnam. Sometimes we exchanged the MPC's for Piasters (Dong), the local money. The beer cost us one hundred Piasters, or about one dollar.

While enjoying the beer, Cooper told me truck convoys going back and forth from Camp Carroll and the Rockpile stopped along this section of the road to get beer and soda from the shops.

After finishing our beer, Cooper said, "Let's go," and Mark went to start the truck. Jokingly I said to Cooper, "What about more beer to take with us?"

He smiled. "Next stop," he said.

The truck stopped in front of an ordinary house in the small village outside the gate to Dong Ha Base.

"You want in on a case of beer?" Cooper said.

"Sure," I said.

"Give me ten bucks."

"Ten bucks! How much is a case?"

"Twenty-five dollars on the black market; the only way to get good beer," Cooper said. Beer was not always available on the base and when it was, the ration was two cans. A minute later Cooper came out with a case of Carlings Black Label on his shoulder.

After dinner, Sergeant Cooper and I sat cleaning our rifles, each enjoying a Black Label. "What do you think about the job?" Cooper asked.

"You're right; it's not rocket science; looks straight forward. I can manage it."

"I'm leaving in three days; then the job will be yours," he said.

"I don't see any big problems. The job is certainly a change from our experience as grunts in a line company," I said.

"We are still grunts!" Cooper said. "The way I see it, any time we are off the base, we are in the bush, and anything can happen. Don't ever get caught on the roads after dark," he said. "The VC own the place after dark. Never let your guard down. When it's you and a driver, he watches the road; you watch everything else. So far, I have been lucky," he said. "Plus, the VC are attacking the base with rockets more often than they used to. This entire fucking country is bad for our health, no matter where you are or what you are doing. A couple of more days and I am gone."

He was a solid Marine and I wondered if Sergeant Cooper planned to stay in the Marine Corps back home. He hated Vietnam (hell, we all did), but he liked being a sergeant. He would make a good drill instructor.

Cooper was correct. In a couple of days, I would take responsibility for the supply runs. I hoped Cooper's luck out on the roads would continue for me.

CHAPTER 32
I TAKE OVER

The next day we delivered supplies to Papa Four. The compound was located out along Highway 9 past Cam Lo headquarters. Papa Four was similar to the other compounds with sandbag walls and bunkers and rows of wire all around. I did not see any hooch-type buildings though, the Marines at Papa Four lived in tents. As we were driving into the compound, near the back bunker Mike was filling sandbags; he gave me the one-finger wave.

After Cooper introduced me to the sergeant in charge, and the guys in the compound unloaded the supplies, I had a chance to talk with Mike.

"What about getting us back together?" Mike asked.

"I don't know; it won't be easy," I said. I told Mike that it sounded like Albert was having a little trouble settling in at Papa Two, but I hadn't had a chance to talk with Terrance and Ernie yet to see what they thought because they were out on patrol.

"How are things here?" I asked Mike.

"No problem, these guys are cool," he said. "I went on an evening patrol last night and sat in an ambush for a couple of hours; nothing happened. I think I can handle the rest of my tour here," Mike said. I was happy to hear Mike was okay where he was.

"How about what you are doing?" Mike asked.

"I'm good with it for now; we load up supplies in the morning then deliver them to the compounds. The hot meals and a cot are a hell of lot better than Chinook."

"I hear that," Mike said.

"We have only been at these assignments for two days. Let's see how things work out before I try to get us back together," I said.

"Elliott, let's go," Cooper shouted from across the compound. I told Mike I would stay in touch. On the way back to Dong Ha, we stopped in Cam Lo at the icehouse, and I bought Cooper a beer. We were now even.

Back on base, my rifle needed cleaning from all the dust riding in the back of the truck. I sat in a chair looking at the rifle disassembled on my cot. I laughed to myself. After all the months in the field sitting under a poncho in the rain, trying to keep the rifle clean, I sat cleaning my rifle in a nice dry hooch with a cold beer sitting next to me. What would my old platoon buddies think about this?

The next day, we made a quick run out to Papa Two. No problems on the road and Albert's mood had improved. I gave him the cigarettes he had asked for. I had a chance to talk with Ernie and Terrance. They said they were getting along fine.

Returning from our run, Cooper received word he could leave the next day for Phu Bai to start his trip home. A day sooner than scheduled, Cooper was one incredibly happy Marine. The first time I met Sergeant Cooper, I noticed, in addition to his rifle, he carried a Model 1911 45-caliber pistol. I asked him where he got the pistol from. He said he had bought it from the guy he took over the supply runs from, than made me an offer I could not refuse. I bought his pistol.

Next morning, I helped him get his gear ready and carried it over to the airfield. I thanked him for showing me the ropes and I wished him luck getting home. He told me to keep a sharp eye on the roads and take care of the guys at the CAP compounds. "No problem," I said. We would never hear from or see one another again.

I did not think his departing early created any problems. After three runs I knew enough to get the job done. The next day, I made my first run with Mark. Now I rode in the cab and not in the back of the truck. Like Cooper, as soon as we drove off the base, I made sure my rifle was loaded and pointed out the window. I wore the 45 for backup.

Heading down Highway 1, I did what Sergeant Cooper had told me to do. I watched everything but the road. When Mark yelled, "Pothole,"

I held on as he swerved to miss it. Now flying down the dusty road with the windows open and my rifle sticking out, the rifle got as dirty as it did riding in the back. Since the M-16 was prone to jamming, I cleaned my rifle every night.

Mark, a lance corporal, was a laid-back guy. He told me he was Cooper's driver most of the time, and that a couple of convoy trucks had hit mines and taken small-arms fire, but so far, they had not run into any major problems out on the road.

Let's hope it stays that way," I said.

While at Papa Two, I talked with Albert, Ernie, and Terrance about how things were going. They had been on a couple of patrols and ambushes and were getting to know the area and the other guys. I told Al that Mike said he was doing okay at Papa Four and was making friends with the guys there. Al asked if I still planned on talking to the captain about us getting back together. "I don't think so," I said. "Let's just see how it goes, we only got a hundred days left."

Albert told me he heard the talk that the VC might be planning something in the area. In case the information was correct, the last couple of days they worked on improving the compound defensives. "Be careful on the roads," he said.

"Don't worry about me," I said. "You're the ones out here at night."

Mark and I finished our run out to Papa Three and returned to the base late in the afternoon. The next day with no supply run to make, I used the time to clean up my gear, take a shower, and write home to tell the family about my change of duty. I hoped Mom would worry less when she found out about my different assignment. Since I was not home and still in Vietnam, my assignment probably made no difference to her.

May 12, before first light, I woke to artillery fire. Outgoing, I lay back down. Ben came in the tent. "Papa Two is under attack," he said. We listened to the radio traffic. The sergeant reported sappers attacked the compound. (VC crawling in with satchel charges trying to blow up the wire and bunkers). We could hear shooting in the background. The sergeant reported one Marine was dead and several wounded. He did not give the name of the Marine killed. The base let Papa Two know a reaction force was on the way to help.

Later in the morning, a truck from the reaction force stopped in front of our tent with the body of the Marine killed in the attack at Papa Two. The Marine killed was Terrance, part of his leg blown off by a satchel charge. I felt terrible; I should have gone to Papa Two with my fire team and not Terrance. Killed after taking my place, his death hit me hard—another "why him and not me" moment that would take some time for me to get over. Eight other Marines were wounded during the attack; fortunately, Albert and Ernie made it through okay.

Three days later, on May 15, Papa Three suffered a similar attack that also allowed the VC to overrun the compound. The attack wounded twelve and killed one Marine. I did not know him.

For the next three days, I was busy running supplies and replacements to Papa Two and Three to help rebuild the compounds. Albert and Ernie told me about the attack on Papa Two and how it scared the shit out of them. We talked about Terrance. Even though we had only known Terrance for a month, we considered him a friend and a fellow Marine who we knew would always have our backs. I still think about that attack and Terrance. I can never know if I had gone to Papa Two, whether it might have been me who was killed.

Not having been there for either attack, I cannot give a detailed account of what took place. A book titled *A Voice for Hope* by Thomas Flynn, a Marine seriously wounded during the attack, gives an excellent account of the attack on Papa Three. Another book titled *Tiger Papa Three* by Edward Palm chronicles the operation of Papa Three after the May 15 attack.

On May 18, it was our turn. Dong Ha Base was attacked by rockets and artillery shells fired by the North Vietnamese from their side of the DMZ. Ben and I ran from our tent to the sandbag bunker. Explosions were going off all around the base. A rocket hit about twenty-five meters from our bunker, shrapnel flying everywhere. We did not know if a ground attack would follow when the rockets stopped. When we ran from the tent, we took our rifles, helmets, and flak jackets with us, so we were ready. When the attack ended, we sat on the sandbag wall of our bunker and listened for more rockets. We also listened for but did not hear any small-arms fire around the base and figured that no ground attack was happening.

In the morning, we found out the base received 150 140 mm rockets, which caused extensive damage to the base. The attack killed eleven Marines and wounded ninety-one. For the next couple of days, no trucks were available to deliver supplies to the CAP compounds. We were all busy cleaning up the base. We filled sandbags and helped clean up damaged buildings. I notified the captain we were okay, and supply runs would start again as soon as a truck and driver were available. After the attack, Albert called in from Papa Two to check on me.

Two of the CAP compounds and the main base had been attacked in a span of six days. A total of thirteen Marines were dead and over one hundred wounded. I did not look forward to my next supply run. I hoped the VC and NVA would leave us alone for a while.

Ben and I found out four or five of the rockets had landed in or near the officers' quarters of tin-roofed hooches located near our tent. For safety reasons in case of another attack, all the officers had moved to a different location on the base, leaving their quarters empty. Ben and I figured the VC, using their base spies, would know the officers had moved and would not bother to attack the same area again. We decided to take over one of the empty hooches, which were a lot nicer than our tent. We grabbed our gear and moved in. There was no one around to tell us we couldn't. That night the base received another short rocket attack. I was used to sleeping on my cot at the end of the tent with the side rolled up for a quick exit. So, when the rocket attack started, and half asleep, I forgot we had moved into the hooch. I rolled off the cot, crashed through the screen wall, and fell three feet to the ground, landing hard enough to knock the wind out of me. I crawled the few feet to the bunker and rolled in, gasping for breath. Ben was in the bunker, laughing his ass off.

Even after the second attack, we decided to stay in the hooch. We learned days later our intelligence people had figured out the Vietnamese who worked on the base as barbers, cleaning people, and doing other jobs had paced off where critical areas were and turned the information over to the North Vietnamese to plot their attacks. After the attack, the base command ordered all Vietnamese workers off the base. It didn't matter much; by now the North Vietnamese had all the information they needed, and the rockets kept coming.

CHAPTER 33
THE FRENCH BUNKER

We continued to receive rockets from the north every couple of days to harass us. Mark and I returned to routine supply runs to the CAP compounds. After a run one day, Ben and I were walking back to our hooch when we passed by an old French bunker. We had seen the bunker before but never thought much about it. Made of concrete and stone, the bunker was two stories high. Attached to one side was a large sandbag bunker to protect the entrance. We looked inside and found the bunker empty; no one was using it. I said to Ben, "We should move in here."

The thick walls made it noticeably cooler inside. We were tired of living in the hot tin-roofed hooch. This place showed possibilities. With the captain living out at Cam Lo, no one was around to tell us we could not move into the bunker. The roof looked solid and did not appear to leak. We moved in and started to fix it up. On the resupply run the next day, I filled the cooler with ice, beer, and coke. I took a couple of empty ammo crates from the dump and talked the supply sergeant out of an old chair I spotted; it cost me two beers. Back at the bunker, we built a table out of the ammo crates and used pieces of the wood to build a cover for the machine gun slot. That helped keep the rats out. We set the backup PRC 25 radio and tape recorder on the table. With the volume turned way up, "Gloria" playing on the tape recorder sounded really good bouncing off the concrete walls.

After chow, I took my chair outside and leaned it against the bunker. I sat enjoying a cigarette and a cold Miller High Life beer, thinking, "This is not bad. We did not have an officer or higher ranked NCO around to hassle us. Like Ben had said, all we needed to do was keep the supplies coming and no one bothered us."

After dark, I lay on my cot playing around with two giant cockroaches, both about four inches long, who lived in the bunker with us. I called them Joe and Ralphie, though I could not really tell them apart. I chased them around the walls of the bunker with a beam of light from my flashlight. We kept our food in an airtight five-gallon can so Joe and Ralphie could not get at it. At night and with no noise from artillery firing, I could hear the two of them chirping as they talked to each other. They probably wondered who that crazy guy was with the flashlight.

The bunker's thick walls kept it fairly quiet inside, which made it good for sleeping. Late one night, we woke to an explosion, followed quickly by another that sounded close by. We realized it was a rocket attack on the base. We were not too sure about the strength of this old concrete bunker, so we grabbed our rifles and went into the attached sandbag bunker. The rockets kept coming, a couple landing close by. We heard a loud crash inside the concrete bunker, but when we looked inside, we did not see anything. After the attack ended, we went to see what had happened. Fires were all around the base, so we went to help.

In the morning, I checked around our bunker and discovered what had caused the loud crashing sound. A rocket had hit the corner of the bunker and glanced off of it without exploding. A fresh chunk of concrete was knocked out of the bunker's corner. Looking around, we found a 140 mm rocket buried in front of the bunker and notified the base. A couple of EOD guys came out, cordoned off the area, and told us to stay away until they could take care of it. One EOD guy told me the rocket must have hit the bunker on the side and glanced off without detonating. He said a direct hit would have blown half the bunker away. I did not want to think about what might have happened if we were inside and the rocket had exploded. Later in the afternoon, the EOD guys came to remove the rocket to detonate it somewhere else.

The French bunker where I lived on Dong Ha Combat Base.
Oval indicates where rocket took a chunk of concrete off the corner.

I continued to make supply runs to the compounds. One day on the way to Papa Two, as we rounded a corner, Mark yelled, "What's that in the road up ahead?" My eyes shifted from watching the side of the road. "Looks like a huge water buffalo. It's blocking the entire road. You think it might be a setup for an ambush?" I said.

"Nah, I have seen this before; the owner is probably in the bushes taking a crap," Mark said and slowed down. As he did, an old guy with a typical pointed-tip straw hat on came out of the bushes. With a long bamboo stick, he slapped the huge animal on the ass. Snorting big piles of snot out of its nostrils, it slowly moved off the road. The old man turned to watch us go by. Mark was laughing. "Told ya," he said. I relaxed my butt cheeks and took my finger off the trigger.

We made it to Papa Two—no problem. While unloading supplies, Albert told me he heard our friend Rick Figueroa from Second Platoon, who had been transfer to the 1-9, had stepped on a mine. His leg was badly torn up and broken in three places. He was flown to Da Nang for medical treatment. The next day, I tried to reach the hospital in Da Nang on the radio to find out more about what had happened but could not get through. He recovered and returned to duty. A few weeks later, Fig was wounded again, and again he recovered and returned to his unit.

As I was leaving Papa Two, Albert handed me a plastic Kodak film container. I thought he wanted me to take the film in for developing. "I took some hash off a VC we killed the other day. Take this out to O'Grady," he said. Great, now I am a drug runner. I kept a little for myself.

At mail call that evening, I received three letters: one from Mom, one from Phyllis, and one from Surfboards Hawaii. Back at the bunker, I grabbed my chair, a cold beer, and went outside. Leaning against the bunker, I opened the letter from Surfboards Hawaii first, the only surf shop that answered my request for an order form. I looked it over and read about design ideas. I filled out the form and ordered a ten-foot-one-inch high performance nose rider with a step-down deck and concave nose, three redwood stringers, and a deep white resin fin. In the morning, I mailed the form. Weeks later, a letter came from the surfboard shop to let me know the board cost $175, expensive for a surfboard in 1967. I sent a money order to pay for the board. When it was ready, Dad picked it up.

We got word from Papa Two that a patrol had been ambushed and Albert was wounded and was being sent to the hospital on the Dong Ha Base. I rushed to the hospital to look for him. When he arrived, he was loaded on morphine. I only had a chance to talk to him for a few moments before the corpsmen took him in for surgery. "I'm going home, Tom," he said, a smile on his face. My hand on his shoulder, I said, "I know, Al, you'll be fine. You're out of this damn war. Stay in touch; Mike and I will see you back home." I was concerned about my friend.

A sniper had shot Al. The sniper's bullet hit one of the rounds on the ammo belt Al wore around his waist, the round exploding into two pieces. One of the pieces was lodged close to his spine. The field hospital at Dong Ha did not have the facilities to manage such a delicate operation to remove the piece of shrapnel. The doctor sent him to Phu Bai for surgery. The operation was a success. The doctor said if the sniper round had hit him and not the belt of ammo he was wearing, it would have killed him. He was lucky. Gravely wounded and nearing the end of his tour, they sent Albert home. I let Mike know about Al. We were glad he survived.

On the third of July, I received a letter from my friend Doug. He told me where to find him on base. After my supply run that day, I managed to find him. Doug's time in Vietnam was getting short, only forty-three days left on his tour. Off duty, we enjoyed a cold one and I said, "Too bad you were reassigned to Dong Ha so near the end of your tour. The NVA are stepping up operations and the base is getting hit by rocket attacks more often."

I told him about my job as the supply NCO for the CAP compounds outside the base. Never having been off base, Doug asked if he could go on a supply run with me one day. He said he felt badly about never going out in the bush. I told him not to worry about what he did in Vietnam. Like Sergeant Cooper had told me, I told Doug, "This entire country is unsafe for everybody; it doesn't matter if you were in the bush or on the base. If there is a bullet or rocket with your name on it, it would find you. Our goal here, no matter where you are stationed or what your assignment, is to stay alive one day at a time."

"You want to go off base; I'll take you off base," I said.

Early the next morning, the North Vietnamese gave us an early Fourth of July show by sending in a bunch of rockets. I wondered if they even knew it was the Fourth of July and what the day meant to us.

The night before the first run Doug was due to go on with me, I found out a patrol around Papa Two was ambushed, one Marine killed and one wounded. Even though it looked more dangerous now to make the supply runs, Doug still wanted to go. Over the next few days, he made two runs with me. Doug got a chance to see about life in a CAP compound, the countryside, and how the local people lived. He took pictures along the way, including one of me passing out suckers to the kids, which I often did. We experienced no problems on the runs, and he was happy he had a chance to get off the base. Those runs were the last time I would see him until we got home. Somehow a reporter found out about us seeing one another in Vietnam and wrote an article about us that appeared in our hometown newspaper.

After the July 4th rocket attack, I became concerned about my R&R request. The next time the captain came into Dong Ha, I planned to ask him about it. Like the Animal's song, "I gotta get out of this place."

Albert wounded on patrol outside Papa 2.
Ernie Hoffman stayed with him until he was Medevac'd to Dong Ha Base.

Tom Elliott passing out suckers to the kids near a CAP unit.
Picture Courtesy of Doug Binkley.

Friends from Childhood Hold Reunion in Dong Ha, Vietnam

By NEL TURNER
Staff Writer

The odds are against it, but it happened.

With some half a million United States servicemen now in Vietnam, two Temple City Marines, close friends from childhood who have been in Vietnam for almost a year, finally met and are currently stationed only 300 yards from each other in the village of Dong Ha, USMC command post for the demilitarized zone.

The two friends are Cpl. Tom Elliott, son of Mr. and Mrs. Richard C. Elliott, 6361 N. Sultana, Temple City and Lance Cpl. Doug Binkley, son of Mr. and Mrs. Richard T. Binkley, former Temple City residents now of 86 W. Birchcroft, Arcadia.

Tom and Doug first became friends when they were in the third grade here and living only three houses from each other. They remained fast friends and neighbors on through elementary and high school and both graduated from Temple City High School in 1963. Both attended Pasadena City College, with Doug leaving there to go to Orange Coast College.

During those growing up years, they were in Boy Scouts together and members of Explorer Post 163, which for many years was headed by Doug's father, Dick Binkley, as advisor. Tom became an Eagle Scout, Doug a Life Scout.

In 1966, they received their draft notices and both volunteered for the United States Marine Corps. Tom officially became a member of the USMC in February, 1966; Doug in January, 1966.

They lost track of each other, but for the past several months have been hoping to meet in Vietnam. Through letters to and from their parents they have been getting information of each other, but with the odds against finding anyone you know in Vietnam, they had almost given up hope of meeting there. When the day finally came a few weeks ago and they were once again together, "such happiness you can't describe," they both wrote their parents.

Doug has less than 40 days to go before he is due to return to the United States. Tom has less than 60 more days.

Cpl. Elliott was on a search and destroy mission in Vietnam for six months prior to his going to Dong Ha. He is now serving in a pacification program with his headquarters in Dong Ha. The Marines live and work with the Vietnamese people, supplying five or six villages around Dong Ha with needed materials, food and services.

Lance Cpl. Binkley is in Logistics Support Unit I of the Marine Corps. He is in general supply and maintenance at the present time with his company also based at Dong Ha.

TOM ELLIOTT

DOUG BINKLEY

Sunday, July 9, 1967 Temple City (Cal.)—3

The story of Doug and Tom meeting up in Vietnam. Article in the *Temple City Times* newspaper, 1967.

CHAPTER 34
R&R

I was still waiting for approval for R&R in Hawaii, which I had requested months earlier. When the ship had stopped in Hawaii nine months ago, I surfed at Waikiki beach. I was anxious to go back and surf there again. The plan was to have Phyllis meet me there as well.

After the July 4th rocket attack, the captain came to Dong Ha for a meeting. After the meeting he found me and said my request for R&R in Hawaii had been approved and would start on July 27 and go through August 3. He said a corporal from a CAP compound outside of Phu Bai would come to Dong Ha to take my place as the supply NCO while I was away. He also told me he needed another radio operator at Cam Lo Headquarters. Because of my radio experience, he wanted me to come to Cam Lo when I returned from R&R. I was tired of making the supply runs and moving to Cam Lo as the radio operator sounded good.

Surfing was extremely high on my priority list for Hawaii. My legs were still in decent shape from all the walking, but I was worried my arms might not be ready for all the paddling. I found an old plank of flat wood and set it on top of a row of sandbags high enough to lie down on and practice paddling. I practiced knee paddling and then standing up and walking back and forth on the plank like surfing a wave. Not having surfed for over ten months, I needed to get ready for Hawaii. I am sure guys walking by who knew nothing about surfing had no idea what I was doing. One guy who did know yelled out, "Hang ten, dude." I also did a couple hundred push-ups every day. After boot camp, I swore I would never do another push-up, but it turned out as the most effective way to build up paddling muscles. After a couple of weeks of training, I felt ready for Hawaii and hanging ten.

Before I left, Ben received his orders to rotate home and I asked him about his tape recorder. I offered him $35 for it and the tapes. "Done deal," he said. I wanted to keep listening to "Gloria" and to Dick Dale and the Del Tones play surf music.

I had not worn my lightweight khaki dress uniform since we were in the Philippines ten months earlier. I took my wrinkled, water-stained uniform to the laundry on base to have it cleaned. I needed my uniform for traveling. At the PX, I bought a set of corporal stripes to replace the lance corporal strips on the sleeves. I polished my shoes and borrowed a small knapsack. When I arrived in Hawaii, I planned to buy civilian clothes and a bathing suit.

About a week before I left, the corporal arrived from Phu Bai. For the next week, I trained him to take over the supply run duties. He picked it up quickly. Returning from a run to Cam Lo headquarters, we stopped for a beer at Cam Lo icehouse. Sitting there enjoying our beer, we heard an explosion and saw a cloud of dust rising high in the air above Dong Ha. "Looks like the base took a few rockets; we better get back to the base," Mark said.

"I hope they didn't damage the runway; I am leaving on R&R in two days," I said.

A couple of rockets hit the base the night before I left. Early the next morning, I reported to the air terminal for a flight to Phu Bai. I was ready to get out of Dong Ha. From Phu Bai, I flew to Da Nang. All the airplane flights I had taken so far were on C-130 cargo planes. I was looking forward to flying for the first time in a commercial jet liner with windows.

I waited overnight in Da Nang. The flight to Hawaii was scheduled to leave at 0500. I found a cot in the transit hooch and then went to see the paymaster to draw some money. Out in the field, there was little need for money except to buy beer when available. I had saved money on the books for Hawaii. Even after paying for my new surfboard, I figured there was enough money left for the trip. At the paymaster's office, I showed my orders to the clerk and asked for $400 in cash. After waiting a long time, the paymaster came out to tell me he did not have my pay records; they must have somehow gotten lost in transit. Great, I am leaving and needed the money.

Phyllis would have money, but I did not know how much. The paymaster saw panic on my face and said, "Don't worry, I'll work something out for you." He told me to come back in an hour.

Civilian clothes were available in the PX on base, but I did not want to spend what little money I had until I found out about my pay. Walking around the PX, I found a place to order a cheeseburger, fries, and a coke over ice. To me this was heaven, and I hadn't even left for Hawaii.

Back at the paymaster's office, the clerk told me the paymaster had set up temporary records and issued me $400 in cash. Now I was ready to party.

Nine months after my discharge from the Marines, I received a letter informing me I owed the government $225. The letter said the Marine Corps had overpaid me when my records were reestablished after the R&R screw up. That really pissed me off; I had spent all that time in Vietnam, shot at by the VC and dodging rockets, and now the fucking government wanted its money back. I told Dad, "They could pound sand; I did not intend pay it." I threw the letter in the trash and forgot about it. Months later, I found out Dad had pulled the letter out of the trash and paid the government their money.

At 0500, I boarded the flight to Hawaii. I scored a window seat. How cool to sit in a real seat facing forward and be able to see out of the plane. Way better than the canvas sling seats in a C-130. As the plane roared down the runway, I watched the countryside fly by. The plane left the ground, and we flew out over the ocean, Vietnam fading quickly behind us. I felt relief being away even if only for seven days. Anticipation of Hawaii, seeing my fiancée, and surfing filled my thoughts.

On the way to Hawaii, we stopped on Wake Island for the plane to refuel. In the air terminal, I enjoyed looking at the walls covered with pictures and a display case full of memorabilia from WWII. Wake Island had been the only place Marines had successfully repelled a Japanese amphibious assault. However, when the Japanese attacked the island a second time, they were able to overrun the Marines. Ironically, years later, I spent fifty-five days on Wake working for a civilian contractor installing an underwater listening system.

A small PX on the island sold alcohol duty free. I bought bottles of vodka, gin, tequila, and Kahlua. I figured five bottles should be enough to get me through a week in Hawaii, and they only cost me nine dollars, including a box to carry the bottles in. I was not the only one getting back on the plane carrying one of these boxes.

During the flight from Wake to Hawaii, I talked to the guy sitting next to me. He said he planned to fly home to the mainland.

"I thought we were not supposed to do that," I said.

"Ya, I know, but I am going to go anyway," he said.

The second day in Hawaii, I ran into the same guy on the street in Honolulu. "What happened to flying home?" I asked.

"MPs stopped me in Los Angles, put me on a plane, and sent me back." He told me two other guys were sent back with him. They did not get into much trouble but were out the money for their plane tickets. I was glad we decided Phyllis would meet me in Hawaii.

As the plane was coming into land, I enjoyed looking at the ocean's colorful coral bottom. There were waves breaking over the reefs. I knew there would be waves for me to ride. I was anxious to get back on a surfboard. I couldn't decide what excited me most—seeing my girlfriend or surfing.

After our plane landed, we had to attend a lecture before we could go into town. The talk was mostly about venereal disease. I did not have to worry about that this time. We were told again we could not travel to the mainland. The last thing said was, if we did not show up at our assigned time to return to Vietnam, we would be considered absent without official leave (AWOL). Not good. After the lecture, a shuttle bus took us to Fort DeRussy. From there it was a short walk to the hotel.

Phyllis had arrived a couple of hours earlier. I had told her in a letter to reserve a room at the Edgewater Hotel, the same hotel I had stayed in when the ship stopped in Hawaii. When I walked into the hotel lobby, Phyllis was waiting for me. She was standing next to a potted giant Bird of Paradise and silhouetted by the sun shining through the window. She looked like an angel. She had changed her hair style; I liked it. Dressed in a cute Hawaiian print sundress, she had a big smile on her face. We gave each other a big hug and a kiss. "I already checked in," she said. "Let's go to the room."

"Lead the way," I said, smiling.

We spent a couple of wonderful hours in the room getting to know one another again. Later, hand in hand, we left the hotel to go shopping. I needed civilian clothes.

The weather was warm, and the trade winds made things pleasant. Enjoying Hawaii and walking along the streets, I still found myself looking around for booby traps, trip wires, and anything that looked out of the ordinary. I felt naked without a rifle in my hand. Being out of Vietnam was one thing. Getting Vietnam out of my head was going to take time.

At a local surf shop, I bought a pair of shorts, long pants, and a couple of Hawaiian shirts. What I was really after were a bathing suit and sunglasses. Even though I brought alcohol, we needed to find a liquor store because Phyllis drank Crown Royal, which was not available on Wake. Back at the hotel, we went to the pool next to the beach for the afternoon. I dove in the pool and floated around trying to relax.

Leaving the hotel later for dinner, Phyllis asked, "What do you want to eat?"

"Steak and spaghetti," I said.

"That might be hard to find in one place," she said.

Not a block from the hotel, we happened upon an Italian restaurant. I looked up and saw a sign in the window that read, "Steak and Spaghetti." "We're eating dinner here," I said. With a bottle of red wine, we enjoyed a great dinner. For an instant, I thought about sitting in the bottom of my fighting hole on Operation Chinook, eating a can of C-Ration Spaghetti.

Though everything went great, the day had been a long one, and I was tired from all the travel. After dinner, we returned to the hotel. Sleeping should not have been a problem, but the quiet kept me awake. No artillery going off all night. What noises I did hear were unfamiliar; I tossed and turned before finally falling asleep.

Phyllis knew what I wanted to do in the morning—well, that too—but, before she woke up, I took off to rent a surfboard. A ten-minute walk to the board rental place and with the sidewalks empty, I enjoyed walking alone. The rental place was opening when I arrived. The cute, young girl in the teeny-weeny bikini who ran the place when I was here before was not there. Nor were the beach boys to carry the boards down to the water. I told the guy running the rental place I was on R&R from Vietnam and wanted to surf every morning. "Pick out a board and I will have it ready for you every day," he said. He gave me a discount on the rental fee.

I picked out a nine-foot ten-inch board and paddled out. Knee paddling, I could already feel my arm muscles starting to ache. I was glad I had spent the time working out. I paddled out to one of the many reef breaks off the beach. Since it was early, only the locals were out surfing. I stayed off to one side to watch waves go by and get an idea how they broke over the reef. I sat on the board and watched the sun come up over Diamond Head. I was so happy to be out on the water and riding waves, I wanted to scream, so I did.

On my first attempt to take off on an unfamiliar board, I realized I was a little too far forward on the board. The wave picked me up and the nose of the board went straight down. I had made a beginner's mistake and I could not believe I had "pearled." I surfaced hoping no one saw me. On the next wave, I jumped up and got a short ride. A couple of more waves and I walked to the nose. Just like riding a bike, you never forget. After about an hour and gaining confidence, I moved over into the better take-off sections to get a longer ride. I took off on the biggest wave of the day and surfed it all the way in. I sat on the board and smiled. I wanted more but my arms were like two wet noodles hanging by my side. I managed to paddle back to shore. I turned in the board and told the guy I'd be back the next morning. Turned out I could not wait that long. I went back and surfed again later in the afternoon.

By the time I made it back to the hotel, Phyllis was ready for breakfast. As we walked into town, a car or truck backfired. To me, it sounded like a rifle shot and I ducked behind a nearby park bench. I stood up quickly when I realized what I had done. Embarrassed, I told Phyllis it would not happen again. She seemed to understand and held my hand as we walked. She never mentioned the incident again.

The week away from Vietnam went by quickly, too quickly. One day we rented a car and drove around the island. I enjoyed watching the surf at Pipeline and Waimea Bay, too big for me to surf.

We shopped for gifts for the family, and I bought two surf shop T-shirts to bring back with me. We enjoyed the beach, spent time in our room, and I surfed twice a day. On my last day, I paddled out beyond the surf and sat looking at Diamond Head and back at the beach. During the past eleven months, some of my friends had been killed or wounded; now I felt lucky I was in Hawaii surfing and hoped to return here someday. I had two more months to do in Vietnam. I rode one last wave to the beach.

Forty-eight years later, I spent my seventieth birthday in Hawaii, staying at the Hyatt Hotel on Waikiki Beach. I surfed twice a day for five days. I surfed the same spots I had surfed while there on R&R.

When I returned to Vietnam, I had about seventy days left on my tour. The last night we were together, Phyllis and I went to dinner at a nice restaurant in Honolulu. We talked about getting married when I returned home. We decided she would work on wedding plans, and as soon as I knew a firm return date, she would set the date for the wedding. Now I really had a reason to survive the next seventy days.

CHAPTER 35
CAP HEADQUARTERS, CAM LO

I hated to end our long goodbye kiss but Phyllis's cab to the airport was waiting. I watched as the cab disappeared around the corner. I could not wait to see her again back home. At Fort DeRussy, I waited with other guys returning from R&R for the shuttle to the airport.

I took one last look at the surf breaking over the colorful reefs as the plane lifted off the end of the runway. I hated to leave. After a week of R& R spent surfing, eating tasty food, lying around the pool and the beach, and the love making, I felt relaxed and refreshed. I did not want to go back to the war. I don't think any of us really wanted to go back to Vietnam. I noticed it was quieter on the plane leaving Hawaii than when we left Vietnam. However, once in the air and Hawaii fading behind us, I started to feel eager to get back. I was ready to tackle the last seventy days of my tour and wanted to see what had happened while I was gone and how the guys were doing.

The plane stopped to refuel at Wake Island again, but no alcohol was allowed on the return trip. Too bad, as real liquor was always hard to get on the base. After landing in Da Nang, I caught a C-130 to fly to Phu Bai and then on to Dong Ha. As I walked off the plane, the smells, the heat, the dust, and the sound of helicopters reminded me of my first day. Welcome back to Vietnam, Tom.

With Ben gone, I moved out of the French bunker and into the CAP living quarters where I had stored my rifle and gear before leaving on R&R. Talking with the guys, I found out the NVA was stepping up attacks, hitting the base with rockets and artillery fire nine times during the week I was gone. No CAP personnel were wounded in the attacks. I wanted off this base.

I radioed the captain to let him know I made it back to Dong Ha. He told me to see about hitching a ride out to Cam Lo. I put on one of my new surf shop T-shirts and changed into my utility uniform, flak jacket, and combat boots.

Sea bag over my shoulder, tape recorder in one hand, and rifle in the other, I caught a ride to the base west gate and told the guards I needed to hitch a ride to Cam Lo. Right after I got there, a convoy of three trucks leaving the base and headed for Camp Carroll stopped at the gate. While they were checking out, I asked the driver in the last truck if he could drop me at Cam Lo. He asked why I wanted to go there. I told him I was reporting for duty at the CAP compound there. "You CAP guys are fucking crazy living in those small villages. Jump in the back; I'll drop you there," he said.

The back of the truck was full of cases of ammunition, grenades, C-Rations, and a pallet of empty sandbags. I squeezed into a corner and sat down on a box of ammo. When the truck hit the first pothole, my ass went up in the air and then down on the hard wooden box. How I wished I was back in the comfortable seat on the airplane! I had made this same run delivering supplies to the compounds and knew it was not far to Cam Lo. The convoy passed by Papa Three where guys were working on one of the sandbag walls. At Cam Lo, the truck stopped in front of the compound gate. I jumped out and thanked the driver. He shouted, "Good luck, man" as he took off to catch up with his convoy.

I stood across the road looking at the entry to the compound and saw a single PF guard on duty. When I crossed the road, he opened the gate for me. I took a deep breath and walked into the compound. As I walked toward the living quarters, the gunny came out of the kitchen shack. He greeted me with another bone-crushing handshake.

Shaking hands, he asked me, "How was your time in Hawaii?"

"Too short," I said.

He laughed, "No doubt. Let's find you a cot."

In the living quarters, gunny told me to throw my gear on the empty cot in the corner. "I'll give you a tour of the compound," he said. "As our new radio operator, I guess the first thing I should show you is where the radio bunker is."

"No, the first thing you need to do is show me where the head is," I said. The head, a small tin-roofed building, sat about a meter outside the first line of fighting trenches.

The radio bunker was constructed of rows and rows of sandbags stacked eight feet high, with openings on both sides and next to the hooch. Inside the bunker, the gunny introduced me to Bob, another radio operator, who was happy to have my help.

In the kitchen shack, the captain and the doc were sitting at a table. Two guys were cooking dinner. In addition to C-Rations, the CAP compounds received other canned meals in bigger cans. Meals like beef stew, spaghetti and meat balls, and SPAM. We also had access to eggs, potatoes, rice, and even fresh vegetables and meat, all depending on who you knew back at Dong Ha. Having been the resupply NCO for the past few months, I knew the right people. I learned we would take turns cooking. Having worked in a deli and a restaurant before getting drafted, I knew my way around a kitchen. The captain welcomed me and introduced me to doc, the headquarters corpsman, and the other two guys.

Back in the radio bunker, Bob showed me the layout. The radios sat on a table; a shelf above held the code books, logbooks, and manuals. Miss March hung on the wall on one side, Miss July on the other. The compound used a generator for power. The generator was not always dependable, and it did not run 24/7. There was a bank of batteries under the desk to provide backup power for the radios. Communications to Papa One were via hardwire. Bob showed me all the procedures and code books, all stuff familiar to me. I told Bob the empty spot on the table by the radio would be a good spot for my tape recorder.

"Any country western music?" he asked.

"Sorry, do you like surf music?" I said.

Bob laughed and said he had never been in the ocean.

Outside the radio bunker was an old observation platform built by the French. Constructed of four concrete columns with a platform and covered lookout post on top, it towered over the compound. Tall radio antennas sat secured to the top of the tower and needed checking every couple of days. On one of the columns was a steel-rung ladder. We climbed to the top of the tower and Bob showed me the routine for maintaining the antennas. With a 360-degree view, I could see the compound's overall defensives.

By the time we finished going over things in the radio bunker, a dinner of rice with slices of SPAM and canned corn was served. Not bad, but after all the great food in Hawaii, a real let down. (I would eat more rice than I wanted over the next couple of months.) At dinner, the gunny asked me if I wanted a beer. Now I knew I would like this duty.

After dinner I cleaned my rifle, unpacked my gear, and settled in. Lying on my cot, I thought, "Seventy days here. I can do that." I was tired from all the traveling and fell asleep. My sleep was cut short by the sound of artillery fire, and I sat straight up. I remembered Camp Carroll was not far down the road on a plateau overlooking our location. When the 175 mm howitzers fired, it sounded like they were right over us. The gunny said, "You will get used to it." He was right, but it took more than one night. A couple of hours later, I stood my first radio watch.

In the morning, Bob showed me around the rest of the compound. A trench with sandbag walls and fighting positions went around the back with a sandbag bunker at each of the four corners. He showed me the ammo bunker built under the concrete tower. Inside were an M-60 and A-6 30-caliber machine guns. If the compound came under attack, we would take the machine guns out to one of the fighting positions. The PF soldiers were supposed to assume the remaining fighting positions. I realized that with only seven or eight Marines in the compound, along with a few Army guys and hopefully the PFs when we needed them, we might be in deep shit if attacked. Seventy days and counting.

Outside the radio bunker entrance.
Tom Elliott with M-60 and Browning A-6, 30-caliber machine guns.

Tom Elliott checking out the radio antennas on top of the French built lookout tower, Cam Lo Papa headquarters.

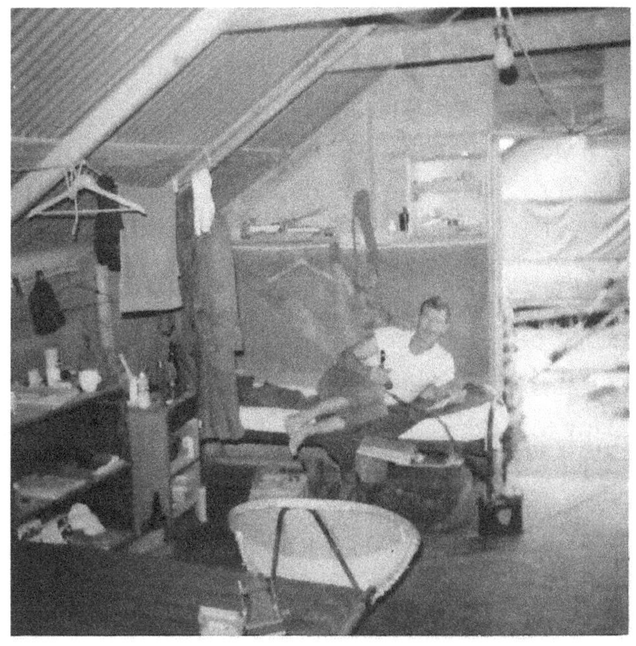

Hooch at Cam Lo Papa headquarters.
Tom Elliott on daytime radio watch.

Gunny Kalani headed for the outhouse at Cam Lo headquarters.

For two weeks, I stood radio watches, took care of the antennas, helped with the cooking, and made repairs and upgrades around the compound. I got to know the guys better and felt comfortable with life at Cam Lo. When there was time, we walked down to the icehouse to have cold 33 beer. Not much going on. I still counted the days.

In the early morning of August 14, Bob was on radio watch when he sent a guard to notify the captain that Papa Three was under attack. On the radio, the sergeant at Papa Three asked for help and reported the compound was under heavy attack from small arms, rocket-propelled grenades (RPG's), and sappers. The captain was immediately on the radio, asking Oscar Company to send a reaction team. He also told Oscar we were not going to wait; we were going to head for the compound ourselves. He told the Oscar force to meet us at the bridge near Papa Three.

We grabbed our rifles and the M-60 out of the ammo bunker along with belts of ammo. We piled into the back of the army's radio truck. With the gunny driving, we headed down Highway 9 toward Papa Three. I held the M-60 machine gun on top of the truck's cab at the ready in case VC were waiting for us. Bob, on the radio, stayed in touch with the reactionary force and Papa Three. The Oscar force reported it was right behind us as we arrived at the bridge. They went by us and directly down the road into Papa Three. Beginning to get light, the Oscar force moved in and ran the remaining VC out the back of the compound.

With the area cleared, we started to help. One Marine, Mark Black, was killed in the attack and five Marines were wounded, including Tom Willey, a friend of mine from Second Platoon. He was a short timer, and his wound was serious, so he was sent home. Doc worked on the wounded while the rest of us helped check the area for VC and any unexploded ordnance. A dozen dead VC bodies hung in the wire and lay around the compound. A couple of the M-16 rifles our guys were using were on the ground with rounds jammed in the chambers. Helicopters came from Dong Ha to pick up the wounded. This was the second time in three months the VC had attacked Papa Three. Obviously Papa Three had been doing an excellent job of patrolling and protecting the village, and the VC wanted them out of there.

A few weeks later nature did what the VC could not. The monsoon rains pushed by a passing typhoon raised the river and flooded out the compound. The compound had to be relocated across the road up on higher ground.

We helped the wounded get to the Medevac choppers. Oscar force left troops at the compound to replace the dead and wounded Marines. Over the next few days, the captain would assign new men to Papa Three. When we returned to Papa HQ, I spent the afternoon cleaning the M-60 machine gun. I wanted it ready in case the VC attacked the Cam Lo compound next.

CHAPTER 36
THE ICEHOUSE

The VC attack and overrun of Papa Three put us a bit on edge at Cam Lo headquarters. Were we next? We had taken a few of incoming mortar rounds lately, but no ground attack. My daily routine was getting old. I wanted this adventure to end.

One duty I did enjoy required me to keep the compound supplied with ice. Due to the process used to make it, the ice was no good in drinks, but it worked well to keep our beer, soda, and food cold. Two or three times a week with one or two guys, I drove the truck to the icehouse. Before returning to the compound, we often took time to sit in front of the store and drink a cold 33 or a Tiger beer. The weather was hot and humid, we wore T-shirts, cutoff utility trousers, combat boots, and soft covers (hats). We leaned our rifles against the table; I wore my 45-caliber pistol. Seeing us sitting with cold beer in our hands, guys riding by in truck convoys on their way to Camp Carroll and beyond gave us odd looks and wondered what the hell we were doing there.

One afternoon Bob and I went for ice. In no hurry, we sat out front to drink a beer. No traffic along the road, it was quiet, and we watched the people across the way working in the rice field. A peaceful setting.

With the ice chest full of ice and loaded in the truck, I told Bob I was going to have another beer. He said he was going to get some sleep on the front seat of the truck. While I was sitting on the porch alone and thinking of home, the owner of the icehouse came outside and sat down across the table from me. He did that occasionally. He had a drink in his hand, likely his homemade rice wine. The owner knew me because I always came to get the ice and he knew us Marines lived in the compound down the road. He considered us his best customers.

The owner whose name I cannot remember spoke limited English. He asked if the captain and I would come have a meal with him the next afternoon. I was surprised by his request and told him I would ask the captain.

"Good," he said and went back inside.

I had eaten rice with the PF troops at our compound a few times but had never eaten a meal with a Vietnamese family in their home. This would be interesting; I hoped the captain would accept the invitation.

Back at the compound, we dropped off the ice and I found the captain in the kitchen shack. I told him the owner of the icehouse had invited he and I to have a meal the next afternoon. "Sure, why not?" the captain said. I went back to the icehouse to let the owner know the captain accepted his invitation. Smiling and with a slight bow, he said, "Good, good." I returned the bow.

The next afternoon, the captain and I walked to the icehouse. The captain carried his 45-caliber pistol. I carried a M-16 rifle, my pistol and the radio. We never left the compound without our weapons.

At the store, the owner was waiting for us out front. He greeted us with a smile, a handshake, and a slight bow to show respect. We returned the bow. The captain thanked him for the invitation.

Inside he showed us to a room I had never seen before. With a table and chairs, it looked like a dining room, clean and neat. The room was separate from the store and the icehouse. I felt privileged the owner had invited us, and to show respect, we left our weapons outside the room, but where we could see them.

The owner introduced us to his wife, whom I had met before when picking up ice. A small woman, she often served us our beer. She was more formally dressed today than when serving us beer. The owner showed us where he wanted us to sit. At CAP school, I had learned local customs for this type of occasion, and I tried to be on my best behavior. Difficult for a Marine, I know, especially for one who had spent five months in the bush.

Before eating, the wife served us tea. Our host began to tell us a little history of the icehouse and how his family started it with help from the

French when they were in Vietnam. The French also had built part of the compound we were using as CAP headquarters.

After tea, the owner poured the captain and me a small glass of his homemade rice wine. Then he poured one for himself. We held the glasses up for a toast. I managed to drink it down though the owner chuckled when he realized we did not enjoy the wine. He then gave me and the captain a cold 33 beer. The cold beer was perfect for washing down the wine.

On the dinner table were small bowls set in front of each of us, and next to each bowl were chopsticks along with a fork for the captain and me. I had learned to use chopsticks while eating rice with the PF troops. The wife set a large bowl of rice next to her husband. In the center of the table, she placed a row of smaller bowls. One held a green leafy vegetable which looked to me like the weeds that grew along the side of the road. In another bowl were small fish, whole and covered with salt. They looked like the little minnows that swam in the shallows of the streams feeding into the river. In the third bowl was a mixture of shredded carrots and bean sprouts. The bowl of most interest to me looked like a bowl of beef chunks in a thick dark sauce.

Before eating, I noticed the man and his wife bowed their heads. The captain also noticed, and we did the same. Our host said something in Vietnamese, ending with an amen. I knew there was a Christian church in the village but did not know the family was Christian. I had not been to church in many months and, in fact, was having a tough time believing lately. At home, we would hold hands around the table and Mom would choose one of us to say the evening meal prayer.

Our host picked up the large bowl of rice and passed it around. I filled my smaller bowl using the flat wood spatula. On top of the rice, we each put a little bit of food from the smaller bowls. I waited for everyone to fill their bowls before starting to eat. The greens had little taste, the carrots and sprouts the same. The little fish were so salty, I did not want to bite one, so I swallowed it whole.

I had taken one piece of the meat from its small bowl. I picked it up with the chopsticks and put it in my mouth. The sauce was like a thick soy sauce with spices I did not recognize. The meat was tender and tasty. With my chopsticks, I reached into the small bowl to take a second piece. As I did, the captain gave me a look.

"Do you know what it is you are eating?" he asked. I noticed the captain had taken only one small piece.

"I think it's beef, tastes like it. What is it; water buffalo or something?"

"Dog," the captain said. Our host looked at me and nodded his head yes.

"Very good," I said bowing my head slightly toward his wife. She smiled. They considered it a delicacy and certainly not an everyday dish. I ate one more piece. I did not want to offend our host's wife, and it actually did taste quite good. I had heard the Vietnamese ate dog. This was my first and last time.

Our host reached over to a shelf and picked up a small bottle of clear liquid. He put drops in his bowl of rice. He motioned we should do the same and handed the bottle to the captain. He put one drop in his rice and passed the bottle to me. I should have watched the captain's reaction as he took a mouthful of his rice. I put one tiny drop in my bowl. That one tiny drop turned my bowl of rice into molten lava. Our host chuckled again at our reaction and offered us another cold beer. One beer would not be enough to put out the fire on my lips. What I had learned in CAP school about leaving a little food on my plate so the family would think I had had enough would not be a problem. No way could I eat more of the rice in my bowl.

When we finished eating, our hostess cleared the table. Her husband offered us another beer. We declined. The captain offered to pay for the drinks, but our host said no. He told us he and the other villagers were thankful for the Marines who were protecting their villages from the VC. He warned us some of the PF troops assigned to our compound were VC sympathizers and told us we should be careful. We already knew that but were grateful that he told us.

"Sir, it's getting late, and we don't want to be out here after dark."

"You're right; we should go."

We picked up our weapons and walked outside. Daylight fading, we shook hands and bowed, thanking the owner for the food and beer. His wife was standing in the doorway, and we turned and exchanged bows with her. Our host thanked us again for coming and for protecting the villages.

Walking along the road, the captain said, “That was interesting.”

“Yes, Sir, but I wish you hadn’t told me I ate dog.”

The captain laughed, “Now you have a story to tell your grandchildren.”

Approaching the compound I said, “I hope the PFs on guard duty at the gate don’t shoot our asses.”

CHAPTER 37
THE POKER GAME

I was waiting outside CAG headquarters at the Dong Ha base for the captain to finish his afternoon meeting. The gunny stuck his head out the door and said, "Elliott, there is a message here for you from Mike O'Grady."

Inside the office, the radio operator handed me a scribbled message. "This came in a couple of hours ago," he said. I stared at the message, seeing words I never wanted to see, my hand shaking.

The gunny took the message and read it. "Pat Cochran was killed yesterday."

"Not Pat, goddamn it; I hate this fucking war!" I shouted. "I'm going to graves registration to see if I can find Pat's body."

"Go," the gunny said, "we will pick you up there."

I ran across the base to graves registration where half a dozen body bags on stretchers were inside the tent. I asked the corpsman if one of them was Pat Cochran.

He said, "They just came in, I'm not sure yet, you can check for yourself if you'd like." I knelt and read the toe tags. No Pat. Upset about the loss of my friend and the other men I did not know lying in the tent, I sat outside on the sandbag wall. I tried to cry but was too mad, so mad I wanted to kill every fucking VC in the goddamn country. More good men's lives wasted in this useless fucking war.

I remembered one evening drinking beer around a fire ring on the beach in Oceanside before leaving for Vietnam, Phyllis made Pat and me promise to always watch out for one another. We told her not to worry; we would always have each other's back. Now I was mad at myself for leaving Second

Platoon, and not being there to watch out for him. I felt I let both my friend and Phyllis down. Now I cried.

The gunny stopped the jeep in front of graves registration, and I jumped in the back. The gunny and captain looked back at me; I shook my head no. I said nothing on the drive out to Cam Lo. At the compound, I went straight to the radio bunker. I felt safe there. Alone with a blank piece of paper in front of me and a pencil in my hand, I thought, how do I tell Phyllis?

The next morning in the radio bunker, the blank piece of paper and pencil were still sitting on the tabletop. In a real funk, no motivation, I wanted to be alone. I had landed in Vietnam over nine months ago. I recalled the Marines watching us new guys enter the Dong Ha base yell out to us "thirty and a wake up." They were letting us know the number of days they had left on their tour in Vietnam. Having recently arrived, I had over three hundred days to go. Now I was down to thirty and a wake up. During my first few weeks in country, I worried about how much time I had left. Over time and with the loss of friends in the platoon killed or wounded, my attitude changed. I found I did not give a damn anymore about how much time I had left. Life became a quest to survive one day at a time. Down to thirty days I knew anything can happen to anybody at any time. This close to the end of my tour, the time passed more slowly each day. I started to worry again if I would survive that one more day. The loss of my friend Pat did not help.

One of the PF troops who spoke English entered the radio bunker. He said there was a problem with the water well pump and asked for help. The local troops asking us for help with projects around the compound was not unusual. They helped us by providing security around the compound taking the defensive positions and standing watch. I never knew the number who were supposed to be on duty, or if all the ones who should be on duty showed up. They came from the local villages and sometimes brought their young sons. One young boy liked to run up to us and say, "Marines number 1, VC number 10," knowing we would give him chocolate. We called him Cowboy because he always wore a camouflaged cowboy hat. We knew a few of the PF troops were VC sympathizers, but it could not hurt to try and make a few friends. When we finished helping the PF troops with a project, they often asked us to sit and eat a bowl of rice with them.

I agreed to help with the water well pump and went to find Bob to help me. We suspected all it needed was a good cleaning. We pulled the pump up, cleaned it out, and put it back down. The pump worked fine. The PFs clapped for us when the water flowed freely again, an equivalent to a bunch of high fives today.

Repairing the well pump brought me out of my funk. Feeling better, I decided to surprise the PFs. Before they asked us to have rice with them, I said, "Let me make the rice today." One guy translated what I said. They all pointed at me, laughed, and nodded yes. I am sure they wondered what I knew about cooking rice. I used a couple of boxes of Uncle Ben's, easy to make, and the rice not sticky like their rice. To liven up the rice, I poured a can of tomato sauce over the cooked rice and added drops of Tabasco. Mixed up, it tasted like a poor man's Spanish rice. With a slight bow, I filled each of their bowls with rice. They laughed at the red color but ate it up. They either liked it or did not want to offend me. The next day I put in an order for twelve cans of tomato sauce and more Uncle Ben's.

Tom Elliott outside the radio bunker, CAP Papa headquarters, Cam Lo, with the kid we called Cowboy.

Tom and Bob helping the PF troops repair the water well pump, CAP Papa Headquarters in Cam Lo.

Now out of my funk, I looked forward to our weekly poker game. Not a big money game, but enough to make it interesting with a few dollars changing hands.

Long before Texas Hold'em, and the now popular phrase "All in," we played seven card stud. After dinner, there were six of us playing a game around the table in the kitchen shack. The guy dealing wore a green plastic dealer's visor. We could have been in a back-room poker game anywhere.

We had played for about half an hour, while I sipped my ration of one beer because in three hours, it was my radio watch.

Starting a new hand, the dealer dealt out the first three cards, two down, one up. I looked at my down cards, both kings, my up card a four. A good start. The other up cards on the table were a ten, an ace, a seven, a five, and a deuce. The player with the ace bet first. I raised. Three guys called. The guys with the five and the deuce folded.

Bets placed between each round of cards dealt before the final down card created a nice pile of cash in the middle of the table. My fifth up card was a third king. I looked around at the other hands and tried to figure out who could have what. The hand with three sevens showing could not have four sevens because another player showed a seven in a possible flush hand. He could not have sevens full of aces because three aces showed in other hands. The guy with two-pair showing, tens and aces could not have aces full of tens. He could not have four tens because a ten showed in another hand. He could have tens full of aces if the last ten was one of his down cards. I did not see how the possible flush hand could make a straight flush. My three kings, well-hidden, might be the best hand.

The player with the three sevens bet. The two-pair hand called and the player with the possible flush folded. I raised; it was time to figure out where I stood. The remaining players called the raise. The dealer dealt the last down card. The player with the sevens looked at his last card and bet again. Did he hit his full house? The two-pair hand looked and raised. Did he have the tens full? If I paired one of my cards, my full house would be best. I turned up the corner of my last down card. I did not pair up. My last card was the fourth king!

Already counting my winnings, I raised and pushed my money to the center of the table. Before the other players could react to my raise, Flash, Boom!!! A huge explosion in the compound. Bob, on watch outside, yelled, "Incoming." Rushing to get out of the kitchen shack, the poker table went up in the air with the money and the cards flying. Two more rockets exploded near the other side of the compound.

I ran to the hooch, grabbed my flak jacket and helmet. Next I ran to the ammo bunker to get the M-60 machine gun. Outside, I jumped into the trench and headed for the bunker to set up the M-60. The other guys ran to their assigned positions. Boom! Boom! Two more rockets landed short of the compound in the wire in front of me. Shrapnel flew overhead. The captain was on the radio requesting illumination. Two more rockets hit, one short, one long.

Illumination lit up the sky around the compound. I strained my eyes to see if the VC were trying to crawl through the wire and hit us with satchel charges like they did at Papa Two and Three. My heart pounding in my chest—damn, I only had a month to go. I did not see any VC. I yelled down the line to Bob, "See anything?"

"No," he answered. None of the defensive positions reported VC in the wire.

We checked on the PF troops around the compound. Oddly some of the troops who were supposed to be on duty did not show up. The PF troops must have known the attack was coming and did not warn us. So much for making friends. There was another problem I found that night. I always kept two belts of ammo for the machine gun wrapped in a poncho in the bunker. When I got to the bunker, I found the belts of ammo lying in dirt at the bottom of the bunker and the poncho was gone. There was no way to prove who had taken the poncho but my trust for the local troops dropped a little that night.

None of the rockets hit anything important. We knew the VC often set up rockets on temporary tripod stands made of heavy bamboo or tree branches, aiming the rockets in the general direction of the target. The rockets were set with timers to go off well after the VC had left the launching area. Not the most accurate method of rocket attack, but sometimes they scored a lucky hit. We figured that is what must have happened this time.

We stood watch for the rest of the night; the adrenaline rush kept me awake. Fortunately, no more rockets and no ground attack followed. In the morning, we stood down from watch and went to check for damage around the compound. Most of the rockets had landed short or overshot the compound. The rocket that exploded in the middle of the compound did minor damage. I searched around the crater left by the explosion and found pieces of shrapnel and the exhaust port from a 102 mm Russian-made rocket. I held up the exhaust port to show Bob. He looked down at me and said, "If that rocket had landed thirty-five meters shorter, it would have hit the kitchen shack where you guys were playing poker."

"That would have really messed up the game," I said.

Back in the kitchen shack, we found the money and cards all over the floor and the table and chairs turned over. Standing around the upturned table, I said. "Guys, I had four kings; I would have won the pot. The money is mine."

"Oh yeah, sure you did," they all said in unison.

I was unable to convince them, so we split up the money fair and square. We were glad the attack had not killed or wounded anyone. We enjoyed a good laugh about the poker game.

I headed back to the radio bunker to finish my letter to Phyllis. I had survived another day. Six days until my twenty-second birthday. I'll throw a party.

The exhaust port from Russian-made 102 mm rocket that landed in the compound during the poker game.

CHAPTER 38
MY BIRTHDAY

My letter to Phyllis was short; I wasn't sure what to say. I did tell her Pat had died, and how badly I felt about not being there like I had promised. Years later, I would read a book describing the battle where Pat was killed. Pat was not the only Marine to die that day. I realized there was nothing I could have done.

The day after the rocket attack on Cam Lo headquarters, the North Vietnamese hit the Dong Ha Base with three separate rocket and artillery attacks, destroying two helicopters, and damaging twenty-four others. Attacked again on September 3, rockets hit the ammo dump, causing a huge explosion. We heard it in Cam Lo and saw the cloud of smoke ten kilometers away. Seventeen helicopters were damaged, and seventy-seven Marines wounded. The attacks in our area were increasing to a point where Marine Command became convinced Dong Ha was too vulnerable to artillery and rocket attacks to continue as a helicopter facility. They moved operations back to Phu Bai. Supply operations moved down to the new Quang Tri Combat Base.

September 8th, 1967, my twenty-second birthday, did not start out as I had hoped. The day dawned cloudy and rainy, and the temperature was climbing to over hundred degrees. Then the captain came to tell me my grandfather had died. My favorite grandfather, Grandpa Frank, was my grandmother's second husband on my mom's side. They lived near us, and Grandpa took me fishing and bowling—his two favorite things to do. I spent more time with him than with my other grandparents who lived in Ohio. My parents had asked the Marine Corps to allow me to come home for the funeral. The Marine Corps denied the request, and I never learned why. With less than thirty days left on my tour, it pissed me off the Marine Corps would not let me go home early. While on radio watch, I wrote a letter to Grandma to tell her how sorry I was Grandpa had died and I would not be able to attend his funeral.

When my radio watch ended, the sun came out and the guys were ready to party. I wanted to do something special for them on my birthday. I managed to pull strings with the supply guys I knew at Dong Ha and scored enough steaks and chicken for all of us. I had already iced down a case of beer. Using locally made chunks of charcoal, I lit the barbeque and threw on the steaks and chicken and opened my first beer. The guys gathered around the compound picnic table; the party was officially under way.

We were all enjoying our beer and eating the steaks and chicken when the captain came out to give me two birthday presents. First, my promotion to sergeant E-5, earning a fifty dollar raise in pay and more money for the new surfboard. But the best part about the promotion was, I now outranked Dad who had been a corporal in the Marines during WWII. I couldn't wait to tell him. No birthday cake, but the guys sang Happy Birthday anyway. I missed the marble cake with sweet butter frosting Mom always baked for my birthday.

A truck on the way to Camp Carroll stopped by our compound to drop off some mail. I received a letter from Mom and Dad with pictures of my new surfboard that Dad had picked up. Seeing the pictures was like getting another birthday present.

The best news of the day was when the captain told me I was to be transferred to Phu Bai on September 22. I would wait there for my orders back to the real world. A year ago, I left for Vietnam on board a ship. Today while enjoying my third beer, I thought of how many times over the past year I did not know if I would make it to twenty-two. Now if I can survive a few more days, this adventure will end, and I can go home. After a bad start, my birthday turned out better than planned.

CAP Papa Headquarters, Cam Lo
September 8, 1967 (Tom's twenty-second birthday)
Left Side: Tom Elliott, Dicky, Gunny Kalini, Lt.
Right Side: Bob, Shaf, Franz, the Captain

I wanted out of Vietnam before the monsoon rains started again. That was not going to happen. A couple of days after my birthday party, the rain came down in buckets, the first really hard rain of the season. We found out later the heavy rain had been part of a typhoon. At one point, it rained for two solid days. The sound of the rain hitting the corrugated metal roof of our hooch was deafening. I woke one morning to hear the gunny say, "Damn, look at all this water." A low spot in the hooch plywood floor had flooded, and water was all around the gunny's cot. He reached up and took his 45-caliber pistol out of the holster hanging above him. He shouted out, "Fire in the hole," and then shot five holes into the floor. The water slowly drained out. Problem solved.

Around the compound, the rains wrought havoc on our defenses. The fighting holes and trenches filled with water, the sandbag walls gave way, sliding into the trenches. After three days of rain, the compound was a mess. To keep as much rain as possible out of our hooch, we rolled the canvas sides down, which made the place smell musty all the time. Years later, I lived in Morgan City, Louisiana, working as a diver on the offshore oil rigs. Living near the bayou and swamp, that same musty smell was always in the air, reminding me of the hooch and my last couple of miserable weeks in Vietnam.

I stood radio watches, worked repairing the compounds trenches and sandbag walls and whatever else I could do to pass the time, and counted the days. On my radio watch one afternoon, Mike called me. Somehow, he found out another friend of ours from Second Platoon, Ray Potter, was killed on September 10th. He was in same area where Pat Cochran had died a couple of weeks earlier. Later that afternoon, the captain told us that the VC had ambushed a patrol near one of the CAP compounds down near Phu Bai and another Marine was killed. Ron Black was also an original member of Second Platoon. I called on the radio to let Mike know about Ron. "Goddamn it, this should not be happening; we've only two weeks left, and we are still losing guys. We've got to get out of this fucking place," Mike said.

"Soon, Mike, soon," I said. In two days, we would lose one more friend from Second Platoon.

CHAPTER 39
BACK TO THE REAL WORLD

My final days passed without incident. My last night of radio watch at Cam Lo, I sat alone in the radio bunker thinking, thirteen months of my life had passed and for what? I came close to dying aboard the *Lenawee* during the typhoon. In Okinawa and the Philippines, I endured long days of training with millions of mosquitoes as the enemy. After landing in Vietnam in less than two weeks, we were in combat. I watched Paul die right in front of me. Gary was killed on New Year's Eve. A sniper round missed me by inches. The next day Hummingbird was not so lucky. On Operation Chinook, we survived countless mortar and rocket attacks, small-arms fire, booby traps, endless days of monsoon rains, leeches, too little food or sleep, and not enough beer.

Transferred to CAP, Terrance had been killed after taking my place, and Albert had been wounded. After I left Second Platoon, Pat, Ray, and Anthony were killed, and Ron died a week ago. Other Marines from Lima Company were also killed and wounded. Again, the thought, "Why them and not me?" Perhaps if I had stayed with the platoon, I might have died as well. Did I let the guys in Second Platoon and Lima Company down by volunteering for CAP? I will never know how things would have been different if I had stayed with the platoon. Over the years, I learned to live with my decision.

I could not wait to get away from this place, this war. I wanted to go home, marry Phyllis, ride my new surfboard, get a job, buy a car, and forget all about the war.

Radio chatter from Dong Ha brought me back to reality, the base was under rocket attack again. I hoped I wouldn't have to stay long or overnight in Dong Ha.

The next morning, with my seabag in the back of the jeep, I waited for the gunny to take Mike and me to Dong Ha. At Papa Four, Mike was waiting in the middle of the road for us with his seabag and rifle to make sure he did not miss his ride. Gary and Ernie were already in Phu Bai.

Before leaving Cam Lo, I said goodbye to the captain, Bob, Doc, and the other guys I had served with the last four months. I would never see or hear from any of them again. I had not developed the same camaraderie at CAP as I had with the guys from Second Platoon. The CAP guys and I worked well together as a team, did our jobs, and watched each other's back, but it was never quite the same as with Second Platoon. Because of my assignment as a resupply NCO and radio operator, I did not spend time at one of the compounds going on patrols or ambushes. I respected the guys who did.

The Marines who lived in the compounds risked their lives every day to protect the villages to which they were assigned. The corpsmen often provided medical assistance to the villagers. All their demanding work and dedication showed the local people they were the good guys. While we were in country, I believed CAP operations were successful. However, years later, I wondered if all the effort and loss of life did any real good overall. I often wondered what happened to the icehouse owner and the people in the villages we helped. I am sure they did not fare very well when the North took over.

At Dong Ha Airfield, we thanked the gunny for the ride and told him to keep his head down. He told us to go home and live long, happy lives; we deserved it. He stuck out his hand for one last bone-crushing handshake.

The clerk at the airfield told us the next flight to Phu Bai was scheduled in the morning and put us on the manifest. Mike and I found a couple of cots in the transit hooch. "Damn, I did not want to stay overnight in Dong Ha," I said to Mike.

"I predict no rocket attack tonight," he said. Outside the hooch, we found the nearest bunker in case his prediction was wrong. No rocket attack that night, and in the morning, I got a big "I told you so," from Mike.

Eager to get out of Dong Ha, we reported early to the airfield. The clerk told us the plane was on its way and escorted us out to a trench dug near the end of the runway. He told us to stay down in the trench until the crew chief signaled us to board the plane. Other guys were waiting in the trench, and we all sat on the edge smoking and talking about going home. All eyes were on the far end of the runway.

Losing altitude fast, a giant C-130 came out of the clouds. When the plane touched down, it bounced once and then sped down the runway, slowing as it approached where we waited. When it reached us, the plane spun around, the back door opened, and Marines went running for the trench on the other side of the runway. With the engines still running, the crew chief signaled us to board. Carrying our seabags over our shoulders, we ran to the back of the plane and took a seat. Before I could fasten my seatbelt, the plane was down the runway taking off. No rocket attack during the brief time the plane sat on the ground. The first leg of the long trip home was underway, but we were not out of Vietnam yet.

At Phu Bai, we checked in at CAP headquarters. Technically in transit home, we did not have to stand watch or perform other duties. We spent our few days there cleaning up, turning in our rifles and web gear, and waiting. Waiting was the hard part.

The next leg home was a flight to Da Nang. Assigned to living quarters in Da Nang, we had to wait four days for our scheduled flight to Okinawa. Mike, always looking for an angle, found out that if we took off our belts and turned our rank chevrons upside down, we could pass as Seabees. The Seabees had a nice bar on their base across the road from the Marine base. We spent our waiting days drinking beer in their bar and eating cheeseburgers and fries at the PX, happy we were out of the bush. The bartender at the Seabee bar knew we were Marines but did not care; we were the paying customers, who needed beer.

With other guys in the terminal heading home, the nervous energy in the room was evident. We wanted this nightmare to end. Outside sat a Continental Airlines jet, its tail painted gold. Continental called their planes, "The proud bird with the golden tail."

The plane was boarded by rank—officers first, followed by noncoms. The stewardesses on board were four of the most beautiful round-eyed women we had seen in a long time. We were all smiles: laughing, joking, and with a few catcalls. The stewardesses took it all in stride; they were definitely in charge. When one of them started to give the safety briefing, the ruckus settled down. The engines started. I twisted and turned in my seat, unable to settle down. Other guys were doing the same. "Let's get the hell out of here," we were all thinking.

When the plane started down the runway, we all held our breaths until the wheels left the ground. Then we let out a collective cheer so loud that I bet the people on the ground could hear us. Plus, a show of middle fingers in the windows let Vietnam know what we thought of the war.

After we leveled off, the stewardesses came through the cabin. One stopped and asked the staff sergeant in front of me if he needed anything. He looked up at her pretty face, her hair under the cute little hat she wore, and said, "How about a little of that golden tail I have been hearing so much about?" Those of us sitting close enough to hear what he had said started laughing, the stewardess right along with us.

She looked down at the sergeant and, with a big smile and a twinkle in her eye, replied, "You'll have to wait a little longer for that, Sergeant," then gave him a pat on the top of his head. That kept us laughing and the sergeant's face turned red.

In Okinawa, we would have to wait two days for our flight to the States. Assigned to the Marine barracks, we stowed our gear and went to a short briefing. At the briefing, we were told we needed to pass an inspection before leaving. We needed to be clean shaven, have a proper Marine Corps haircut, and be dressed in clean, pressed uniforms. Not standing for inspection in months, there was work to do.

I also found out our flight to the real world would land at El Toro Marine Air Station in California. My orders stated when I returned, I would receive a twenty-day leave. I lived less than a two-hour drive from El Toro, so Mom and Dad could pick me up.

After the briefing, I took my uniform to the cleaners and went to the barber shop. In the barracks, I polished my shoes and brass. I picked up my uniform from the cleaners. After a good shave in the morning, I'd be ready for inspection.

Mike and I knew other guys who were waiting for their flight home. A bunch of us took off for the nearest club on base. I was tired of drinking beer and wanted something else. At the club, I ordered a gin and tonic. In the partying mood, ready to unwind, and thankful I was out of Vietnam, one G and T led to another and then another.

The next thing I remembered was Mike holding me up in the shower and the chilly water running over me. Mike kept yelling at me to wake up and sober up. They had moved up our flight, and inspection was in one hour. Hearing that, I sobered up enough to stand on my own. A little shaky, I passed inspection. Not long after, we boarded our plane for the last leg home. I took a seat by the window. My head against a pillow, I slept half the trip home. When I woke up, I lit a cigarette. Mike was sitting beside me, and I thanked him for making sure I did not miss the plane.

"We've have had each other's backs all this time; no reason to stop now," he said.

"I owe ya big time, Mike."

I knew we were getting close to home when the pilot announced heavy fog around the El Toro Air Station. Disappointed, we diverted to Travis Air Force Base near Sacramento to wait until El Toro cleared. On the way north, the pilot announced the coast of California was visible from the right side of the plane. The plane took a slight dip to the right as all the guys on the left side jumped up and moved over to look out the other side. All of us were cheering again.

Another loud cheer erupted when the plane touched down at Travis. We taxied up near the terminal but were disappointed again when the pilot told us we had to stay on the plane. After thirty minutes, a civilian guy came on board and said it was okay for us to disembark but we could only stand under the wings, and no smoking. Off the plane we laughed and joked, happy our feet were standing on home ground again. A couple of guys bent down and kissed the ground. We did wonder why we could not go inside the terminal.

Finally, the civilian guy announced we could go inside and to please follow him. He was walking too slowly and four or five of the guys started to get ahead of him, so he walked faster. We moved faster, he moved faster, and finally a couple of guys started yelling and took off at a full run for the terminal. We all followed. We hit the double glass doors so hard the glass shattered all over the floor. Guys headed for the bar, or the restaurant, or the bank of pay phones along the wall. Other guys simply stood around in a daze; we were home! I headed for the phones to call home. Mom answered and I told her I was home. Crying so hard she handed the phone to Dad. "Where are you?" he asked,

I told him we were at Travis but about ready to fly to El Toro. "Can you pick me up in a couple of hours?" I asked.

"We are on our way," he said.

The plane refueled; it took time to round up everyone, especially the guys in the bar. Back aboard, a stewardess told us why we were not allowed in the terminal when we first landed. A plane load of Army guys was waiting inside for their flight to Vietnam. We needed to wait until they boarded their plane and not be in the terminal at the same time with them. A wise choice.

The flight to El Toro was short, at least compared to the flight from Okinawa, but the anticipation of getting home for real made it feel like it was taking forever. As the plane came into land and before the wheels touched down, I was holding my breath again. We all were. As soon as the wheels hit, we clapped and cheered. Now we were really home.

Inside the terminal, I showed my orders to the officer who looked at them and said, "Sergeant Elliott, you have twenty days' leave."

"Yes, Sir. My parents are waiting out front for me."

"Well, why are you still here?" he asked.

Straight out of the bush and no debriefing, just go home. No argument from me, I was out of Vietnam. What more could the Marine Corps do to me?

They weren't done yet.

CHAPTER 40
MY LAST 100 DAYS

After the officer asked, "Why are you still here?" I picked up my sea bag and walked toward the door leading to the terminal. Away from home for thirteen months, my Marine buddies and the Marine Corps had become my family. We fought the enemy together, watched each other's back, and saw friends die. Now home, how would I react when I see my mother, father, brother, Phyllis, and friends? How would my family and friends react when they see me? Who will watch my back? Scared and afraid of the change, I hesitated before going through the terminal door.

Entering the terminal, my younger brother Tim, ran up and grabbed my heavy sea bag. He had a tough time dragging it along the floor. I hugged Dad and Mom. Mom was crying. "Let's get out of here," I said, "before they change their minds."

I had called Phyllis from Travis to let her know I made it back. She had passed her registered nurse's test the day after I left for Vietnam. She worked at a hospital in Eagle Rock. She said she would wait for me at our house. I was anxious to get home to see her and my new surfboard.

My last couple of weeks in Vietnam, I had stopped writing letters home. The drive to our house was nonstop talking. Mom was the happiest she had been in a year. When we arrived at the house, Phyllis was waiting in the driveway along with neighbors welcoming me home. I gave Phyllis a big hug and a kiss. Everyone clapped! I was a bit overwhelmed, lucky to have friends and family actually welcoming me home from the war.

After the neighbors left, Phyllis and I sat on the back porch talking. Dad brought my new surfboard out of the garage and laid it on the grass.

With no wax on the board's deck the clear fiberglass over the white foam glistened in the sun. I checked out the step-down on the deck, the concave bottom and deep white fin, and the three redwood stringers. Everything I wanted. The next day, Roger and I went surfing at Huntington Pier. That surfboard hangs on the wall in my garage to this day as a reminder of my time in Vietnam.

At the briefing in Okinawa, they told us that if we had less than ninety days left on our enlistment when we returned, we were eligible for early discharge. The day I returned to the real world, I had 120 days to go, including twenty days' leave. The Marine Corps made me do the last one hundred days. I would spend all of it at Camp Pendleton near San Clemente and close to Trestles. Al and Mike were also stationed there; we were back together again. With one year left on his enlistment, our friend Rick Figueroa was assigned to a recon company stationed at another camp on the base. We were all out of Vietnam!

My twenty days' leave was over before I knew it. I surfed as much as possible. I was also trying to get used to life around civilians again. I managed not to screw up by asking my mother to pass the "fucking butter." Phyllis and I moved in together, renting an apartment in Tustin. Plans were underway to get married after my discharge. Mom was not happy we were living together and not married.

After leave, I reported to Camp Pendleton assigned to what the Marines call a casual company. Every man in the company, including most of the officers, had already served in Vietnam and had less than one hundred days until discharge. Few of us planned to stay in the Marines. As a sergeant, I could keep my surfboard on top of the wall lockers in the squad bay where I lived during the week. In the evenings, I surfed at Trestles. On the weekends, many starting on Thursday afternoon, I went home to our apartment.

For more than a month, we trained daily in the classroom and in the field where we threw hand grenades or practiced on the rifle range. We were just going through the motions and counting the days.

In early December, the company commander told us we were going to participate in a battalion-sized training exercise. The plan was to make everything as real as possible. Command assigned officers to each company to observe, evaluate, and judge us during the exercise. A few days later, we were riding in cattle cars (truck and trailer rigs) on our way to the navy base in San Diego.

"I don't like it," Al said. "This is too much like the day we left for Vietnam."

"Don't worry, Al, the Marine Corps wouldn't lie to us. Would they?" I said.

"I really hope we don't have to climb down the cargo nets again," Mike said.

At the harbor, the battalion boarded three ships. Our company boarded a new ship with nice accommodations and much better than the *Lenawee*, the ship we had taken to Vietnam. That night, we cruised up the coast.

The next morning, the companies made amphibious and helicopter landings across different beaches along the coast of Camp Pendleton. We did not have to climb down cargo nets. Instead, the ship we were on opened at the stern. Enclosed tracked amphibious vehicles transported us to the beach, landing on the beach at, of all places, Trestles. Landing there, I had a flashback to the day the MPs had busted Roger and me for surfing.

From the beach, we moved into the hills. Almost dark, we set up a company perimeter. We dug fighting holes, slept on the ground, and ate C-Rations again, reminding us of our days in Vietnam. Al, Mike, and I wondered what in the hell we were doing out here with less than two months until our discharge. We realized that until our last day, our asses still belonged to the United States Marine Corps, and we needed to follow orders. At least this time it was only for a couple of nights, and we did not have to worry about the incoming mortars and rockets.

The next morning, my squad started up a creek bed along one side of a hill, assigned to attack from the right flank. Marines from a recon company were on the hill acting as the enemy. They were armed with rifles and shooting blanks. Another squad attacked the hill from the front. All of us were shooting blanks at one another while the judges watched us. As we neared the top of the hill and were about to declare victory, a judge pointed to me and said, "Stop; you have been wounded, lie down."

One of the guys called for a corpsman. When he arrived, the judge told him shrapnel had fractured my leg, causing arterial bleeding. When the corpsman reached for the pressure point, I gave him a dirty look, and we both laughed. He applied a tourniquet and started to bandage my leg. When he finished, the judge told the corpsman he had done a decent job, but I died anyway. "Manage it like a real situation," the judge said.

"I'm dead?" I asked, thinking I went through a full tour in Vietnam, made it home alive, and now on a practice exercise, a judge tells me I am dead. I laughed out loud. The judge told me again to play dead. Al and Mike came over wondering what happened. "I'm dead," I said. They started laughing.

The corpsman filled out the toe tag (which I still have) and tied it to my boot to show I was dead. The officer who told me I was dead said I could not get up to walk down the hill. He told the corpsman to arrange for a stretcher. Guys from the platoon, including Al and Mike, carried me down the hill. Now it was my turn to laugh. I should not have laughed; the guys dropped me hard on the ground at the bottom of the hill. Laughing again, Al said, "Shouldn't make any difference; you're dead, right?"

The radio man, my old job, called for a Medevac chopper. The guys laid my pack and rifle on my stretcher and carried me to the chopper. I waved goodbye to Al and Mike as the chopper flew away. I got the finger. What's next, I was thinking.

The chopper took me to the beach where the operation command post was. When the chopper landed, guys carried me to a tent identified as graves registration. I thought of my friend Pat and wanting to see his body at graves registration in Dong Ha.

Everyone was going through all the steps of field operations, getting a chance to do his job as if it were a real situation. Even at graves registration, the priest looked down on me, waved his hand up and down and across his chest, and said words I did not understand. When the priest finished, a clerk standing by said, "You can get up now."

"What am I, undead?" I asked.

"You are now a new replacement," the clerk said.

With the time well past noon, and now undead, I was hungry and asked the clerk if there was a place to eat. He took me outside and pointed to a large tent on the beach. "That is the mess tent," he said. "When you finish eating, go to the replacement tent." He pointed down the beach and said, "They will reassign you back to your company." I grabbed my pack and rifle and headed for the mess tent. I was in no hurry to rejoin the company, so I took my time enjoying a sandwich, chips, and a coke.

At the replacement tent, the clerk told me it might be hours before a ride was available back to my company. "Just hang out," he said. Looking out at the water, I noticed nice waves breaking. What the heck, what can they do to me? (Hopefully not send me back to Vietnam.) I took off my boots, flak jacket, and utility shirt and went bodysurfing. No one stopped me. Guys on the beach must have wondered who the crazy guy in the water was.

As I dove under a wave, I thought what it must have been like for the families of the guys we lost when they found out their loved ones had died in Vietnam. I could not imagine the pain. I know it would have been extremely hard on my mom had I died during my service. I decided that even if I told her I played dead on a practice exercise, she would be upset. I never told my parents what happened that day.

I bodysurfed a couple of good waves, but the water in December was cold, so I did not stay out for long. Getting late, the clerk told me there was no ride available back to my unit until the morning. The exercise was scheduled to end the next day, so I found a cot in the replacement tent and headed back to the mess tent for dinner. I liked this, being dead.

Late the next morning, I caught a ride back to my company. The captain assigned me to the same platoon. The boys asked where I had been. I told them all about being dead and going bodysurfing. O'Grady said, "Elliott, you are the luckiest bastard I know." The platoon commander came around and told us to get our gear ready; the exercise was over. Trucks would take us back to our barracks. The timing was perfect, a Thursday afternoon. Back at the barracks, the captain said, "See you at 0800 Monday."

For the next couple of weeks, we continued with our boring training and received weekend liberty. For the holidays, we received ten days' leave. With only a month to go, I spent my leave surfing and looking for a civilian job.

Since my return from Vietnam, Phyllis and I talked about what I wanted to do after my discharge. I had been a poor student and did not want to go back to school. Yet I could not figure a way to make any money surfing. My only other talent was drawing, so I decided to look for a job as a draftsman. The company where I worked when drafted had told me to come back after I finished my service. The drive was over an hour from our apartment, so I decided to look for something else. I put in a few applications nearby and got a call from an architect's office in Newport Beach. After the interview, the boss asked when I would be available to start work. "At the end of January, when I get out of the Marines," I said. That turned out to be a mistake. On my interview, I noticed the draftsmen working in the office all wore shirts and ties. I owned one good shirt, one tie, and a dated sports coat. Phyllis and I went shopping the next day.

With one week left until the end of my "Two Years to serve," the captain called me to his office across the street from the barracks.

"Sergeant Elliott reporting, Sir." I saluted; the captain returned my salute. My records sat on his desk.

"Have a seat, sergeant."

"Yes sir," I said.

"I reviewed your records."

I knew what was coming next.

"We want you to stay in the Marine Corps." Yep, that's what I thought he wanted; A couple of the other sergeants told me the captain had told them the same thing. They both declined his offer.

He gave me the "We need men like you who have been to Vietnam and know how it works" speech. I am sure the look on my face did not show I agreed. He tried to sweeten the deal with an offer of a $10,000 cash bonus to re-up for four more years.

"I have one question," I said.

"What's that?" he asked.

"Will I go back to Vietnam?" I had enjoyed being a sergeant in the Marines and might have stayed, except I did not want to return to Vietnam.

"Yes, in six months you'll be eligible to go back," the captain said.

I did not take long to think about it. "Sir, I am not interested. One tour in Vietnam was enough."

"I understand Sergeant, but if you change your mind let me know," he said.

"Yes, sir. Thank you, sir," I stood up, we saluted each other. I turned around and walked out of his office.

I walked across the street to the barracks, took my surfboard off the top of the wall lockers in the squad bay. I put the board in the back of my dark green 1957 Ford Ranchero and drove off. As far as I was concerned, my adventures in the Marine Corps were over.

Ten minutes later I paddled out at Trestles.

A week later while driving off the base on my last day in the Marines, I was ready to get back into civilian life of sleeping in and surfing. Then I remembered I was going to work in the morning. The next morning, with my new suit and tie on, I drove thirty minutes to Newport Beach. When I arrived, the boss assigned me a drafting table and gave me the job of lettering notes on finished drawings. Very tedious and boring work.

Every day at lunch, I drove to the beach to watch the surfers. Another mistake. The middle of my second week, I drove to the beach at lunch like I did every day. Wishing I was out surfing, I said screw this. In the Marines, I had worked outside all the time, wearing a utility uniform, getting dirty, carrying a rifle, and surviving a year in Vietnam. What the hell am I doing wearing a tie and working in an office all day?

I drove home, called the boss, and told him I quit. Being stuck in an office was driving me crazy. I told him he did not even have to pay me. He said he understood my decision and paid me anyway. A week later, I went to work driving a soda pop truck. A few weeks after that, I started commercial diving school. I worked the next fifty years all over the world in the offshore diving industry. A great career, but that's another story.

THE END

EPILOGUE

Twice I have traveled to Washington, D.C., to visit the Vietnam Memorial known as "The Wall." The first time, I stood on the hill across from The Wall. Looking down over the sloping grass, I was able to see the entire memorial with the names of those lost as if they were staring at me. Stunned, I stared back. I don't know how long I stood there until I worked up the courage to walk down to the wall and look for Panel 13-E. There on line 71, I found Paul Evan's name; the first man I saw killed in Vietnam. I remembered the day he died. I touched his name and read it aloud. That is when I started to cry. I slowly moved along the panels, finding, touching, and saying the names of the seven other platoon mates I had lost in Vietnam. The thought I had many times in Vietnam and have had since hit me hard. "Why them and not me?"

Returning from Vietnam, I was lucky to have had incredibly support from family and friends, mostly my surfing buddies. Other returning veterans were not so lucky, suffering ridicule and outright hostility from clueless people, much of it happening on the college campuses. While proud of my service in the Marines and having served in Vietnam, when I first returned home I did not make a big deal about being a Vietnam veteran. After my discharge, I let my hair grow out and I never wore anything that would identify me with the Marines or Vietnam. I tried to blend in as much as possible.

I never went to college. After completing commercial diving school in 1969, I moved to Morgan City, Louisiana, and then Northern Scotland to work the offshore oil rigs until the end of the war. My friends and workmates were supportive, and I had few encounters with those who protested the war.

Phyllis and I had married shortly after my discharge. Our marriage lasted four years. Unlike other Vietnam veterans, I do not think I suffered problems with PTSD; however, my current wife of over forty-five years may have a different opinion.

Sometime after returning from Scotland, I joined Chapter 218 of the Vietnam Veterans of America (VVA) in Santa Barbara, California, where I was living. After a couple of years, I dropped out. The meetings had become nothing but bitching sessions. No one really tried to understand what may have been troubling us. Many of the veterans figured the government somehow owed them a living simply because they had fought in Vietnam. None of it helped me. I stayed away for years.

The first time the VVA chapter brought the traveling Vietnam Memorial "The Wall" to Santa Barbara, I went to see it. I reconnected with some of the veterans and became active in the chapter again. I currently serve on the board as the secretary/treasurer. We have brought the traveling "Wall" to Santa Barbara three times.

Everyone serving in Vietnam had a job to do. The politicians said our job was to stop the spread of communism. Everyone but the politicians knew that was bullshit and was never going to happen. The percentage of veterans who actually took part in combat operations in Vietnam was around forty to sixty percent. Combat jobs like grunt rifleman, radio operator, tank driver, helicopter pilot, door gunner, artillery battery crewmen, and many more. A considerable number of in-country veterans provided support for the men in the field. There were hundreds of combat and noncombat jobs. The men and women who served in Vietnam did their jobs and did them well. Our country asked us to serve, and we served with honor. As far as I am concerned, it was the politicians and protesters back home who lost the war.

Even though we all had different jobs, everyone in country was in harm's way one way or another, and we all had one goal. That goal was to stay alive for one day at a time, and make sure we did whatever possible to see that our buddies stayed alive one day at a time. If you were able to stay alive one day at a time for about 385 days, your tour would be over, and you would go home. Nine hundred and ninety-seven men lost their lives on their first day in Vietnam. 1,448 were killed on their last day. I will be forever grateful I survived that one more day at a time.

Guarding the traveling "Wall" late one night with no one else around, I found Paul's name. He had died only twelve days after we landed in country. I then found Ron Black's name, the last man in my original platoon killed, eighteen days before our tour ended. I counted the number of names between them. In that time span alone over 7,000 men were unable to survive that one more day. "Why them and not me?"

After I volunteered for duty at a CAP unit, Second Platoon and Lima Company began operations west of Dong Ha near the DMZ. During these operations, my friend Pat Cochran was killed by enemy fire on August 21, 1967. The battle he died in is described in the book titled *Lima 6*, written by Marine Colonel Dick Camp, commanding officer of Lima Company. Ray Potter and Anthony Sawicki were killed on September 10, and Ron Black on September 11, 1967. All were original members of Second Platoon. Eighteen days after Ron died, the surviving members of our platoon left for home.

Albert Drotar, Mike O'Grady, and I stayed together to the end, spending our last one hundred days at Camp Pendleton waiting for discharge. We saw each other two or three times after that and at the battalion reunion in Ennis, Montana in 2002. Albert had recovered from the wounds he received while on patrol at Papa Two but struggled with PTSD the rest of his life. He died on March 12, 2011. Mike died on May 23, 2004, from the effects of Agent Orange. Neither died in the war; they died because of their participation in it.

In 2003, we held our first platoon reunion at Doc Miller's cabin outside Harrisburg, Pennsylvania. Eighteen members attended. We enjoyed our time together hearing about each other's lives and reminiscing about our tour in Vietnam. Stories told at that reunion and others helped establish the framework for this memoir.

Over the years, the platoon held three more reunions at Doc's cabin; I attended one. Eight of the original members held a small reunion at Tom Willey's house in 2019, as Doc Miller had died the year before.

The battalion holds a reunion every two years. I have attended three, the last one in 2016 the fifty-year anniversary of the formation of the battalion. That reunion was held in San Diego, California near Camp Pendleton. Only Rick Figueroa and I from the Second Platoon attended. On the last day, everyone at the reunion attended a service at the Mount Soledad Veterans Memorial. There, we dedicated a plaque to honor the 391 men killed in action during the time the battalion had fought in Vietnam. Once again, "Why them and not me?"

None of us, the men of Second Platoon Third Battalion 26th Marines, will ever forget that time in our lives or the brothers we served with, or the Marines we lost. Serving with my fellow Marines, especially in combat, developed a lifelong bond. I am proud, happy, and humbled to have served my country with these men.

Semper Fi Marines. Sgt. Thomas Elliott

Second Platoon Reunion at Doc Miller's Cabin September 2003.
Standing: Tony Benedetto, Tom Willey, Lt. Jaak Aulik Weapons Platoon commander, Russ Helton, Jim Cooper, Doc Bill Miller, Lt. Frank McCarthy Third Platoon commander, Doc Cutright.
Sitting: Jim Mulhall, Al Drotar, Tom Carey, Tom Elliott, Sgt. Jim Strange, Lt. Harry Dolan (Turk) Second Platoon commander, Rick Figueroa.
Photo Courtesy of Phil Balint

Plaque dedicated in 2012 to the 391 Marines from the battalion whose lives were lost in the Vietnam War. Mount Soledad Veterans Memorial, San Diego, California.

IN MEMORY OF

Paul Evans: Lance Corporal
Sioux Falls, South Dakota, Age 21
Killed In Action on Operation Chinook
December 22, 1966
His name appears on the "Wall" Panel 13E - Line 71.

Gary Schneider: Corporal
Ft. Jennings, Ohio, Age 19
Killed in Action on Operation Chinook December 31, 1966
His name appears on the "Wall" Panel 13E - Line 105.

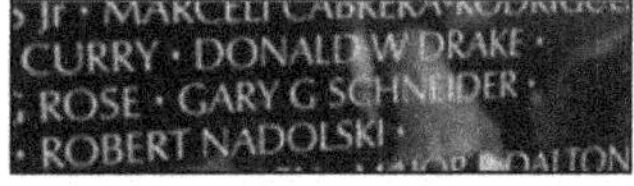

Ferrell Hummingbird: Lance Corporal
Oakland, CA, Age 20
Killed in Action on Operation Chinook
January 14, 1967
His name appears on the "Wall" Panel 14E - Line 27.

Patrick Cochran: Corporal
Del Rio, Texas, Age 20
Killed in Action August 21, 1967
His name appears on the "Wall" Panel 25E - Line 23.

Raymond Potter: Corporal
Campbell, Ohio, Age 25
Killed in Action September 10, 1967
His name appears on the "Wall" Panel 26E - Line 50.

Ronald Black: Sergeant
Jacksonville, Illinois, Age 21
Killed in Action September 11, 1967
His Name appears on the "Wall" Panel 26E - Line 54.

Anthony Sawicki: Lance Corporal
Philadelphia, PA, Age 19
Killed in Action September 10, 1967: Bronze Star Awarded
His Name appears on the "Wall" Panel 26E - Line 51.

"THE WORST CASUALTY OF WAR IS BEING FORGOTTEN."

I WILL NEVER FORGET.

CPSIA information can be obtained
at www.ICGtesting.com
Printed in the USA
LVHW101627081122
732650LV00008B/1068

9 798885 909419